Digital Age

Teaching Skills

A Standards Based Approach

3rd Edition

Constance Wyzard, Ph.D.
Boise State University

Barbara Schroeder, Ed.D.
Boise State University

Chris Haskell, M.S.
Boise State University

ERC Publishing
Boise, Idaho
ISBN: 978-0-9758723-8-3

Textbook Website:
http://dats.boisestate.edu

Table of Contents

Introduction: Digital Age Teaching Skills

Welcome to the exciting and challenging world of teaching in a Digital Age. This textbook, *Digital Age Teaching Skills,* will be your guide in learning about the role of technology in teaching and learning and building the necessary technology skills to be an effective teacher. You will become acquainted with current research about using technology in education and be able to provide a comprehensive answer to the question, "What are the benefits of technology integration for teaching and learning?"

Throughout the process, you will plan instruction, build lesson plans, craft presentations, develop documents, and evaluate technology-enhanced curriculum. You will demonstrate your Digital Age teaching skills by creating letters, lessons, rubrics, assessments, and other teaching artifacts using technology. In short, you will create and model "real world" technology-enhanced teaching skills.

This textbook is arranged to help you complete a culminating project, a Technology Teaching Portfolio based on the International Society for Technology in Education standards (NETS-T) for teachers (ISTE, 2008). The portfolio will be a valuable professional resource for yourself and potential employers. You can preview how your portfolio should look and how you will build it in Appendix A.

Practice exercises and instructions for completing technology artifacts will be provided for both Windows Vista and Mac OS X operating systems. Mac OS X instructions are also included in the textbook and appendices.

National Educational Technology Standards for Teachers

The International Society for Technology in Education (ISTE) released the NETS for Teachers (NETS-T) in 2000, which set standards for integration of technology in education. The NETS-T 2000 defined the fundamental concepts, knowledge, skills, and attitudes for applying technology in educational settings.

ISTE released an update of the NETS-T in 2007 and unveiled the new NETS-T in 2008. The new ISTE NETS-T provides a framework for educators to use as they transition schools from Industrial Age to Digital Age places of learning.

As you progress through this textbook, you will become very familiar with the ISTE NETS-T standards, creating artifacts that demonstrate competencies in these standards. The five standards (ISTE, 2008) state that teachers:

1. Facilitate and Inspire Student Learning and Creativity
2. Design and Develop Digital Age Learning Experiences and Assessments
3. Model Digital Age Work and Learning for applying technology to maximize student learning
4. Promote and Model Digital Citizenship and Responsibility
5. Engage in Professional Growth and Leadership

By exploring the possibilities of technology for teaching and completing the exercises presented in this text, you will be gaining the skills and concepts necessary for teaching in a Digital Age. In order to demonstrate and document those competencies, you will prepare a portfolio rich with examples (artifacts) of your ability to use technology for teaching and learning

A Technology Teaching Portfolio

The use of portfolio assessment has become increasingly valued in education as a means of measuring the performance of a student. The portfolio not only provides a more comprehensive view of a student's attainment of standards, but also enables a student to assume ownership of learning. As an alternative to more quantitative methods of assessing performance, a portfolio requires students to collect and reflect on examples of their work. In essence, students have the opportunity to select representative artifacts and then reflect on their choices. As Jones (1994) notes: "By viewing learning as a construction of the individual, not something to be absorbed from teachers and texts, they are experimenting with a 'portfolio assessment' approach to education." In this approach, "problem-solving and student reflection, and their appropriate portrayal or documentation, receive primary attention" (p. 23).

Many educators advocate the use of portfolios for enhancing the assessment process and providing an authentic means of measuring student progress in meeting educational goals. Using portfolio assessment encourages student participation in learning outcomes and can be used for a variety of purposes including:

- Encouraging self-directed learning.
- Enlarging the view of what is learned.
- Fostering learning about learning.
- Demonstrating progress toward identified outcomes.
- Creating an intersection for instruction and assessment.
- Providing a way for students to value themselves as learners.
- Offering opportunities for peer-supported growth (Prince George's County Public Schools, 2008).

A Technology Teaching Portfolio is a purposeful collection of work that clearly demonstrates your skills and ability to use technology for teaching and learning. The portfolio should contain artifacts that represent your growth in meeting each of the five ISTE NETS Standards for Teachers.

As you progress through the chapters and individual exercises, you will begin to experience the power of technology as a teaching and learning tool. The exercises you complete and the instructional products you produce will be your first steps in integrating technology. Showcasing your work in a Technology Teaching Portfolio will demonstrate your growth in technology and in reaching the National Educational Technology Standards.

Overview of Digital Age Teaching Skills

This textbook is designed to guide you through the development of the necessary Digital Age skills crucial for today's teachers and students. As you progress through the book, you will discover ways to use your new skills in teaching and assist your students in becoming problem solvers and skilled users of technology. Each chapter provides fundamental concepts as well as exercises designed to help you acquire the technology skills to meet one or more of the ISTE NETS for Teachers Standards (NETS-T). Website links in each chapter of the book provide research and background information necessary to expand conceptual understanding. Additionally, individual exercises are identified as required or possible artifacts for the Technology Teaching Portfolio you will be creating. A basic overview of the chapters and appendices follows.

Chapter 1: Technology in Education

In this chapter, you will explore reasons for integrating technology and examine standards for teachers and students in technology and all academic areas. You will find out more about the Millennial Generation, college and workforce skills needed today, and why standards are important. You will begin your technology skills training with file management exercises, learning how to organize digital files and folders (NETS-T Standards 3 & 5).

Chapter 2: Designing Learning Environments

In this chapter you will examine the planning and designing of learning environments with a focus on the role of technology in enhancing higher order thinking skills, collaboration, and communication. Of particular interest is the discussion of assistive technology and technology solutions available to people with disabilities. You will examine course management systems and determine best uses of common course management components. You will also learn how to integrate word processing software, using both desktop software and online, collaborative applications (NETS-T Standard 2).

Chapter 3: Planning Instruction Using Technology

In this chapter you will create basic lesson plans using technology as a primary teaching strategy and plan a technology-supported lesson outlining the standards to be addressed, technology tools to be used, and evaluation methods to be employed. You will use technology to evaluate, assess, and support learning by creating and integrating spreadsheets to explore concepts and transform numbers into visual charts that enhance and simplify your students' understanding of abstract concepts (NETS-T Standard 2).

Chapter 4: Evaluate and Assess Using Technology

This chapter focuses on assessment, what it is and how technology can assist in the assessment process. The role of evaluation in the teaching process, the kinds of assessments available to measure learning, and the role of technology in assessment are primary topics of discussion. You will have an opportunity to design assessments using rubric and test generators available on the Internet (NETS-T Standard 2).

Chapter 5: Digital Age Work and Learning Skills

In this chapter, you will explore the second generation of Internet-based services (Web 2.0) that have transformed the web from a collection of websites to an infrastructure supporting user participation, social interaction and collaboration. You will use Web 2.0 tools to extend the walls of the classroom and provide an e-learning workspace that brings another dimension to teaching and learning (NETS-T Standard 3).

Chapter 6: Digital Citizenship

Although the advent of technology has brought about exciting opportunities for teaching and learning, it has also brought about an advent of dangers. Concerns such as Internet predators, cyberbullying, pornography, and identify theft require that teachers be proactive in protecting their students. This chapter of the book discusses the need for Internet safety education, guidelines for acceptable use policies, and other safeguards.

The Digital Divide, the gap between those who have access to technology and those who do not, is highlighted in this section as well as possible ways to address digital inequities. Other issues investigated in this chapter are the rise in copyright and plagiarism abuses (NETS-T Standard 4).

Chapter 7: Professional Practice, Growth, and Leadership

As you are just beginning your professional teaching career, it is especially important that you become familiar with professional organizations and professional development. The role of technology in keeping abreast of current teaching issues, trends and concerns is examined in this chapter, with a focus on RSS technology. You will subscribe to and publish RSS feeds tailored to professional interests and needs. Additionally, the common components of student information systems (SIS) and the management of student data are also examined (NETS-T Standard 5).

Chapter 8: Engagement and Creativity

There are many ways to inspire and facilitate student learning and creativity through technology. In this chapter, you will explore one tool, presentation software, and how it can be used to enhance teaching and learning. You will learn how to create effective, engaging presentations along with other meaningful learning activities (NETS-T Standard 1).

Appendix A: Technology Teaching Portfolio
This helpful appendix provides information you will need to get started using Google Sites to build your Technology Teaching Portfolio. We provide a template to facilitate this process.

Appendix B: Google Docs Word Processing Basics
There may be times when you and/or your students won't have access to Microsoft Office products. Using Google Docs can provide the needed tool and also empower learners through its collaborative and publishing features. Many of the exercises and activities can be completed using Google Docs.

Appendix C: Google Docs Spreadsheet Fundraising Activity
This fundraising activity example uses the free and collaborative Google Docs spreadsheet software to create a fundraising spreadsheet for your class.

Appendix D: Technology Skills: File Management (Mac OS X)
All software tools and skills are now provided for the Mac OS X operating system. If you are a Mac user or want to learn about additional operating systems, please use the helpful information and tutorials provided in appendices D, E, F, and G.

Appendix E: Technology Skills: Word Processing (Word for Mac 2011)

Appendix F: Technology Skills: Spreadsheets (Excel for Mac 2011)

Appendix G: Technology Skills: Presentation Software (PowerPoint for Mac 2011)

Appendix H: Creating an Annotated Video Playlist
Create a customized and annotated video playlist using the features of YouTube.

Appendix I: Artifacts Table
In this handy table, you can refer to and find all of the exercises and artifacts you will prepare for your Technology Teaching Portfolio. We have placed this table on the last page of the book, for easy and quick reference.

Getting Started

In order to get the most from this textbook, you will need to have the following hardware/software configurations, basic technical skills, and access to our companion website (http://dats.boisestate.edu) to download needed data files and easily access all Internet links included in this book.

Hardware/Software Requirements		
	PC	**Apple**
Operating System	Windows Vista or Windows 7	Mac OS X
Application Software	Microsoft Office 2007 or 2010	Microsoft Office: Mac 2011
Preferred Web Browsers	Firefox http://getfirefox.com Chrome http://www.google.com/chrome Safari http://www.apple.com/safari	Firefox http://getfirefox.com Chrome http://www.google.com/chrome Safari http://www.apple.com/safari
Accounts	Gmail account with at least the following services: • Gmail • Google Docs • Google Sites • Blogger	
Technical skills	• Can navigate the Internet • Can download and install programs	
Companion Website	http://dats.boisestate.edu You can download data files for some of the exercises in this textbook, access all websites mentioned in the book, link to our sample Technology Teaching Portfolio, and receive updates on book corrections or additional exercises offered.	

References

ISTE. (2008). *NETS for Teachers*. Retrieved from http://www.iste.org/standards/nets-for-teachers/nets-for-teachers-2008.aspx

Jones, J. E. (1994). Portfolio assessment as a strategy for self-direction in learning. *New Directions for Adult and Continuing Education, 1994*(64), 23-29.

Prince George's County Public Schools. (2008). *Portfolio assessment*. Retrieved from http://www.pgcps.org/~elc/portfolio

Introductory Exercise

Your Technology Teaching Portfolio provides the structure and navigation to help you create a dynamic   demonstration of your work and progress. It is essential you begin to build this structure at the beginning and continually add to it. You will, therefore, begin by creating your Technology Teaching Portfolio and adding information to your welcome (home) page.

Exercise 1: Create Your Technology Teaching Portfolio

In this activity, you will begin the process of building your Technology Teaching Portfolio. We recommend using Google Sites (http://sites.google.com), a free, collaborative, browser-based website building tool. Google Sites is included as part of your Gmail account, so all you need to do is login to Gmail and then access Google Sites.

Please refer to **Appendix A** and set up your Technology Teaching Portfolio using the Google Sites template created for you: https://sites.google.com/site/techportfoliotemplate

Add information to the welcome (home) page to get started.

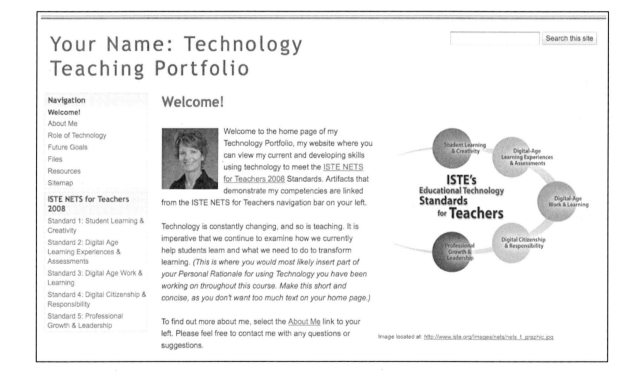

In this chapter, you will examine reasons and benefits for integrating technology and then demonstrate proficiency in digital file management skills. ISTE NETS-T Standard 5 states "teachers continuously improve their professional practice, model lifelong learning, and exhibit leadership in their school and professional community by promoting the effective use of digital tools and resources." NETS-T Standard 3 addresses the need for teachers to "demonstrate fluency in technology systems and the transfer of current knowledge to new technologies and situations" (ISTE, 2008). Both of these standards can apply to the exercises and technology skills included in this chapter.

Being a teacher involves staying current with research on teaching with technology and applying best practices of technology integration. By evaluating and reflecting upon current research and professional practice, you can help create and maintain engaging and productive learning experiences for you and your students. You can, as NETS-T Standard 5 states, "contribute to the effectiveness, vitality, and self-renewal of the teaching profession." In the first part of this chapter you will discover more about the importance of technology in teaching and about standards in teaching and learning. Then, you will practice essential computer skills in the Technology Skills: File Management section that all teachers should know and be able to teach to their students.

Why integrate technology?

The reasons for integrating technology into classroom instruction are many, and include the benefits technology affords for teaching and learning, the nature of today's digital natives, and the needs of the future workforce. An overview of these topics is provided here, but you will also be using the Internet to further examine the reasons for integrating technology.

Benefits for Teaching and Learning

Since the introduction of the computer into education in the 1970s, educators have investigated its effects on students, teachers, and learning environments. Early studies were focused on demonstrating the impact of a particular technology or software on student achievement and student motivation. With increased access to computers and the Internet, researchers extended their efforts to investigate the role of technology in the educational setting including its impact on teachers and the learning process. In the past decade, the study of the computer as an instructional delivery medium has been expanded to investigating technology as "a transformational tool and an integral part of the learning environment" (Fouts, 2000, p. 9).

Much of the research investigating the impact of technology indicates that the use of technology in K-12 education is indeed having a positive effect on student learning, motivation, and success. When teachers are properly trained to use technology to enhance instruction, student learning is improved. Student attitude and motivation are lauded as direct benefits to integrating technology; benefits that help keep students on task and even affect school attendance and classroom behavior. Many researchers have concluded that integrating technology is particularly effective in the differentiation of instruction, thus making it an ideal strategy for assisting students with special needs.

One of the greatest benefits of using technology in education is in the development of higher-order thinking skills. These skills require more complex cognitive abilities and are dependent upon a learner's mastery of lower skills. To best illustrate this concept, a taxonomy, a hierarchical classification of cognitive skills, was first developed by Benjamin Bloom in 1956 and recently revised (Anderson &

Krathwohl, 2001). Anderson, a former student of Bloom, revised Bloom's Taxonomy using verbs rather than nouns for each of the categories and rearranged the sequence within the taxonomy. The image below helps illustrate this new taxonomy:

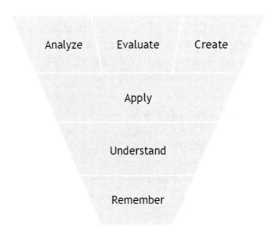

Public Domain image, retrieved from http://commons.wikimedia.org/wiki/File:BloomsCognitiveDomain.PNG

Adding Digital Age terminology to Bloom's taxonomy has been proposed by Andrew Churches, which he calls "Bloom's Digital Taxonomy" (Churches, 2008). For instance, "blogging" might be a new verb used for Bloom's "evaluating," and "conducting Boolean searches" might apply to "understanding." By adding technology terminology to this taxonomy, teachers can more easily identify the hierarchy of learning in their instruction and design appropriate lesson sequencing to more effectively enable learning.

Using technology to investigate and examine complex problems allows students to develop higher-order cognitive skills and become more independent, analytical thinkers. Students construct their own learning through the use of technology tools and resources. Instead of the traditional teaching model where the teacher lectures and serves as the primary dispenser of knowledge, with technology the teacher's role is that of a guide who assists student learning. Studies reinforce the role of teacher as a guide and advocate the essential need for skills such as problem solving, synthesizing information, and communicating via technology (Barron, Harmes, Kalaydjian, & Kemker, 2003; Brown & Campione, 2002, Hopson & Knezek, 2001; Lyle, 2008; Meyer, 2003; Miller, 2006). With the advent and increased accessibility of many of the new Web 2.0 applications, the opportunities for enhanced student interaction and collaboration have also increased possibilities for promoting higher-order thinking skills.

The Center for Applied Research in Educational Technology (CARET), a funded project of ISTE, includes a comprehensive review of research evidence on the impact of technology in education (http://caret.iste.org). The CARET website includes common questions posed about the effectiveness of technology in teaching. One of the questions is, "How can technology influence student academic performance?" You can find answers to this question, along with relevant research by clicking the "questions and answers" link on the CARET website.

For teachers and administrators, technology provides a means of improving productivity and efficiency. Data obtained through technology drive decision-making, allowing educators to make timely, informed decisions. Technology makes it possible to access real time information and use this information to help students learn and achieve at higher levels.

Benefits of Technology for Teaching and Learning

National Education Technology Plan 2010
http://www.ed.gov/technology/netp-2010

Technology: A Catalyst for Teaching and Learning in the Classroom
http://www.ncrel.org/sdrs/areas/issues/methods/technlgy/te600.htm

Research on Computers and Education: Past, Present and Future (PDF format)
http://www.portical.org/fouts.pdf

U.S. Department of Education, Benefits of Technology Use
http://www.ed.gov/about/offices/list/os/technology/plan/national/benefits.html

Why Technology in Schools?
http://www.edtechactionnetwork.org/why-technology-in-schools

Center for Applied Research in Educational Technology
http://caret.iste.org/

Critical and Creative Thinking: Bloom's Taxonomy
http://eduscapes.com/tap/topic69.htm

Using the new Bloom's Taxonomy to Design Meaningful Learning Assessments
http://www.lincoln.edu/assessment/planning/usebloom.pdf

Bloom's Digital Taxonomy
http://www.techlearning.com/article/8670

Millennial Generation - Digital Natives

Today's students, the Millennial Generation, have grown up with computer technology, experiencing innovations in everything from electronic games to the Internet. Acknowledging that the "millennials" see the "potential for computers to revolutionize the classroom," the U.S. Department of Education solicited their input in developing the National Education Technology Plan.

This generation, first described as digital natives by Marc Prensky (2005), are the "native speakers of the digital language of computers, video games and the Internet" (p. 1). Today's students are the first generation to grow up with technology, the first generation that prefer graphics to text, and the first generation accustomed to receiving information really fast. Prensky, in describing digital natives, states:

> Our young people generally have a much better idea of what the future is bringing than we do. They're already busy adopting new systems for communicating (instant messaging), sharing (blogs), buying and selling (eBay), exchanging (peer-to-peer technology), creating (Flash), meeting (3D worlds), collecting (downloads),

coordinating (wikis), searching (Google), reporting (camera phones), programming (modding), socializing (chat rooms), and even learning (Web surfing). (p. 2)

Realizing the learning characteristics of the digital native, teachers are encouraged to explore ways to actively engage these tech-savvy students in the learning process through technology. However, a report (Center for Policy Studies, 2005) describes students' frustrations with our nation's still text-dominated schools. Today's teachers must learn to employ technology as a means to actively engage the Millennial Generation, transform educational practices, and foster student achievement. Employing technology as a teaching strategy will help bridge discrepancies between the technology-rich lives of our students and their learning experience in the schools.

The National Education Technology Plan 2010, *Transforming American Education: Learning Powered by Technology*, calls for applying the advanced technologies used in our daily personal and professional lives to our entire education system to improve student learning, accelerate and scale up the adoption of effective practices, and use data and information for continuous improvement (National Education Technology Plan, 2010).

This plan presents five goals with recommendations for states, districts, the federal government, and other stakeholders. Each goal addresses one of the five essential components of learning powered by technology: Learning, Assessment, Teaching, Infrastructure, and Productivity.

Millennial Generation – Digital Natives

U.S. Department of Education: National Education Technology Plan
http://www.ed.gov/technology/netp-2010

Listening to Student Voices – On Technology (PDF format)
http:// www.educationevolving.org/pdf/Tech-Savvy-Students.pdf

The Digital Disconnect: The widening gap between Internet-savvy students and schools
http://www.pewinternet.org/Reports/2002/The-Digital-Disconnect-The-widening-gap-between-Internetsavvy-students-and-their-schools.aspx

Learning in a Digital Age: Listen to the natives
http://www.siprep.org/prodev/documents/Prensky.pdf

Creating and Connecting (PDF format)
http://www.nsba.org/site/docs/41400/41340.pdf

College and Workforce Technology Skills

The global economy is directly impacting the nature of work and the kinds of jobs that will be available to the next generation. With globalization, the need for high-skilled workers able to cope with increasingly complex technology is growing; however, there is a real concern that the K-12 education system is not preparing students for the jobs of tomorrow. Technology plays a major role in the development of the technical and learning skills necessary to succeed in higher education and the workplace.

College and Workforce Technology Skills
The Skills Gap http://cdn.americasedge.org/clips/WA-Skills-Report.pdf Workforce Literacy in an Information Age http://outreach.lib.uic.edu/www/issues/issue5_7/slowinski/index.html

What are standards and why are they important?

The standards movement in education was initiated with the publication of *A Nation at Risk* (1983), a report that dramatically advocated the reform of American education.

> Our Nation is at risk. Our once unchallenged preeminence in commerce, industry, science, and technological innovation is being overtaken by competitors throughout the world. This report is concerned with only one of the many causes and dimensions of the problem, but it is the one that undergirds American prosperity, security, and civility. We report to the American people that while we can take justifiable pride in what our schools and colleges have historically accomplished and contributed to the United States and the well-being of its people, the educational foundations of our society are presently being eroded by a rising tide of mediocrity that threatens our very future as a Nation and a people. What was unimaginable a generation ago has begun to occur--others are matching and surpassing our educational attainments. (Retrieved from: http://www.ed.gov/pubs/NatAtRisk/risk.html)

Of course, this was just the beginning of the educational reform movement, which gained momentum with the passing of the No Child Left Behind (NCLB) Act (2001). NCLB, advocating the increase of standards of accountability in American schools, was the impetus behind standards-based education reform. By the time NCLB was enacted, many states and professional organizations had already begun the process of identifying standards in an effort to improve education. This standards-based movement, beginning with the 1983 *Nation at Risk* report, has shaped American education at every level, mandating teacher accountability for student learning.

ISTE National Education Technology Standards

The International Society for Technology in Education (ISTE) provides the leadership for the development of technology standards for teachers and students. The ISTE website describes their role:

> ISTE's National Educational Technology Standards (NETS) have served as a roadmap for improved teaching and learning by educators throughout the United States. The standards, used in every U.S. state and many countries, are credited with significantly influencing expectations for students and creating a target of excellence relating to technology.

The NETS for students were first released in 1998 and recently updated (ISTE, 2007) with new standards that "identify several higher-order thinking skills and digital citizenship as critical for students to learn effectively for a lifetime and live productively in our emerging global society." Below are the 2007 NETS that define "what students should know and be able to do to learn effectively and live productively in an increasingly digital world:

1. Creativity and Innovation
2. Communication and Collaboration
3. Research and Information Fluency
4. Critical Thinking, Problem Solving, and Decision making
5. Digital Citizenship
6. Technology Operations and Concepts (NETS for Students)

Technology standards for teachers were first released in 2000 and were updated in June 2008. The NETS for teachers (ISTE, 2008) list five areas in which teachers should be proficient:

1. Student Learning and Creativity
2. Digital Age Learning Experiences and Assessments
3. Digital Age Work and Learning
4. Digital Citizenship and Responsibility
5. Professional Growth and Leadership (NETS for Teachers)

ISTE describes the 2008 technology standards for teachers as a way to "provide a framework for educators to use as they transition schools from Industrial Age to Digital Age places of learning." The standards reflect changes in the role of technology in teaching and learning and will enable teachers to better prepare their students for global learning in a Digital Age.

ISTE Standards for Students and Teachers

ISTE 2007 NETS for Students
http://www.iste.org/standards/nets-for-students/nets-student-standards-2007.aspx

ISTE 2008 NETS for Teachers
http://www.iste.org/standards/nets-for-teachers/nets-for-teachers-2008.aspx

---

References

Anderson, L., & Krathwohl, D. R. (2001). *A taxonomy for learning, teaching and assessing: A revision of Bloom's taxonomy of educational objectives*. New York: Longman.

Barron, A. E., Harmes, C., Kalaydjian, K., & Kemker, K. (2003). Large-scale research study on technology in K-12 schools: Technology integration as it relates to the national technology standards. *Journal of Research in Technology Education*.

Brown, A. L., & Campione, J. C. (2002). Communities of learning and thinking, or a context by any other name. *Contemporary Issues in Teaching and Learning, 120-126*.

Center for Policy Studies. (2005). Listening to student voices - - on technology. Hamline University.

Churches, A. (2008). Bloom's taxonomy blooms digitally. *Tech & Learning*. Retrieved from http://www.techlearning.com/article/8670

Coley, R., Cradler, J., & Engel, P. (1997). Computers and classrooms: The status of technology in U.S. schools. Princeton: Educational Testing Service, Policy Information Center.

Fouts, J. T. (2000). Research on computers and education: Past, present and future. Bill and Melinda Gates Foundation Report.

Hopson, M. H., Simms, R. L., & Knezek, G. A. (2001). Using a technology-enriched environment to improve higher-order thinking skills. *Journal of Research on Technology in Education, 34*(2), 109-120.

ISTE. (2008). NETS for Teachers. Retrieved from http://www.iste.org/standards/nets-for-teachers/nets-for-teachers-2008.aspx

Lyle, S. (2008). Dialogic teaching: Discussing theoretical contexts and reviewing evidence from classroom practice. *Language and Education, 22*(3), 222-240.

Marston, D., Deno, S. L., Dongil, K., Diment, K., & Rogers, D. (1995). Comparison of reading intervention approaches for students with mild disabilities. *Exceptional Children*, 20-37.

Meyer, K. A. (2003). Face-to-face versus threaded discussions: The role of time and higher-order thinking. *Journal of Asynchronous Learning Networks, 7*(3), 55-65.

Miller, J. P. (2006). *Educating for wisdom and compassion: Creating conditions for timeless learning*. Corwin Press.

National Education Technology Plan (2010). Washington, DC: U.S. Department of Education, Office of Educational Technology. Retrieved from http://www.ed.gov/technology/netp-2010

Prensky, M. (2005). Listen to the natives. *Educational Leadership, 63*(4), 8-13.

Technology in Education Exercises

The following exercises are intended to introduce you to the many roles of technology in education, what research says about the best ways to integrate technology in the classroom, and how to find more information about technology in education. You will research studies about technology in education, begin to compose your "Personal Rationale" for technology use in your future classroom, and then practice and learn basic file management skills, essential to efficient computer use. You will finish this chapter by creating a plan for teaching file management skills to your own students.

Exercise 1: Research Technology in Education

ISTE NETS-T Standard 5

You need to be knowledgeable about research in the field of educational technology, citing studies that prove the effectiveness of technology in teaching in learning. In this exercise, you will locate research studies that support the use of technology in education.

✓ Navigate to the ISTE Center for Applied Research in Educational Technology (CARET) http://caret.iste.org to learn more about what research says about effective uses of technology for teaching and learning.

✓ Search using your content area as keywords and select three articles to read.

✓ Write a summary about each of these articles and key points you would use to support the use of technology in the classroom.

✓ Include the APA-formatted references of the articles from the CARET website.

*Could be used as an artifact for Standard 5

Exercise 2: Personal Rationale for Technology Integration

You will begin to develop your personal rationale for integrating technology in your future classroom. Incorporate information you found on the CARET website, the National Education Technology Plan, ISTE NETS for Teachers, this chapter, and any other research you have conducted.

✓ Compose and post this rationale on your welcome (home) page of your Technology Teaching Portfolio.

✓ Make this rationale concise and succinct, about one paragraph.

✓ Adjust this rationale as you continue to learn about technology and its uses in the classroom.

✓ **Optional:** Produce a video using your webcam or portable device, upload to YouTube (make your URL unlisted), and embed on the front page of your Portfolio.

This technology skills section and file management exercises were adapted from *Educating Teachers* (2007) – Pollard, C., VanDehey, T., and Pollard, R.

Y ou will find that even the most accomplished of your computer savvy students may need direction in how to locate, organize, and manage their files and folders. ISTE NETS-T Standard 3 states teachers should "exhibit knowledge, skills, and work processes representative of an innovative professional in a global and digital society." Certainly an understanding and modeling of practical digital file management skills demonstrates this standard. File management skills demonstrate "fluency in technology systems" and "model and facilitate effective use of current and emerging digital tools" (ISTE, 2008).

 File Management Basics in Mac OS X (See Appendix D)

File Management Basics in Windows Vista

Windows Explorer provides an efficient way to view, organize, and edit all the drives, folders, and files on your computer. A drive is the hardware used to store software applications and information. Computers can have many drives located physically within the computer or on shared drives made available across networks. The primary hard disk is usually designated as the C: drive and other letters assigned for additional drives. You can think of a drive as a filing cabinet drawer full of folders to organize information.

Windows Explorer displays the drives and folders on your computer in a hierarchical file system called a directory tree. The hierarchical organization of drives, folders (also called directories), and files can be compared to the branches and leaves of an upside down tree. The nodes (branches) of the hierarchy are called directories while the leaves are the files themselves. The main directory is called the root directory, or the top-level directory. The root directory is the directory by which all others are created. Any directory (folder) can be divided into subdirectories (also called subfolders). Subdirectories (subfolders) can be further divided into additional subdirectories (subfolders).

Not only are you able to view this hierarchical arrangement of folders and files on your computer using *Windows Explorer*, you are able to copy and move files and folders, as well as perform other necessary organizational and management functions.

The following exercises will help you apply good digital file management skills and integrate ways to help your own students become fluent in managing and integrating technology systems.

Starting Windows Explorer

1. Right-click the **Start** button at the bottom left corner of the task bar.
2. Select **Explore**.
3. Click the maximize icon in the upper right hand corner of the window.

Notice that the window is divided into two parts with the **left folder pane** displaying **Favorite Links** in the top half and a **Folders** section displaying a hierarchy of directories and folders in the bottom half. The contents of the current item selected in the left pane will be displayed in the right contents pane. In the previous illustration, the contents of the Desktop can be viewed in the right contents pane.

Windows Explorer Layout

The Favorite Links section in the left pane provides quick access to folders that are typically accessed often. When you click any of these links in the left pane, you will be able to view the contents in left pane in the **Folders** area and in the right contents pane. You are able to open files by double-clicking on them. When you run your cursor over the items in the bottom **Folders** section on the left, small triangular shaped icons become visible indicating that there are folders and subfolders available. Clicking on the triangles allows you to collapse and open directories and folders and view any subfolders.

Viewing Directories, Folders, and Files

1. Select the **Documents** folder in the left folders pane.

The right contents pane will display any subfolders and/or files located in the selected **Documents** folder. Clicking on a subfolder, either in the right or left pane will disclose the subfolders and/or files located within each of these folders.

2. Click each of the directories and folders in the left folders pane to view the folders located on your computer.
3. Double-click the subfolders in the right contents pane to further view the organization of folders and files.
4. Click the triangle to the left of **Documents** in the left folders section.

Now the indented list of folders is collapsed. This navigational system allows you to graphically display the directories, folders, and files on your computer.

Windows Explorer Features

The menu bar in *Windows Explorer* presents the following categories of functions to access: **File**, **Edit**, **View**, **Tools**, and **Help**. A dropdown list appears as you click each menu option presenting specific commands available within the category. In this section, you will examine the commands that are the most necessary for you and your students to use to effectively manage and organize your work.

When you click the **File** option on the menu bar, a dropdown list appears allowing you to perform operations such as making a new folder, creating a shortcut, deleting a file or folder, and renaming a folder. It also gives you a means of determining the properties of the file/folder you currently have selected. You are able to see the type of file or folder, location, size, contents, and the date when it was created, modified, and accessed. This can be very valuable information for you and your students.

The commands available in File on the menu bar are also available by selecting the file or folder and right-clicking your mouse in the highlighted area. You must right-click with your cursor in the highlighted area, as commands are context sensitive. A different dropdown menu may be available depending upon where your cursor is when you right-click.

Explore Menus

1. Select a folder in the left folder pane of *Windows Explorer* and click your right mouse button (also called a right-click) in the highlighted area.

You are presented with commands that allow you to explore, open, and search the contents of the folder. You are also able to cut, copy, delete, and rename the selected folder.

2. Select a folder in the right contents pane of *Windows Explorer* and right-click in the highlighted area.

Notice that most of the commands are the same, but that now you are able to create a shortcut in the right contents pane menu, but not in the left folder pane.

3. Place your cursor in the white area of the right contents pane.

4. Click the right mouse button.

Different commands are now available including the ability to make a new folder and change your view and arrangement of the contents.

Creating folders and saving pertinent work in those folders will keep your students' assignments organized and easy to locate. Each time you save your work, you will want to make sure that it is stored in an appropriate folder with a title that you recognize for that work. In this next exercise, you will make a new folder on your USB flash drive (also called a thumb or jump drive).

Insert a Flash Drive

1. Insert your flash (also called a thumb or jump drive).

2. As soon as you insert it, you will notice a new icon located on your task bar in the lower right hand corner of your screen, which allows you to safely remove the flash drive when you have completed using it.

3. If you do not have *Windows Explorer* open, right-click the start button and click explore to open it.

4. Select **Computer** in the left window and you will see the drives available (your screen will not look exactly as the one in this exercise since your computer may have different drives, such as network drives, available).

As soon as the flash drive is available, then proceed with creating a new folder as described below.

Flash Drive

Create a New Folder

1. Double-click the Flash drive icon in the right window pane. If your flash drive is new, there may be some files that you do not recognize from the manufacturer or there may be no folders or files visible in the right contents pane.

2. Right-click in the white area of the right contents pane.

3. Move your cursor to the **New** command.

4. Click **Folder** [Folder]

5. Type your **First Name** in the highlighted **New Folder** area.

If you decide that you want a different name for your folder or file, you can easily rename it in *Windows Explorer*.

Rename a Folder

1. Click the folder that you just created and labeled as your first name.

2. Right-click the folder.

3. Click **Rename**.

4. Now type your **Last Name** in the selected area.

Now that you have a folder for your class work, create appropriate subfolders to save your work.

Create Subfolders

1. Double-click your **Last Name** folder.

2. Right-click in the white area of the right contents pane.

3. Select **New**.

4. Click **Folder**.

5. Type **Word Processing** in the new folder name box.

Repeat the directions located below to make seven additional subfolders for your work files. Use the following titles for your subfolders: **Graphics, Audio, Newsletter, Spreadsheets, Presentations, Internet and Teaching Resources.**

1. Right-click in the white area of the right contents pane.

2. Select **New**.

3. Click **Folder**

4. Type in the title

Make sure that folder titles are spelled correctly; if you make an error, use the Rename command to correctly name the folder. Effective file management procedures sometimes require the need to delete files or folders that are no longer necessary. After reviewing the eight folders you created today, you decide that you really don't need a **Newsletter** folder.

Delete Folders or Files

1. Select the **Newsletter** folder (this can be done in either pane).
2. Press the **Delete** key on your keyboard or right-click and choose delete.
3. Click **Yes**.

Remember, when you delete a folder, you are deleting all of the contents. As you work through this book, you will want to add appropriate folders and subfolders within each of the seven folders you have created.

Commands available to users in the Edit option on the menu bar include the ability to **Cut**, **Copy** and **Paste** as well as **Undo**. As with the File menu, some of the most common commands are available with a right-click of your mouse. When you want another copy of a file or folder, you use the Copy command. For this part of the exercise, you will copy your **Last Name** folder and place it in your **Documents** folder (if you are working on your home computer or have permission to copy to the Documents folder on your class lab computer) or copy it to another directory (such as your class lab directory). The exercise below directs you to save to the **Documents** folder, but you can use the same procedure to copy to any directory simply by substituting **Documents** with the appropriate directory.

Copy A Folder or File

1. Select your **Last Name** folder on the flash drive (either pane).

2. With your cursor in the highlighted area, click the right mouse button.

3. Click **Copy**.

4. Select the **Documents** folder in the left folder pane.

5. Click the right mouse button and click **Paste**.

You now have a copy of your **Last Name** folder and subfolders located on your flash drive and the hard drive of your computer in the **Documents** area.

 File Management Tips

✓ It is always a good idea to make backup copies of your work. You can easily paste a copy of the folder on another storage medium.

✓ You can also easily move folders and files to other locations with the **Cut** command. You simply select **Cut** instead of **Copy** and then follow the procedure outlined above to move a folder or file to a different location.

✓ Another common command available through the Edit option on the menu bar is the **Select All** command, which allows you to select all the files or folders in any given folder or drive.

✓ If you are copying or moving all of the files/folders, this speeds up the copying and moving process. If you want to select some, but not all of the folder/files, hold down the Control Key on the keyboard as you select each individual item.

✓ If the folders or files you wish to select are located adjacent to each other, then you can select by clicking on the first file or folder you want to select, hold down the Shift Key and then select the last file or folder in the adjacent group.

Copy vs. Move Using Drag and Drop

In the *Windows* environment it is possible to move files by simply clicking on them and dragging them to a new location. This action is better known as **drag and drop**. When you are moving a file(s) from one location on a drive to another location on the same drive, the file(s) will simply move. This means they will no longer be available in the original location after the drop has been completed (the mouse button released). However, if you are dragging the file(s) from a location on one drive to a location on a different drive, the items will copy. This will leave the file(s) in the original location as well as place a copy in the new location.

Using Keyboard Shortcuts

In the *Windows* environment it is possible to move files by simply clicking on them and dragging them to a new location. This action is better known as **drag and drop**. When you are moving a file(s) from one location on a drive to another location on the same drive, the file(s) will simply move. This means they will no longer be available in the original location after the drop has been completed (the mouse button released). However, if you are dragging the file(s) from a location on one drive to a location on a different drive, the items will copy. This will leave the file(s) in the original location as well as place a copy in the new location.

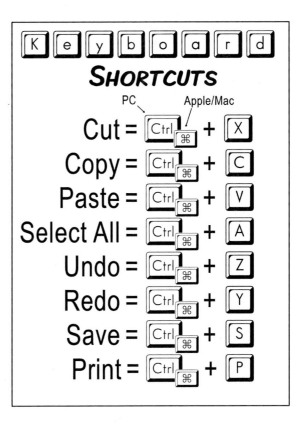

Shortcuts

A feature that facilitates navigation to frequently used files, folders, and programs is the shortcut. Since you will be accessing your **Last Name** folder often, you will want to create a shortcut to that folder on the desktop so that you simply click the shortcut icon and go directly to the folder. Because you want the shortcut to appear on the desktop, make sure that you have the Desktop selected in the left folder pane for the following exercise.

Create a Shortcut

1. Select **Desktop** in the left folder pane.

2. Right-click in the white area of the right contents pane.

3. Select **New**.

4. Click **Shortcut** .

5. Click **Browse** to locate your **Last Name** folder in documents.

6. Select your folder.

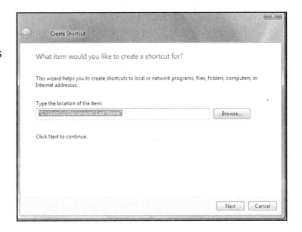

7. Click **Next**.

8. Keep the name for your shortcut and click **Finish**.

9. You will now see a shortcut to your **Last Name** folder on your desktop.

Remember, any of the commands covered in the **File** menu can be accessed through the menu bar as well as with a right-click of a mouse in the context appropriate area.

Other Features of Windows Explorer (Vista)

Other features are available in *Windows Explorer* that facilitate organizing, viewing and searching files and folders. Simply clicking on the Organize button 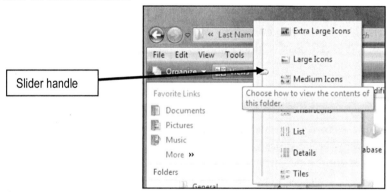 provides a number of options including commands to cut, copy and paste. Also available is the ability to change screen layout and folder options.

When you click the Views button, you are presented with viewing options that become visible as you run the slider over the option. Run the slider handle over each of the options and get a **Live Preview** of each selection.

Notice that while all options display the files and folders available, some choices give more information. Explore some of the folders and files available on your computer. Use the **Details** View to determine the most comprehensive information about your files. This view provides the name, size, type, and date modified. *Windows Explorer* indicates a file type by a distinguishing icon and provides a text description of the file.

Files are also identified by the **file extension**. The list below gives the extensions for *Microsoft Office 2007* files, two graphic files, and compressed files or folders:

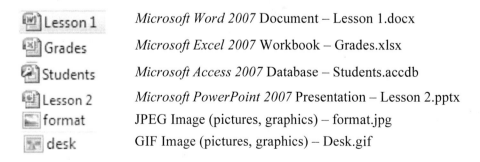

Microsoft Word 2007 Document – Lesson 1.docx

Microsoft Excel 2007 Workbook – Grades.xlsx

Microsoft Access 2007 Database – Students.accdb

Microsoft PowerPoint 2007 Presentation – Lesson 2.pptx

JPEG Image (pictures, graphics) – format.jpg

GIF Image (pictures, graphics) – Desk.gif

Compressed file or folder (common extension is .zip)

File extensions not only tell us what program can open the file, but they can also tell us something about the file itself. By knowing the file extension we know the contents of the file (text, sound, picture) and may even know the relative size. Now that you can distinguish among the types of files on your computer, you can also arrange and sort them.

Arranging Files and Folders

1. Right-click in the white area of the right content pane.

2. Select **Sort By**.

3. Click **Size**.

Your files are now arranged by size with the smallest file at the top of the list. Examine each of the arrangement orders to determine the one most suitable for the task at hand.

Remove a Flash Drive

1. Click the **Safe to Remove** icon at the lower left hand corner of your task bar.

2. Click the **Safely Remove Hardware** message to see if you can now remove the flash drive.

3. Remove the flash drive when you receive the message that is it safe.

Searching for Files and Folders

You can be sure that there will be times when your students will not be able to locate their work. Teaching them how to use the search function will enable them to locate their assignments and then save them in the appropriate folder.

Search – Type item here

1. Click in the **Search** box at the top of the *Windows Explorer* screen.

2. To locate a file, type in a word or a phrase from that file.

3. If you did not find the file for which you were searching, you can go to **Advanced Search** and further refine your search.

4. If you are looking for a specific file type, such as looking for all of the presentations you have created, then you would need to type in the file extension in the search bar and you will be presented with all the files that match that search criteria.

Compressing and Opening Compressed Files

You will experience working with compressed (zip extension) files in some of the exercises in this textbook. For instance, you will be asked to locate a compressed file on our companion website, download it to your computer, and then open (or unzip) that file/folder. Windows XP and newer and Mac OS X operating systems both include easy ways to compress and also open compressed files.

Compressing a file makes it smaller. A compressed file can contain just one file, a number of files, files and folders, just about any combination you can think of. By compressing files, you can put several files and folders into one file. You should always think of file size when you are sending attachments by email, for instance. Sometimes compressing a file will save your recipient time in downloading your file. You might want to compress a file or folder to send multiple files and folders in one compressed package.

> **How to right-click with Mac OS X:**
>
> You can adjust your mouse settings to allow it to right-click (System Preferences>Keyboard & Mouse) or use Apple Command + Click.
>
> On a laptop, you can use a simple "two-finger tap" in place of a right click (System Preferences> Keyboard & Mouse).

1. To **compress** a file or folder, simply select the item and right-click. Scroll down to **Send to** and then **Compressed (zipped) Folder**. Another file will appear in the same folder location, with the extension of **zip**. You have created a compressed file, which you can send to others.

2. To **open** a zip file is easy with newer operating systems (Windows XP and newer) and Mac OS X. Simply double-click the file to open it and the contents will be displayed. If you want, you can discard the original zip file, since you now have the contents of that zip file.

Summary

This technology skills section has presented an overview of the most common functions associated with effective file management. Learning to successfully navigate among windows and use the many Windows operating system features will improve your productivity and your students' performance. The necessity of introducing file management operations as early as possible in the school year cannot be over-emphasized. Your students will need direction and practice in organizing and managing their assignments on the computer.

Next you will have the opportunity to practice various file management skills and produce an artifact that demonstrates your competency in ISTE NETS-T Standard 3.

File Management Exercises

Exercise 1: Exploring File Properties

In this practice exercise, you will learn how to locate and identify files and be able to determine file properties including file size and location. You will discover how easy it is to determine when a file was created and modified, add archiving and indexing information, and discover how to compress or encrypt a file.

✓ **Right-click** the **Start** button  at the bottom of the window and click **Explore** to open *Windows Explorer.*

For the first part of this exercise, you will be locating files on your computer by the type of file.

Locating Files by Type

1. Click the Search box at the top of the Explorer window.

2. Type **.docx** Searching **D**ocuments

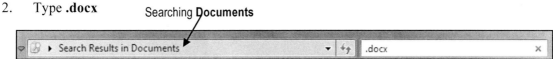

3. All of the docx (Word 2007 and above documents) that are located in your Documents on your computer are displayed.

4. Click your flash drive directory, and then redo the search for .docx or other files such as .doc (*Word 2003* extension).

Exploring File Properties

1. Select any file and right-click.

2. Click **Properties.**   Properties

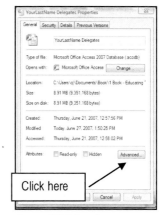

The Properties menu opens with the **General tab** visible.

The **Properties** menu displayed on this example describes an Access 2007 file created at 12:57:56 PM on June 21, 2007 and last modified at 12:58:02 PM on June 27, 2007.

The location of the file is provided (C: drive) and neither the **Read-only** or **Hidden** boxes are checked in this example.

If the **Read-only** box is checked on the file on your screen, then the author selected this attribute to specify that the file is read-only and it cannot be changed or accidentally deleted.

If you check the **Hidden** box, then the file will be hidden and no one could see or use it unless (s)he knew its specific name.

The **Advanced** button 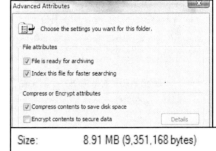 allows you to set attributes for archiving, indexing, compression or encryption.

The default options have the file ready for archiving and indexed for fast searching. Typically, you will want to keep the default options.

If you choose to compress your files, you need only click the **Compress contents to save disk space** option and then click **OK**.

By selecting this option, the file now requires only 112 KB of space on disk.

(*Note*: You will need to close out of the Properties menu and then select and view the properties of the file to view the change in file size.)

Encrypting a file can be done by selecting the **Encrypt contents to secure data** option.

Encryption is the conversion of data into a form that cannot be easily understood by unauthorized people. *Decryption* is the process of converting encrypted data back into their original form, so it can be understood. If you choose to encrypt a file, it is recommended you encrypt the whole folder in which the file is located. Encryption is transparent to the user who encrypted the file. This means that you do not have to manually decrypt the encrypted file before you can use it. You can open and change the file as you normally do. However, be aware that an encrypted file or folder cannot be compressed.

Exercise 2: Identifying File Properties

This exercise will help you identify file properties.

1. Download and open the **Exercise2 Worksheet** and the **File Management Exercise 2 Files.zip** files located in the Textbook Data Files on the textbook companion website http://dats.boisestate.edu

2. To open a zip file (compressed folder) you will need to double-click the file. Once you open the compressed folder, you will be able to view its contents, which can contain folders and other files. Current Windows and Mac OS X operating systems include built-in support for opening zip files.

3. Record the following information for each of the 4 files you find in the **File Management Exercise 2 Files** folder (answers may vary based on computer settings and file location).

	File 1	File 2	File 3	File 4
Name of File				
Type of File				
Location				
Size				
Created				
Modified				
Last Opened				
Read-only (yes/no)				

| Exercise 3: Organizing Files and Folders |

If you have not saved your files in appropriate folders as you created them, it becomes increasingly difficult to locate a particular file. In this exercise, you will organize files into appropriate folders and subfolders for easy retrieval. To complete the exercise, you will need to access our companion website, http://dats.boisestate.edu and click the Textbook Data Files link. Many of these files contain additional information you can use in your resources list and other research.

1. Click the link to **File Management Exercise 3.zip** on our http://dats.boisestate.edu/files link and download the file to your computer.

2. Double-click the **File Management Exercise 3.zip** file to open and display the contents. (It will be a folder called **File Management Exercise 3**).

3. Depending upon your operating system, either drag the folder to your flash drive or other location, or right-click and copy the folder and then navigate to the target folder and right-click and paste. (Also, remember your keyboard shortcuts, **Apple Command + C** for copy and Apple **Command + V** for paste.)

4. Once the copy of the **File Management Exercise 3** folder is in an appropriate location, rename it as, **YourLastName File Management Exercise 3**.

There are 18 standards-related *Word* document/PDF files located in the **YourLastName File Management Exercise 3** folder. Your task is to organize the files by creating new folders and subfolders. Next, you will copy and move files to their appropriate folder(s).

Complete the following steps:

1. Move (cut) the **ISTE NETS** file into a folder named, **Standard 1**.

2. Move (cut) the **Assistive Technology** file into a folder named, **Standard 4**.

3. Move the **Lesson Plans** and **Technology Teaching Strategies** file into a folder named, **Standard 3.**

4. Move the **Course Management Systems** and **Learning Environments** files into the **Standard 2** folder.

5. Move the **Professional Development** and **Life-long Learning** files into a folder named, **Standard 5.**

6. Copy the following files into a folder titled, **Standard 4.**

   - **Digital Divide**
   - **Cyber Bullying**
   - **Firewalls**
   - **Acceptable Use Policies**

7. Move the **Assessment, Student Information Systems,** and **Rubric Generator** files into a folder named, **Standard 2**

8.   Move the **Digital Natives** file and the **Technology Benefits** file into the **Standard 1** folder.

9.   Move the **Workforce Technology Skills** file into the **Standard 3** folder.

10. Since you copied the **Digital Divide, Cyber Bullying, Firewalls,** and **Acceptable Use Policies files**, they are located in the **Standard 4** folder and in YourLastName File Management folder.

11. Move the original **Digital Divide, Cyber Bullying, Firewalls,** and **Acceptable Use Policies** files (the ones located within **YourLastName File Management folder**) into a folder named **Ethical Issues.**

12. Take a look at the structure of your files and folders and compare it with a classmate's if possible.

Exercise 4: Teaching File Management

ISTE NETS-T Standard 3

This exercise provides an opportunity for you to plan a strategy for teaching file management to your students.

✓   Create a new page on your Technology Teaching Portfolio (name it "Teaching File Management") and write directly to that page.

✓   Be specific and describe in detail how you might introduce the concept of file management and how you would approach teaching proper file management strategies. Include the following components:

1.   Class Grade Level (grade level of the class to whom you will be teaching the exercise)

2.   Subject Area (if you are a secondary teacher)

3.   Rationale for lesson (why would you teach these students about file management)

4.   Description of the process you will use – directions you might give your students to assist them in proper file management

*Could be used as an artifact for Standard 3.

This chapter focuses on how teachers design and develop Digital Age learning experiences using technology. ISTE NETS-T Standard 2 encourages teachers to design and develop authentic learning experiences to "maximize content learning in context and to develop the knowledge, skills, and attitudes identified in the NETS-S" (ISTE, 2008). According to NETS-T Standard 2, teachers are to "design or adapt relevant learning experiences that incorporate digital tools and resources to promote student learning and creativity." This can be accomplished in many ways, but one very effective way is to include collaborative activities, which provide easy access for students to view each other's work.

Standard 2 also includes the requirements that teachers "develop technology-enriched learning environments that enable all students to pursue their individual curiosities and become active participants in setting their own educational goals, managing learning, and assessing their progress." In this chapter you will learn about and investigate assistive technologies and how they can be used to provide all learners with the opportunity to participate in activities in their homes, schools, work environments, and communities.

You will need to know various strategies for teaching in a traditional classroom versus an online classroom, as well as cooperative learning and cooperative tools. Included in this chapter are ways teachers can apply technology to support students' multiple intelligences and to effectively manage student learning in a technology-enhanced environment. You will also practice and develop your skills in word processing applications, both computer-based and online, and apply them to effective uses in the classroom, creating useful artifacts for your Technology Teaching Portfolio.

The Learning Environment

A comprehensive definition of what constitutes a learning environment includes not only the physical classroom characteristics but the virtual learning setting as well. In fact, the learning environment is affected by not only those elements in the classroom but by communication with parents and interaction in and beyond the classroom. Teachers are expected to use a variety of communication techniques to foster inquiry, collaboration, and supportive interaction.

In designing the optimum learning environment, whether online or in a traditional classroom, teachers must take into account the individual needs of their students and provide appropriate accommodations for those with special needs. Although integrating technology enhances instruction, it also presents challenges of which teachers need to be aware.

Planning for technology-enhanced lessons requires that the teacher manage student use of computers as well as have an alternate plan if technical problems occur. For an environment to enhance the teaching/learning process successfully, teachers must be proactive in supporting instruction, managing student learning, and communicating with parents.

Classroom Management – Traditional Classroom

In the best of worlds, every classroom would have enough computers for every student but this is the exception, not the rule. In fact, you may only have one computer in your classroom and may be faced with the seemingly overwhelming task of integrating technology into instruction. What are some management strategies that may help in planning computer use for your students? Listed next are suggestions for incorporating technology-enhanced lessons in a one-computer classroom:

- Make sure the computer is in an easily accessible place, one where you can supervise that area while working with other students in the classroom.
- Use the learning centers approach where students move from one center to another in a scheduled manner.
- Devise a system that makes a computer use schedule clear to students.
- Use an LCD projector or a computer to TV connector (these are relatively inexpensive) to project the screen for all students to see.
- Limit use of the computer by one student by encouraging the printing of articles so that the student can return to his/her desk to read through material.
- Instruct students to plan and/or outline papers or presentations by hand before coming to the computer so that their computer time is more effectively used.
- Employ cooperative learning strategies so that more than one student is using the computer at a time.

A one-computer classroom is not ideal, but by advance planning and organization, students can use technology. Additionally, most schools have computer labs or access to a mobile computer carts allowing computers to be brought to your classroom. This, too, requires advanced planning, as you will need to schedule computer time with other teachers in the school. Be aware that there are grant opportunities available to acquire computers for your classroom, and that many teachers have been successful at obtaining four to five computers which greatly expands the possibilities for integrating technology.

Classroom Management – Online

For a number of reasons, many students and parents prefer online learning to the traditional classroom resulting in a tremendous growth of online classes and schools. Establishing an effective "virtual" learning environment requires very structured organization and planning. Course management systems, such as Blackboard, Moodle, Sakai, and others are commonly used to facilitate the online learning environment and/or as a supplement to the traditional classroom.

Course management systems are structured, online systems that enable teachers to provide course materials online as well as a means of communicating with students through discussion boards and other features. Additionally, the assessment features in a course management system track student progress and enable instructors to give quizzes and tests online.

Teachers who have access to a course management system report that it is an effective way to support students' learning. Students, and their parents, over the Internet can access class materials online and monitor student performance.

Classroom Management

How to Thrive—Not Just Survive in a One-Computer Classroom
http://www.educationworld.com/a_tech/tech/tech092.shtml

Ideas for the One Computer Classroom
http://webtech.kennesaw.edu/jcheek3/onecomputer.htm

Tip Sheet: Classroom Management
http://www.lburkhart.com/elem/tip4.htm

Outside the Walls: Bringing the K-12 Classroom Online
http://www.techlearning.com/story/showArticle.php?articleID=177100343

A National Primer on K-12 Online Learning (PDF format)
http://www.nacol.org/docs/national_report.pdf

K-12 Online Instruction for Teaching and Learning
http://www.netc.org/digitalbridges/online/essentials/

Assistive Technology

In planning the optimum learning environment for those students with disabilities, schools are required by the Americans with Disabilities Act (ADA), the Individuals with Disabilities Education Act (IDEA), and the Assistive Technology Act to make provisions for students with disabilities by providing assistive technology. A comprehensive definition of the term (Partner's Resource Network, 2008) is as follows:

> Assistive Technology is technology designed to be utilized in an assistive technology device or assistive technology service. An assistive technology device is any item, piece of equipment, or product system, whether acquired commercially, modified, or customized, that is used to increase, maintain, or improve functional capabilities of individuals with disabilities. Examples include: Braille readers, motorized wheelchairs, and specialized keyboards.

It is essential that you have an understanding of the legislation and tools for providing assistance in the classroom. Following are some links that provide more information:

Assistive Technology

Assistive Technology, University of Washington
http://www.washington.edu/accessit/articles?109

Types of Assistive Technology Products
http://www.microsoft.com/enable/at/types.aspx

Assistive Technology to Meet K–12 Student Needs
http://www.ncrel.org/sdrs/areas/issues/methods/technlgy/te7assist.htm

Section 508
http://www.section508.gov

Center for Applied Special Technology (CAST)
http://www.cast.org

Parent-Teacher Communication

To ensure a positive learning environment, there must be effective communication between teachers and parents. Research studies consistently reveal that high student achievement and self-esteem are closely related to positive parental participation in education. Parents and schools need to work together so all children can succeed in school. Parents are their children's first and most important teachers. But even though studies show that most parents want to be involved in their children's education, they may not be exactly sure how to go about it, especially if they work during the school day. With technology, regular communication can be established.

The importance of communication with parents cannot be overstated. Parental involvement is a key factor in ensuring the success of children in the educational environment. The question is, "How can we as teachers facilitate parental communication/involvement through the use of technology?"

An easy way to enhance parent-teacher communication is through email. Teachers can easily contact parents through email to discuss their child's progress, invite collaboration in the students' education, and provide class highlights. Unfortunately, not all parents have Internet access so teachers must be proactive in reaching them through other means. A common mechanism is the class newsletter, which can be sent on a weekly, monthly, or semester basis. Although the newsletter would take a little time to create, with advanced planning, it could be designed as a class project with students composing much of the content using a word processing or desktop publishing program.

School and classroom websites improve communication by keeping parents informed of activities and events, posting assignments, and featuring student work. Parents are able to access these online sites for daily updates about their child's grades, attendance, and homework. They can easily obtain information without interrupting their workday to phone a teacher or attend a conference.

Parent-Teacher Communication

The Effects of a Teacher-Created Web Page on Parent Communication: An Action Research Study (PDF format)
http://chiron.valdosta.edu/are/vol1no2/PDF%20article%20manuscript/nelms.pdf

9 Techniques for Building Solid Parent-Teacher Relationships
http://www2.scholastic.com/browse/article.jsp?id=3748289

Cooperative & Collaborative Learning

A well-designed learning environment is one in which students are able to develop academic self-esteem and social skills. Cooperative learning is a strategy that has been shown to be effective in promoting student learning and academic achievement as well as in enhancing student satisfaction with the learning experience. Although there are a number of instructional models employing cooperative learning techniques, common conditions include the need for each group member's efforts to be required and necessary for the success of the group, on-going communication, and collaboration among members. One popular cooperative learning strategy developed by Elliot Aronson (2010) is called "Jigsaw." Information about this strategy and how to implement it in your classroom can be found at http://www.jigsaw.org.

Technology affords many opportunities to engage students in cooperative and collaborative learning that extend beyond the traditional walls of the classroom. With the Internet, students can collaborate with other students from around the world and/or with experts in every discipline area. Teachers can structure an organized, collaborative project on the Internet called a WebQuest. First invented by Bernie Dodge and Tom March (Dodge, 2007), a WebQuest is an inquiry-oriented, research activity using the Internet to locate information. Teachers design WebQuests to meet curricular goals, and of course, there are many examples of WebQuests on the Internet.

New social media technologies, the second generation of Internet-based services, have provided a multitude of programs that facilitate communicating, collaborating, creating and reflection. Weblogs and wikis in particular have become more popular as mechanisms for enhancing class communication and collaboration. Anyone with an Internet access has a profusion of online tools available that once were only available when installed on a computer. These tools make it possible to create documents, spreadsheets, databases and presentations. Additionally, it is possible to store and share files online. On the surface, these tools provide access to students to complete assignments that require specific applications, but the added ability to share makes it possible for students to collaborate on projects – actually sharing files and editing them.

A more complete discussion of social media technologies is presented in Chapter 5 of the text with ideas for incorporating these technologies as teaching strategies. The capability of these tools for extending the walls of the classroom and providing an e-learning workspace brings another dimension to teaching and learning. The web-enhanced environment provides a multitude of possibilities for student interaction and collaboration as well as a means of providing a web-enhanced instructional environment.

Cooperative & Collaborative Learning
WebQuests http://webquest.org Jigsaw Cooperative Learning http://wwwjigsaw.org

Summary

This chapter has provided background information on some of the major factors to consider when designing and planning learning environments. Next you will practice and develop word processing skills in desktop and other applications of your choice, creating useful artifacts for your Technology Teaching Portfolio.

References

Aronson, E. (2010). *Jigsaw Classroom*. Retrieved from http://www.jigsaw.org

Dodge, B. (2007). *Webquest.org*. Retrieved from http://webquest.org

ISTE. (2008). *NETS for Teachers*. Retrieved from http://www.iste.org/standards/nets-for-teachers/nets-for-teachers-2008.aspx

Partner's Resource Network. (2008). *Special Education Definitions*. Retrieved from http://www.partnerstx.org/SpecialEducation_Definitions.htm

Exercise 1: Jigsaw Classroom Activity
ISTE NETS-T Standard 2

✓   Research more about Jigsaw Cooperative Learning (http://www.jigsaw.org).
✓   Design a Jigsaw activity you might use in your future classroom.
✓   Include the following components, posting directly to a new page on your Technology Teaching Portfolio, named "Jigsaw Activity" (For an example, please visit http://edtech2.boisestate.edu/sabaa/502/jigsaw.html):

    1.   A description of Jigsaw
    2.   Jigsaw activity and instructions for students.

*Could be used as an artifact for Standard 2

This technology skills section on Windows 2007 word processing was adapted from *Educating Teachers* (2007) – Pollard, C., VanDehey, T., and Pollard, R.

One of the most common tasks students and teachers do on the computer is to create a "word processed" document. The powerful editing features available in a word processing program facilitate the writing process and help students modify and revise their documents with ease. However, some students frequently use word-processing much the same as a typewriter without ever discovering the capabilities of these powerful programs.

This technology skills section will help you discover the myriad possibilities word processing presents for teaching and learning opportunities. With *Microsoft Word 2007* you are able to produce basic documents of all kinds including letters, memos, reports and manuals. More than that, however, *Word* provides features that enable teachers and students to produce desktop publishing materials, web pages, and interactive worksheets.

 Word Processing with Microsoft Word 2011 for Mac (See Appendix E)

 ## Word Processing with Microsoft Word 2007 for Windows

When you open *Microsoft Word 2007*, a window displays with a new blank document on your screen. The window you see is standard for *Office 2007* applications featuring the **Ribbon**, a highly graphical way to use program features, standard tabs, contextual tabs, the *Microsoft Office* button and a quick access toolbar. Since word processing will be the tool that you use most often, it is important to become familiar with as many of the features as possible and be able to use them in other applications.

The open *Word* window displays a blank document with the *Office 2007* ribbon presenting a collection of tabs along the top of the window. The Home tab, which is selected when you open a document, contains a group of commands on the home ribbon that users of an application most often need. The Home ribbon in *Word 2007* displays the basic formatting and editing commands readily available to the user.

Microsoft Office Button   **Ribbon**

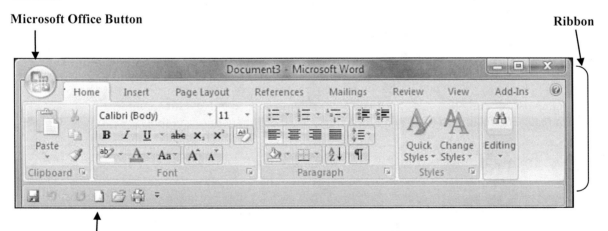

Quick Access Toolbar (Note: the toolbar can be set above or below the ribbon.)

Clicking the *Microsoft Office* button allows you to access the menu of commands you use to work with the total document including opening, saving and printing files.

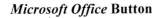
***Microsoft Office* Button**

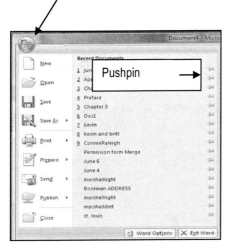

A list of recent documents is presented making it easy for you to return to your most recent projects. A pushpin icon appears next to the file names; you can set the pushpin if you want that file to remain in the recent documents list.

In addition to the basic commands to **open**, **save** and **close** a document, you are able to prepare (security and document permissions), send and publish documents. Using the **send** command, you can email or Internet fax a document. The **publish** command provides an option to publish your document as a blog.

By running your cursor over the commands with the arrow at the end of the button, you are provided with a dropdown list of options relevant to that command.

The **Save As** command is one of the most important commands you and your students need to access each time you start a document. Notice that by placing your cursor on this command, you are provided with several options for saving the document. You then select the format for saving the file; be sure to save the document as *Word 97-2003* if it is to be opened in an earlier version of *Office*.

By clicking any of the tabs at the top of the ribbon, you are presented with a functionally related set of commands. For example, click the **Insert** tab and you are presented with a number of common insert commands including inserting graphics, tables, word art, shapes and symbols.

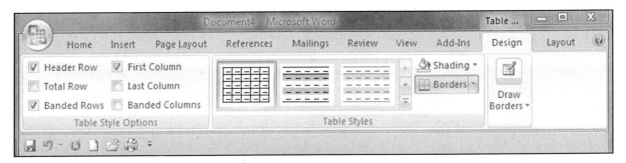

Contextual tabs appear on the ribbon when you select a specific command such as inserting tables. These tabs contain commands that relate specifically to the object with which you are working. These allow you to format your table including the table style, shadings and borders.

Microsoft Word 2007 also provides galleries, which are sets of thumbnail graphics that represent different formatting options. Given a set of these thumbnail graphics, you can run your mouse over each graphic and through the **Live Preview** feature actually see the formatting changes.

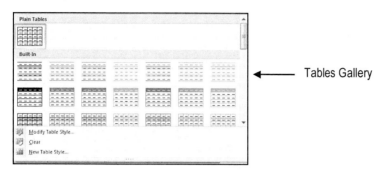 ← Tables Gallery

Although you are able to access all the commands you need through the *Microsoft Office* Button and the ribbon, you will want to create a custom **Quick Access Toolbar** for your most frequent commands. This is easily accomplished by a right-click of your mouse next to the Quick Access Toolbar, selecting the *Customize Quick Access Toolbar* option and then simply choosing those commands that you want to quickly access.

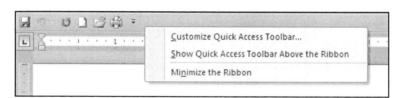

Another feature common across all of the *Microsoft Office 2007* applications is the status bar located at the bottom of the window. It contains more controls and information including a **Zoom** slider to adjust the magnification of a document and buttons for selecting how you view documents. You can also customize your status bar by right-clicking the bar and choosing options. Selecting the grammar and spelling option, for example, will display an error icon indicating possible spelling and/or grammar errors in the document.

Document Information   View Options

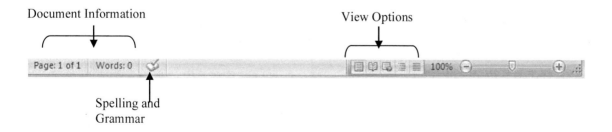

Spelling and Grammar

Now that you have had a brief overview of the main elements of *Microsoft Office 2007*, open *Word 2007* and take time to explore the commands available to you.

Starting Word

1. Click the **Start** button on the task bar in the lower left corner of your screen.

2. Move the mouse pointer to **All Programs** to display the submenu.

3. Click *Microsoft Office,* and then click the program you want to access, in this case, *Microsoft Office Word 2007*.

Viewing Options

Microsoft Word 2007 offers a number of ways for you to view your document each with specific features to facilitate your task. Views can be accessed by either clicking on one of the icons located on the status bar at the bottom of the window or by clicking on the **View** tab located at the top of the ribbon. Once selected, commands become available to you related to viewing options including the ability to view windows in multiple modes, show/hide elements on the screen, adjust the magnification of the document, and enable/disable macros (a series of commands that you group together as a single command to accomplish a task automatically).

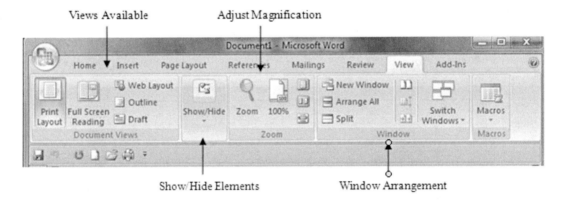

Layout Views

You would choose a layout view based on the document you are producing and on your own individual preferences. When you place your cursor over each of the viewing options, you are presented with a concise definition of the view.

✓   **Print Layout** - Work in print layout view to see how text, graphics, and other elements will be positioned on the printed page. You might choose to work in this view if your document makes use of headers and footers, columns and drawing objects.

✓   **Full Screen Reading** - Work in full screen reading view for typing and editing text. The layout is simplified so that you can type and edit quickly and easily.

✓   **Web Layout** – Work in web layout view to see how your page will look in a Web browser. In this view, you can see backgrounds and graphics as they will appear on a webpage.

✓   **Outline** – Work in outline view when you are working on a document (such as a book or a long report) and want to be able to easily organize by headings.

✓   **Draft** – This view may be preferred when you are working on a draft and want to quickly edit the text.

Viewing Modes

The Show/Hide tab provides options for viewing modes including the following:

- ✓ **Ruler**– This viewing mode is used to assist in measuring and lining up objects in your document.

- ✓ **Gridlines** – A viewing mode that is useful in lining up objects.

- ✓ **Document Map** – This viewing mode displays an outline of the document's headings in a vertical pane along the left edge of the document window. Use the document map to quickly move through documents.

- ✓ **Thumbnails** – This viewing mode displays small renderings of each page in your document displayed in a separate pane. Clicking on a thumbnail image allows you to jump directly to a page in a document. Thumbnails are available in normal, print layout, outline, and reading layout views.

Help Viewer

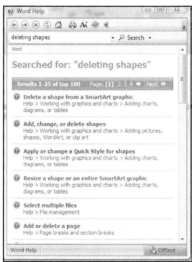

Another feature that will prove to be invaluable to you, and your students, is the **Help Viewer**. With the many commands available within the office applications, no one can be expected to know them all. The **Help Viewer** provides instant instructions on how to use any and all of the features.

A help icon featuring a question mark surrounded by a circle is located in the far right hand corner of the ribbon. Clicking on the help icon takes you directly to the *Microsoft* Help Viewer making it easy for you and your students to find an immediate answer to queries.

Using Microsoft Office Help Viewer

1. Click the help icon and type **deleting shapes** in the help box.

2. Hit **Enter** or click the **Search** button.

3. The results of the search are displayed with hyperlinks to pertinent information. Notice that there are a total of 100 pages of search results available, all dealing with some facet of working with shapes. Typically, the most useful results are listed on the first pages, but you may want to scroll through the pages to locate the most appropriate information for your question or to expand on the topic.

Remember, when your students ask how to delete a shape or to perform any other word processing commands, you can simply direct them to the **Help Viewer**. In this way, they will become more independent computer users (and your time can be used to assist with the content of the assignment, not the program commands).

Saving Documents

With a blank document on your *Word* screen, you are ready to begin a word processing document. Each time you start a document (or spreadsheet or other application, etc.) you should save it as soon as possible, making sure that you save it in the right directory and folder. This is called a **Save As** command and it is one of the most important operations for you (and your students) to perform. Beginning your word processing document by saving it in a specific folder is simply a good file management procedure. It will ensure that the document will be easily located at a later time.

The first document you will prepare is a parent newsletter so you begin by saving the document on the drive of your choice (if you are working at home, you will probably save in Documents on your hard drive; if you are working in a lab, you will want to save on whatever storage device you are currently using).

Save As

1. Click the *Microsoft Office* button [ ].

2. Click **Save As** [Save As ▶].

You now need to choose the file format for the saved file. If you do not make a choice, the default is *Word 2007*. That means that the file will be saved as a *Word 2007* file and can easily be opened in *Word 2007;* however, there may be compatibility issues with earlier versions of *Word* and other word processing programs. For most users of this text, saving the document in the Word 2007 format (the default) will be the chosen option.

Once you have decided on the format in which to save your document, then make sure that you are saving it in the right location. If you do not choose a location, then your document would be saved with the title of Doc1 in the Documents directory on the hard drive of the computer you are currently using. As you want to be able to easily locate this in the future, you decide the drive, folder and subfolder in which to save the Parent Newsletter document.

1. Click your chosen file format and hit enter. The **Save As** window becomes available.

2. Create a new folder by clicking on the **New Folder** icon [New Folder].
3. Name the New Folder, **Word Processing Exercises**. You can save all of your word processing exercises from this book in your folder.

4. Click in the **File name** box, and type **YourLastName Parent Newsletter**.
5. Click [Save] in the lower right hand corner.

Now you can save frequently by clicking on the save icon [ ] on the Quick Access bar and know exactly where your document is located. Also note that the title of your document, **YourLastName Parent Newsletter**, is now displayed in the *Word* title bar.

Parent Newsletter: Planning Your Document

Your next decision involves the actual physical layout of the document. The newsletter you will create will look similar to the one below. You will use the **Page Layout** command tab located on the ribbon to set the size of your document's margins and the physical orientation. Selecting the Page Layout command provides you with themes, page setup options, backgrounds and borders as well as indentation and spacing options.

Page Layout Commands

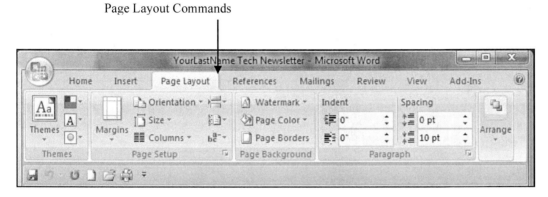

Page Layout

1. Click the **Page Layout** tab located at the top of the ribbon.

2. Click the **Margins** command. A dropdown box appears giving some of the more common choices for margins including the default margin of 1 inch margins as well as an option for setting custom margins.

3. Click the **Narrow** margins option

Narrow		
Top:	0.5"	Bottom: 0.5"
Left:	0.5"	Right: 0.5"

4. This will give you more text and graphics area and less white space in the margins.

5. Click the **Orientation** command. There are two choices, portrait and landscape. The default orientation, portrait is already chosen and is an appropriate orientation for your newsletter

In determining the layout of the newsletter, you decide to add a page border.

Creating a Page Border

Page Border Tab

1. Click **Page Borders**
    [⬜ Page Borders] on the ribbon.

2. Click the **Page Border** tab.

3. **Click** the **Box** setting.

4. Click the down arrow on the **Width** and select **3 pt**.

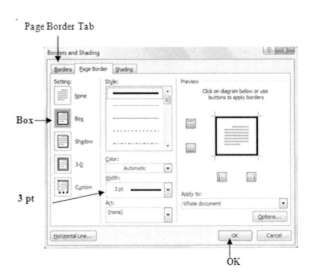

5.   Click **OK**.

With your margins and border set and your document saved, you begin your parent newsletter by using some of the features of the Insert tab. Commands available to you include the ability to insert any form of graphic, hyperlinks within the document and to the Internet, as well as headers, footers, and tables.

The first graphic you will insert in your newsletter is WordArt to write the title. Since you want your title to be located within the top two inches of your document, hit the enter key 8 times and you will see your cursor's location on the *Word* status bar.

Inserting WordArt

1.   Click **WordArt** command [WordArt] on the insert ribbon.

2.   Choose a design from the WordArt Gallery by clicking on your choice.

If you want to use the style shown in the example, click this choice.

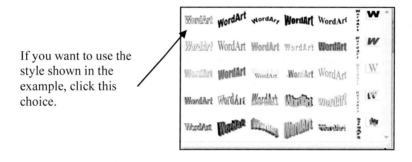

The **Edit WordArt** Text screen appears and you can change the font type and style now or you can always return to the WordArt Tools ribbon and change it later.

3.   Enter the title of the newsletter: **Standards Update**.

4.   Click **OK**.

Now that you have selected WordArt, you are presented with contextualized tabs that contain commands relating specifically to WordArt. These tools will allow you to actually see the changes you make to your word art through a feature called **Live Preview**. Your editing options include the ability to edit the text, change the style, color, font, size and other effects of your word art title.

WordArt Tools   Styles   Position

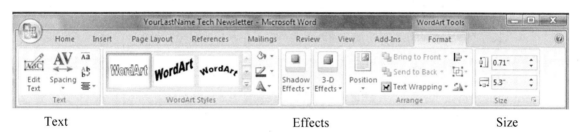

Text   Effects   Size

Make sure that you still have your Standards Update graphic selected and try out the **Live Preview** feature.

1. Click each of the styles in the **WordArt Styles** gallery and visually see your title as it appears in each of the styles. Choose the one you think looks the best

2. Click the **shadow** and **3-D** effects. Decide if you want to use one of these effects for your newsletter title.

3. Click the **Position** icon located on the ribbon. The default for your WordArt graphic is **In Line with Text**. In essence the graphic is treated as text would be treated and moving a graphic formatted in line with text could be done in the same way that you move text on a page. Typically, however, you want to be able to move the graphic freely anywhere on the page.

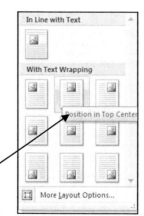

4. Select the **Position in Top Center** option you see chosen in the example since this is where your title will go.

Notice that your Standards Update graphic now has handles as the one does below. These make it easy for you to rotate or resize your graphic. Additionally, you can easily position the graphic on the page.

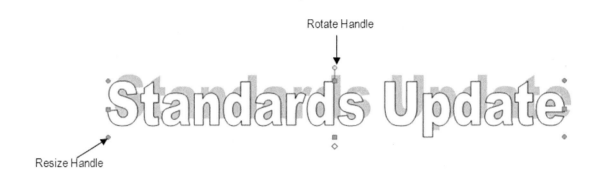

Rotate Handle

Resize Handle

Your newsletter will be more visually appealing when you add other graphics such as pictures, text boxes and shapes. You will again be choosing a command from the **Insert** ribbon.

Inserting Clip Art

1. Click the **Clip Art** icon on the Insert ribbon.

2. The clip art task pane opens.

3. In the **Search for** box, type **school**

4. Click the down arrow at the end of the **Search in** box. Make sure that **Everywhere** is checked (All collections will now be listed).

5. Click in the **Results should be** box and select **Clip Art** and **Photographs** to limit your search. (Selecting the **All media file types** option will result in searching all the files available including movies and sounds.)

6. Click the **Go** button.

A variety of pictures are presented in the task pane. Position your cursor over the one you want to insert and notice that a bar with a down arrow appears.

7. Right-click the bar located at the right of the picture, and click **Insert**. (Clicking on the picture will also insert it.)

8. To close the Insert ClipArt task pane, click the in the upper right corner of the pane.

Once you have inserted, the graphic, the **Picture Tools** ribbon containing commands related to the use of pictures becomes available. These tools allow you to easily adjust, size, arrange and apply styles and effects to your clipart.

Picture Tools

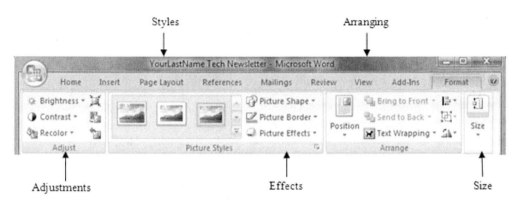

Positioning Pictures/Graphics

1. Make sure your graphic is selected and the picture tools are available..

2. Click the **Text Wrapping** icon on the ribbon. [Text Wrapping ▾]

3. Click the **Tight** option so that you can move the graphic close to the text.

Once the graphic is formatted, it is easier to manipulate by dragging on the handles to resize and holding down the left mouse button and moving it around the page.

Next, you will add a horizontal line to separate the title from the rest of the page.

Inserting Lines

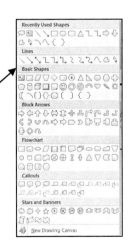

1. Click the **Shapes** icon [Shapes ▾] on the Insert ribbon.

2. Select the first line on the left under the **Lines** heading.

3. Move your cursor to the location on the page where you want your line to begin.

4. Notice that your cursor now looks like two crossed lines +

5. Click the spot where you want your line to begin.

6. Hold down the left mouse button as you move your cursor across the page to the other border.

7. Release the left mouse button when your line is positioned as you want it to be.

If your line is not where you want it to be or if it is sized incorrectly, select it and move it by holding down the left mouse button and/or position your cursor on the end and move the line.

Notice that once your line was placed in the document, the **Drawing Tools** ribbon became available. The command tabs located on this ribbon make it easy to insert shapes, apply styles and effects, and to arrange and size your shape. And, as always, you are provided with **Live Preview** to see the effect of the changes you make to your shape.

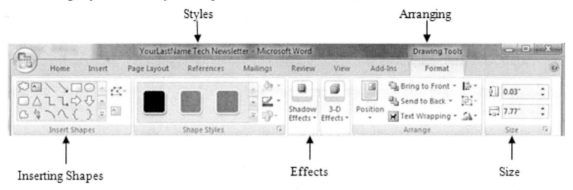

The horizontal line you just inserted is not thick enough so you will resize it.

1. Click the **Size** icon

2. Click the **Colors and Lines** tab.

3. Click the up arrow at the end of the **Weight** box and choose 1.5 pt.

4. Click **OK**.

Now that the banner for the parent newsletter is completed, you will type the text for the first article about the new ISTE National Education Technology standards for students. Type the text located in the box below; the text should go directly below the horizontal line you just inserted.

The International Society for Technology in Education (ISTE) has recently released the *National Education Technology Standards for Students* providing guidelines for student technology concepts and skills in a Digital Age. ISTE, a professional organization that has provided leadership in technology for over a decade, reports that, "As foundational ICT skills penetrate throughout our society, students will be expected to apply the basics in authentic, integrated ways to solve problems, complete projects, and creatively extend their abilities. *ISTE's National Educational Technology Standards for Students* help students preparing to work, live, and contribute to the social and civic fabric of their communities."

You will want to italicize the "*ISTE's National Educational Technology Standards for Students*" text. Applying formatting to text is easily accomplished by using the commands on the Home ribbon or simply with a right-click of the mouse.

Formatting Text

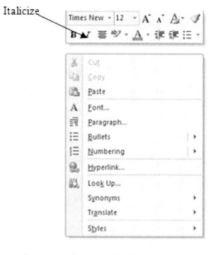

1. Select **Microsoft Office 2007** and right-click. A mini toolbar containing basic formatting options and common commands appear.

2. Click the **Italicize** [I] icon.

The mini toolbar makes it easy to apply formatting options and perform common word processing operations.

Formatting Commands

As you have already seen, most of the formatting commands can be accessed on the formatting mini toolbar; these commands, and a few others, are also available on the Home ribbon. These commands make it easy to change the **format**, the way the text looks on the page, by simply selecting text and then clicking on a formatting icon. There are numerous formatting features available including the ability to change the placement of the text and to add numbering/bullets and borders.

It is a common practice to type your word processing document and then apply formatting features to selected text. You can select text and graphics by holding down the left mouse button as you run the mouse over the desired text and/or objects. A word can be selected by double-clicking on the word; triple clicking within a paragraph allows you to quickly select the whole paragraph. You can even select items that aren't next to each other. For example, you can select a paragraph from one page of your document, hold down the control key and then select a paragraph on another page.

Keyboard Shortcuts you should know for quick formatting

Crtl+B (Bold)

Ctrl+I (Italics)

Ctrl+U (Underlined)

You will be using many of these features to enhance your newsletter. Your article title is, **National Education Technology Standards**. Type your title above the article (you may have to hit enter a few times at the top of your text). The article title should be a different font style and size to set it off from the article.

Changing Font Style and Size

1. Select the title you just entered, **National Education Technology Standards**.

2. Right-click in the selected area and the formatting mini toolbar will appear.

Font Size

Font

3. Select a font style (the example shows Cooper Black, but you can choose any style).

4. Click the down arrow at the end of the font size box.

5. Select a larger font size (this example will use a 20 font for the title). You may have to adjust the size of the font once you see how your title appears in the new font style.

Text Alignment

You have several choices for aligning your text: **left justification** (text aligned on the left side); **right justification** (text aligned on the right side); **full justification** (text aligned on both sides); and, **centered** (text centered). The title will be centered and the text of the article will be aligned on both sides. This time use the commands located on the Home ribbon to apply the alignment-formatting feature.

1. Select the title, **National Education Technology Standards**

2. Click the center icon on the Home ribbon.

3. Select the entire article (not the title).

4. Click the full justification icon on the Home ribbon.

Another formatting feature that will make your newsletter more attractive is the use of columns.

Creating Columns

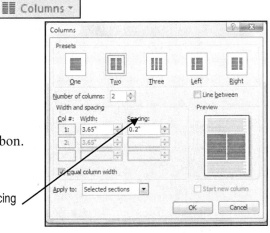

1. Select the article text (not the title).

2. Click **Page Layout** tab.

3. Click **Columns** in the **Page Setup** section of the ribbon.

4. Click **More Columns…**

5. Click **Two** at the top of the box.

Spacing

6. Click the down arrow at the end of the **Spacing** box until it is **0.2**

7. Click **OK**

Since you do not want the whole newsletter to be in a 2-column format, then you will need to insert a section break and set columns back to one.

Inserting Breaks

You can use section breaks to vary the layout of a document. You create a new section when you want to change such properties as line numbering, number of columns, or headers and footers. A section break is a mark inserted at the end of a section, which stores the formatting elements. Placing a section mark at the end of the National Education Technology Standards article will ensure that only the text within the section has two-column formatting.

1. Place your cursor at the end of the paragraph (communities).

2. Click the **Breaks** command ⌐Breaks ▾ on the **Page Layout** ribbon.

3. Select **Continuous** (this inserts a section break so that you can start the next section on the same page).

4. From the **Break** tab, you have the ability to apply page breaks, column breaks and text wrapping breaks as well. If you want to see where breaks are placed, you can use the

    Show/Hide button ¶ on the Home tab.

Clicking the button activates the feature and will disclose exactly where you have placed a section break in your document, which appears as below:

Now that you have set the section break, let's add a horizontal line below the article with a width of 1.5 pt. Your newsletter will look similar to the one below.

Add a horizontal line here.

The next article to place in your newsletter is a preview of the student technology standards. Type the title, "**Skills for a Digital Age**" in your choice of font and font size. Then type in the following article:

A national research study, "*Listening to Student Voices*," conducted by the Center for Policy Studies reports that today's students are frustrated with the lack of technology in the classroom. The tech-savvy generation that has grown up with technology is disappointed in traditional classroom instruction. The report recommends technology standards be a focus of K-12 instruction.

With the article already entered, you decide to add a text box and include a listing of the student technology standards for your readers.

1. Click the **Text Box** icon on the **Insert** ribbon.

2. Click **Simple Text Box** and immediately a textbox section appears on the page instructing you to use the Text Box Tools tab to change the text box.

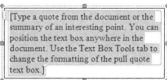

3. Click the **Text Wrapping** command located on the format tab (it becomes available when the text box is selected. Choose the **Tight** option

    ☒ | Tight

4. Try some of the styles, text, effects and arrangement options for your text box.

Now that you have formatted the text box, you can move it easily on the page and have the text wrap closely to the text box. Move your text box to the right of the Skills for a Digital Age article.

Inserting Symbols

Enter the title **Student Technology Standards** in the text box with a checkbox symbol at the end of the title (you may have to adjust your box to fit the text and symbol).

1. Click the **Insert** tab.

2. Click **Symbol** Ω Symbol ▾

3. Click More Symbols Ω | More Symbols...

4. Click the down arrow in the **Font** box and select **Wingdings**.

5. Scroll down and select the checked box symbol ☑.

6. Click **Insert.**

7. Click **Close.**

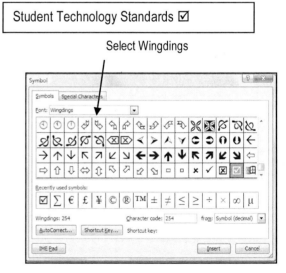

The Student Technology Standards text box will contain a listing of technology standards for students. You will create a bulleted list of the categories. A **bullet** is a dot or other symbol placed before to text to add emphasis. They are used when there is no specific sequence to the items. If order is important, a numbered list should be used in place of bullets.

Enter the following list in your text box (adjust the box borders as necessary):

Student Technology Standards ☑

✓ Creativity and Innovation
✓ Communication and Collaboration
✓ Research and Information Fluency
✓ Critical Thinking, Problem Solving, and Decision making
✓ Digital Citizenship
✓ Technology Operations and Concepts

Creating a Bulleted List

1. Select the list.

2. With the bulleted list selected, click the **Bullets** icon on the **Home** tab.

3. Click one of the bullets from the bullet library.

The list is now indented with bullets emphasizing each of the lines of text. Move the text closer to the left border of the textbox.

Hold down left mouse button and drag.

4. Click the first bullet.

5. When all the bullets appear highlighted, hold down the left mouse button and drag the bullets closer to the left border.

You can adjust the bulleted list and apply formatting features to enhance your text box. Now that you have completed your textbox, adjust the middle section of your newsletter so that the article title is well placed. Add a graphic to enhance the appearance of the article and add a horizontal line to separate this article from the last section of the newsletter.

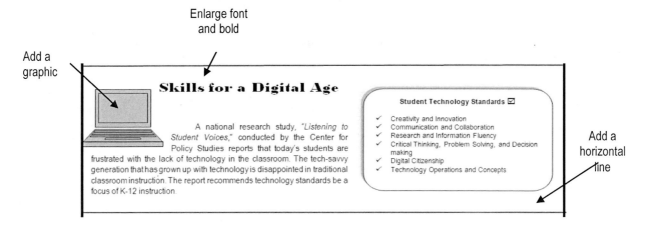

For the last section of your newsletter, you will write a request to the parents to volunteer their time in the after school technology program. To make scheduling easy, you supply a form for parents to complete and return to their child's school. Type the following text.

> Parents,
>
> We are asking for volunteers to help in the computer labs in our after school technology program. Please write your name in the "I Can Help" column for the day(s) for which you might be available this semester and send the form to your child's school.

Beneath the text you will create a form by inserting a table. Tables are an excellent means of organizing and presenting information. A table consists of rows and columns of cells that can be filled with text and/or graphics. Your newsletter table will contain three columns and five rows.

Creating a Table

1. Click **Table** on the **Insert** tab.

2. Click **Insert Table**

3. Enter **3** for the **Number of columns** and **5** for the **Number of rows**.

4. Click **OK**.

Designing a Table

With your table selected, click the **Design Tab**. This makes **Table Tools** available that affect design features including styles, shading and borders.

1. Click the different **Table Style Options** and see how the gallery of Table Styles changes. Pick a table style. (The example uses Banded Rows and Banded Columns).

2. Center the titles using the formatting mini toolbar (right-click).

3. Enter the information in each cell as shown below.

Place your cursor in the top row and enter the column titles. Use your tab key or arrow keys to move from cell to cell.

Column

School	Days/Times	I Can Help
East Elementary School	Mondays (3-5 pm)	
West Middle School	Tuesdays (3-5 pm)	
Central High School	Wednesdays (3-5 pm)	

Cell ⟶   ⟵ Row

Columns and rows can be resized by positioning your cursor on the edge of a column or row and dragging the border by holding down the left mouse button.

Merging the cells in the last row will provide an area large enough to include parent name and contact information.

Make sure your table is selected and then click the **Layout** tab. The table tools available on this tab allow you to merge cells, insert rows and columns, size cells and align text.

Layout Ribbon

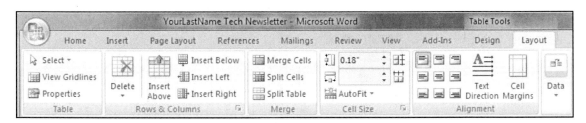

Merging Cells in a Table

1. Select the last row in your table (all three cells).

2. Click the **Layout** tab and select **Merge Cells** [Merge Cells].

Once the cells are merged, enter the following information:

| Name: _____ |
| Phone: _____ Email_____ |

Table borders can be adjusted and/or eliminated by selecting the table and then clicking the **Design** tab. Options include having borders at the top, bottom, outside, and inside as well as having no borders at all.

Printing

As school budgets are limited, it is always a good idea to discuss the school's printing policy with your students and make sure that they know how to print single pages of a multi-page document. Insuring that students view documents before printing will assist in this process as well. If you choose to print using the

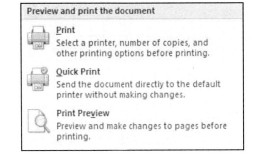

Quick Print icon 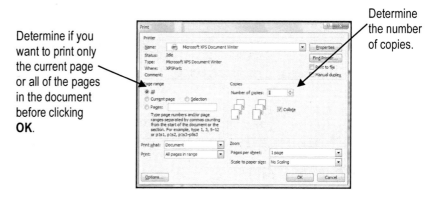 on the Quick Access toolbar, then the whole document will print. Knowing that many students will use that quick method of printing, you will need to direct them in when and how to use the Quick Print, Print and Print Preview commands.

Previewing and Printing Documents

1. Click the *Microsoft Office* button located at the top of the window.

2. Click **Print** [Print] and you are presented with three options shown to the right.

3. Select **Print Preview**. You are given an opportunity to change margins, view your document one page or more pages at a time.

4. Make any editing changes necessary before you print.

5. Click **Print**.

Determine if you want to print only the current page or all of the pages in the document before clicking **OK**.

Determine the number of copies.

You can also print just parts or pages of a document through the **Select** option. This will save paper, as this option will print the exact pages and/or sections instead of automatically printing an entire document.

Summary

This technology skills section has presented many of the features in *Microsoft Word 2007* that are most commonly used by teachers and students. Many of the word processing activities and exercises that follow can also be completed using Google Docs, a free, collaborative, online word processing program.

Complete details on how to use Google Docs are included in Appendix B.

Word Processing Exercises

The following practice exercises are provided to introduce you to other *Word* features and suggest ways in which they can be used for curricular purposes. You might try completing them in another application, such as *Microsoft Office 2011 for Mac*, *Google Docs*, or *OpenOffice* (http://www.openoffice.org) *Writer*.

Next, application exercises are provided for you to apply the skills you have learned to create useful artifacts for your Technology Teaching Portfolio.

Exercise 1: Using Word Features

✓ Always begin your document by saving it in the appropriate directory and folder.

✓ Title this document, **YourLastName Word Practice Exercise**. (*Microsoft Office* button, **Save As**)

✓ Keep your margins at the one-inch default setting. (**Page Layout, Page Setup, Margins**).

With your margins set and your document saved, you begin your word processing practice. Type the following words exactly as they appear:

Word Processing Practice
Here is my opportunity to practice the many functions available through word processing. By becoming adept in word processing, I can be a more productive teacher and better guide my students. Word processing skills that I will need to practice include: formatting, editing, and other useful skills.

Copying and Moving Text or Graphics

1. Select a line of text in the word processing practice paragraph you entered. (Click with your cursor at the beginning of the line and then click at the end of the line while holding the shift key down – this selection method works regardless of the amount of text that you want to select).

2. With your cursor in the highlighted area, click the right mouse button (right-click).

3. Click **Copy**.

4. Position your cursor to the spot where you want the text or graphic to be copied.

5. Right-click and select **Paste**.

Now you have copied the text and/or graphic material and placed it in the same document or in another open document. Moving the text can be accomplished using the same procedure, but by choosing **Cut** from the dropdown menu instead of **Copy**. When you cut or copy items, *Word* places them on an office clipboard, which can be opened in a task pane while you work. You can paste or delete the items on the clipboard without going through the copy/cut process.

Using the Office Clipboard

1. Click the **Home** ribbon.

2. Click **Clipboard** Clipboard ⌐ and the Office Clipboard task pane opens.

3. Cut and copied items can be pasted with clicking on the item.

4. There is only one item on the clipboard at this time – the text that you just copied and pasted. Click the item and it will be pasted in the spot where your cursor last was placed.

5. Click the undo icon ⌐↰ ▾⌐ on the Quick Access toolbar to undo the text that you just pasted. This command can be used anytime that you change your mind about a word processing action.

6. To close the Clipboard task pane, click the X ⌐▾ X⌐ in the upper right hand corner of the task pane.

The *Microsoft Office 2007 Clipboard* allows you to collect multiple items (text and graphics) from any document or other program and then paste them into any document. For example, you can copy data from *Microsoft Excel 2007*, a graphic from *Microsoft PowerPoint 2007*, and a datasheet from *Microsoft Access 2007*, then paste any or all of the collected items in a *Word* document. The collected items stay on the Office Clipboard until you exit *Office*.

The Review Tab

The commands available on the Review Tab are designed to assist in writing and feature editing and reviewing tools. One tool particularly useful to teachers is the ability to insert comments into *Word* documents. For this exercise, you will insert an editing comment into your Word Processing Practice document.

Inserting a Comment

1. Place your cursor at the end of the paragraph you just wrote.

2. Click the **Review** tab and select the **New Comment** icon

A comment box opens to the right of the paragraph. Write the following message to your student: **Great opening paragraph. Now focus on useful word processing commands**.

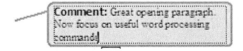

The comments can be read and then deleted by your students as they make the suggested corrections/modifications. You can save the electronic document to make sure that you have a copy of your editorial comments as well. To delete a comment, place the cursor on the comment box, right-click, and then click the delete command.

The proofing commands located on the **Review** tab are also excellent tools for teachers. With spelling and grammar tools available, a misspelled word will appear with a wavy red line beneath it. To correct the word, simply place your cursor on the word and right-click the mouse. A list of possible words will be presented and you need only click the correct word. At this time, you are also able to ignore the suggestions or add the word to the dictionary. Additionally, you can select the AutoCorrect command, which brings up a menu of options allowing you to set the program so that certain errors are automatically corrected.

Checking for Spelling and Grammar Errors

1. Type this sentence: **the girl with the books have left the rom with hour pencils.** (Hit **Enter**)

2. Position your cursor on the word with the wavy red underline, rom and right-click it. A drop down list of several choices is displayed. Click "**room**" (the correct spelling).

3. Position your cursor on the word with the wavy green underline, the and right-click.

4. Click **Grammar**. Grammar...

5. Click **Explain**.

An explanation and reasons for capitalizing are presented; you can accept the suggested change or ignore it.

The Insert Ribbon

One of the most helpful commands available on the **Insert** tab is the ability to insert hyperlinks within the document, to other documents or files and even to the Internet. *Word* allows you to insert hyperlinks within your document through the use of headings and/or bookmarks. Set a bookmark in your Word Processing Practice document so that you will be able to link to that location.

Inserting a Bookmark

Place your cursor in the last sentence of your Word Processing Practice document directly in front of the "**f**" in formatting. This is the spot you will place a bookmark.

1. Click the **Insert** tab and then select Bookmark on the **Links** tab.

2. Select **Bookmark**.   Bookmark

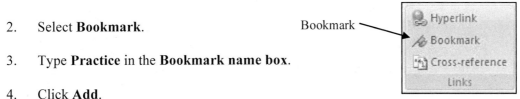

3. Type **Practice** in the **Bookmark name box**.

4. Click **Add**.

Now that you have a bookmarked spot in your document, you will be able to hyperlink to that location.

Inserting a Hyperlink Within a Document

1.   Select the word **Practice** in the title.

2.   Click **Hyperlink** on the **Links** tab of the Insert ribbon.

3.   Click ![Hyperlink] **Hyperlink**.

4.   Click the **Place in This Document** box.

5.   Click the **Practice** bookmark.

6.   Click **OK**.

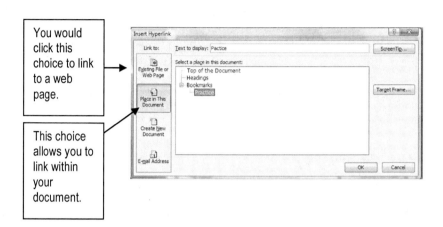

Although your practice document is too short to require a hyperlink, you are able to direct your students directly to the practice skills by clicking on the **Practice** hyperlink. Placing hyperlinks to the web or other files requires a similar process, but then you will choose the **Existing File** or **Web Page** box.

Useful Formatting Commands

A common formatting decision is to determine the line spacing for your document.

Setting Line Spacing

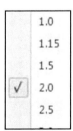

1.   Select all of the text.

2.   Click the **Home** tab.

3.   In the **Paragraph** section of the ribbon, select the **Line Spacing** icon.

4.   Click **2.0** to make your document double-spaced.

5.   Click **OK**.

This practice exercise has presented some basic word processing functions. The next exercises provide opportunities for you to apply the word processing skills you have learned to create artifacts for your Technology Teaching Portfolio.

Exercise 2: Vocabulary Cards

ISTE NETS-T Standard 2

For this exercise, you will create vocabulary study cards (use either *Microsoft Word* or Google Docs) for your students. You can easily create a table with rows and columns and add a word to each cell. Then, simply cut and distribute to students to work in study/review groups.

✓   Save the study sheet as **YourLastName Study Cards** in an appropriate folder if using *Word*.

Design a Word or Google document that is easy to read, and includes the following components.

- ▪   Minimum 10 words or concepts

- ▪   Appropriate font to fit within table cell

*Could be used as an artifact for Standard 2.

Exercise 3: Class Centers Schedule

ISTE NETS-T Standard 2

For this exercise, you will design a schedule (use either Microsoft *Word* or Google Docs) to ensure that each of the four groups of students in your class has an opportunity to work at all four of the class centers including the computer center. You will use the table feature to prepare the schedule to make sure that each group works in all four of the centers for the week (Monday – Thursday).

✓   Save the centers schedule as **YourLastName Centers Schedule** in an appropriate folder.

Design a table that includes the following components:

- ▪   Title it **Centers Schedule** in merged cells in the top row of the table.

- ▪   4 groups (group names of your choice)

- ▪   4 centers – computers (3 others of your choice – i.e., graphing, math, reading, spelling, research, maps, etc.)

- ▪   4 days (Monday – Thursday)

*Could be used as an artifact for Standard 2.

Exercise 4: Collaborative Back to School Newsletter

Required: ISTE NETS-T Standard 3

For this exercise, you will collaborate with a small group using Google Docs and produce a newsletter that will be designed to send to your students' parents or to be given to the parents on "Back to School" night. "Back to School" night is a common practice at middle and secondary schools at which time parents go to each of their student's classes and listen to the teacher who describes class activities and expectations. Often the teacher gives the parents a newsletter to further explain activities and class expectations.

- ✓ Save the newsletter as **YourLastName Back to School Newsletter** in your Google Docs folder.
- ✓ One in the group should create the Google Doc and share it with others in the group.
- ✓ Work together and design a newsletter that is visually appealing and contains the following content components:
    1. Class expectations (description of your vision of your classroom).
    2. The role technology will play in your class (how might your students use technology to reach curricular goals).
    3. Parent involvement (how can parents be involved in your classroom).
    4. Standards – (review state and/or national standards to determine concepts and skills for each curricular area and grade level). Remember, each school district curriculum is based on the state's standards and are more specific in nature than the standards. Locate a school district curriculum on the Internet, go to the grade level and/or subject area you plan to teach. In this way, you will be able to see the specific content and skills your students will be learning. For the brochure, you will want to focus on some of the major areas to be covered in the first month(s) of school.
    5. Highlights of the month or quarter/semester
    6. No spelling, punctuation and/or any other mechanical errors (your newsletter is an external communication to be given to parents).

Your newsletter must be visually appealing and contain the following formatting components:
- WordArt
- Text Box
- Line, border or AutoShape (at least one of these elements)
- Graphic (at least 3)
- Two pages

To share a Google Docs file

1. Select the file you want to share and click the **Share** button.
2. Select **Invite people**
3. Enter the email addresses of the people that you would like to add.
4. Select **To edit**.
5. If you'd like to add a message to your invitation, enter some text and click **Send**. To skip sending an invitation, click **Add without sending invitation**. Your collaborators and viewers will still be able to access the doc from their Docs lists, but won't receive an email invitation. Even if you've previously shared the document with the people to be notified, they'll still receive the invitation you send.

---

*Required artifact for Standard 3.

Exercise 5: Correcting Student Papers Electronically

ISTE NETS-T Standard 3

For this exercise, you will be using the Comment function in *Word* to correct a student's research paper. (Optional collaborative activity: Use Google Docs comment/discussion feature).

1. Open the file **Student Paper** provided in your Textbook Data Files link on our textbook companion site (http://dats.boisestate.edu).

2. Save the file as **YourLastName Student Paper** in an appropriate folder.

3. Read through the student paper on your screen at least once before you begin to insert comments.

4. Make at least 5 comments in the student paper using the following guidelines:

    ▪   General comments concerning the opening and closing paragraphs
    ▪   Any grammatical/spelling and/or mechanical errors - provide the correct construction for the student
    ▪   Suggestions for improvement
    ▪   Overall quality of the research paper

*Could be used as artifact for Standard 3.

Exercise 6: Fund Raiser Flyer

ISTE NETS-T Standard 3

Teachers are often sponsors for school clubs and/or classroom fundraisers, and work with parents in raising funds for school-related functions. For this exercise, design a flyer for the club you sponsor or for your class. Use a flyer template in *Word* or Google Docs.

 Optional: Create this flyer with another classmate using a Google Docs template.

(Save the file as **YourLastName Fundraiser** in an appropriate folder if you are using *Word*.)

✓   Design a flyer advertising your fundraiser and be sure to include the following:

    ▪   Pertinent fundraiser information – date/time, location, type of activity, purpose, cost
    ▪   Formatting requirements:

        1. use of varied font styles and/or sizes
        2. at least one graphic
        3. text and graphics well placed on the page

*Could be used as an artifact for Standard 3.

Exercise 7: Special Event or Project Brochure

ISTE NETS-T Standard 5

For this exercise, you will produce a brochure that will be designed to showcase a special event or project that you have planned. Perhaps you are a music teacher who wants to advertise an upcoming concert, an athletic trainer who wants to recruit students for his/her nutrition class, or an environmental science teacher who is recruiting students for a science study trip to Belize.

Tip: Use a brochure template in *Word* or in Google Docs to save time.

(Save the brochure as **YourLastName Event Brochure** or **YourLastName Project Brochure** in an appropriate folder if you are using *Word*.)

✓ Design a brochure that is visually appealing (should contain at least one image) including the following content components:

1. Description of the special event or project.
2. Purpose of the project.
3. Date/Time (if appropriate)
4. Costs/Deadlines (if appropriate)
5. Eligibility Requirements (if appropriate)
6. Special Highlights
7. Benefits
8. No spelling, punctuation and/or any other mechanical errors (your newsletter is an external communication).

*Could be used as an artifact for Standard 5.

Exercise 8: Class Schedule Using Google Calendar

ISTE NETS-T Standard 3

✓ Create a Google Calendar and add events and class schedules. For information on how to create a class calendar, go to https://sites.google.com/a/googleapps.com/edu-training-center/Training-Home/module-3-calendar/chapter-7/1-2

✓ Share your calendar with a classmate. Think of ways you might use this calendar to share events and assignments with students and parents.

✓ Embed your Google Calendar on a page on your Technology Teaching Portfolio: https://sites.google.com/a/googleapps.com/edu-training-center/Training-Home/module-3-calendar/chapter-7/1-4

*Could be used as an artifact for Standard 3.

The teacher as the planner of instruction has many ways of presenting instructional materials and conducting instructional activities. When deciding on the teaching strategies to be used, teachers consider the content and skills to be taught as well as the manner in which they are to be taught. Research on how people learn clearly shows that students must be active participants who are engaged with the material.

Knowing that learning preferences vary, the teacher must make every attempt to reach all students and engage them in learning. The active process of creating, rather than acquiring knowledge, is a key concept of constructivism, a learning philosophy fundamental to technology integration. Therefore, ISTE NETS-T Standard 2 includes directives for teachers to "customize and personalize learning activities to address students' diverse learning styles, working strategies, and abilities using digital tools and resources" (ISTE, 2008).

Teaching Strategies and Technology

Teaching strategies should include all types of learners: visual, auditory and kinesthetic, and their preferred learning styles. Incorporating various learning strategies in your teaching will help students in retaining information and applying that information. The teacher's goal is to create learning environments that facilitate multiple learning styles and are interactive in nature. Integrating technology into the learning experience can be an effective way to assist in reaching that goal. Through the use of technology, the process of learning in the classroom can be enhanced as students have increased access to visual and auditory information as well as the ability to manipulate that information.

Methods of incorporating technology into lesson planning cover a broad spectrum of technology including software application programs, instructional software and web-based technology strategies. Software applications include database programs, word processors, and spreadsheets, which have no content of their own. Teachers and students use the software applications in a variety of ways in the instructional process.

In contrast, instructional software is a term that encompasses drill and practice, tutorial and simulation software programs. These programs are targeted to specific content and skills and allow for students to move at their own pace. Drill and practice instructional software provides sequential repetition and practice of skills, while tutorials are focused on a specific topic and/or subject allowing students to explore information and provide practice as part of the instruction. Simulations provide a real-world experience for learners that require analysis and evaluation skills. Students are presented with problems and the ability to judge situations and make decisions. The students' decision and subsequent choices affect the outcome of the simulation and resulting consequences.

Table 1 on the next page lists some of the many ways for teachers to integrate technology. As you read through the various ways technology tools can support learning, see if you can identify several tools that you might use in your future classroom and how they might support learning.

Table 1: Using Technology to Enhance Teaching/Learning	
Technology	**Ways to Support/ Enhance Learning**
Word Processing	Create, proofread and edit documents Determine readability of text Improve the writing process Desktop publishing uses Encourage creative writing Organize, present and summarize data
Spreadsheet	Organize and report numerical data Create mathematical formulas Test mathematical relationships Demonstrate mathematical concepts Graphically present mathematical relationships Present numeric data visually
Presentation	Present information in an organized manner Provide visually rich materials Organize information Provide immediate feedback – review, electronic flashcards Display information in different formats Prepare oral reports Provide instructional materials with audio and visual feedback
Tutorials Instructional Software	Provide specific content and skills instruction Enable students to move at their own pace Provide sequenced instruction Document student progress
Drill and Practice Instructional Software	Provide specific skills instruction Provide for repetition and practice of skills Enable students to move at their own pace Provide sequenced instruction Document student progress
Simulations Instructional Software	Engage in real-world experiences Analyze situations Decision making skills Evaluate decisions and resulting consequences
Internet, Mobile, and Social Media	Retrieve, interact with, and manipulate information Create and present to a wide audience Use applications – word processing, spreadsheet, etc. Communicate locally and around the world Collaborate locally and around the world Publish – web pages, blogs, wikis, etc. Provide visual and audio materials Engage in simulations and interactive lessons

Developing Lesson Plans

As you continue through your career in education, you will be introduced to a number of lesson plan formats depending upon your discipline area and school district requirements. For this course, you will use a simplified lesson plan template available in Google Docs—one you will modify as you grow in your understanding and experience as a teacher. The steps involved in developing a lesson plan are as follows:

- Become familiar with the standards you are to address in your subject and/or grade level. Select the subject and/or grade level, topic, concept or skill you will be teaching in your lesson plan.

- Thoroughly examine the topic and concept(s) you will be teaching to determine the best technology strategy to use to teach the topic. For this course, you will be thinking about how to use technology to assist in teaching that topic, while also realizing that technology may not necessarily the best choice for teaching all topics, concepts or skills.

- Provide clear and specific objectives for your lesson. Examine at least one school district curriculum website to determine specific goals and objectives for your lesson plan. Remember you will always align instruction with the state and school district guidelines. You do not have to rewrite objectives. You may use the exact wording of the school district curriculum in writing your objectives, but be sure you cite the school district in your lesson plan.

- Provide a description of learning activities. In this section, be sure to identify in what manner students will be interacting with computers. Will they be working individually in a computer lab or classroom? Will they be working with partners? Is the lesson a group activity? You should be specific in describing the computer configuration as well as the activities in which students will be participating. Table 2 on the following page provides links to information about various teaching strategies, which can provide more help in this area.

- Describe how students will be evaluated. This does not have to be a formal assessment such as a quiz, test, report, etc. You need only describe how you will know the students have reached the lesson objectives. So, if your objective was for students to name the parts of a flower, then how will you determine that they have reached that objective? Perhaps, evaluation will be questions and answers through discussion, a worksheet they complete as they view a presentation, etc.

Table 2: Teaching Strategies

How People Learn: Brain, Mind, Experience, and School [Online Book]
http://books.nap.edu/openbook.php?isbn=0309070368

Constructivism and Technology, On the Road to Student-Centered Learning (PDF format)
http://www.sedl.org/pubs/tapinto/v1n1.pdf

Technology-Supported Lesson Plans
http://edtech.boisestate.edu/bridges/tslessons.htm

Gardner's Multiple Intelligences
http://en.wikipedia.org/wiki/Theory_of_multiple_intelligences

As you learn more about your specific content area, you will become more skilled at developing lesson plans and include other aspects of planning including special adaptations for students, materials needed, expected timing for activities, background planning information, and even specific questions/answers you may have for student discussion.

The following **Technology-Supported Lesson Plan** activity will help you begin this process of becoming familiar with writing lesson plans, collaborating with others, and using Google Docs to publish your work.

Planning Instruction Exercise

Exercise 1: Technology-Supported Lesson Plan[*]
Required: ISTE NETS-T Standard 2

For this activity, you will be using the **Simple Lesson Plan template** available through Google Docs. Your instructor may encourage you to work with a partner on this activity. (For more detailed information and tutorials on how to use Google Docs, see Appendix B.) In this lesson plan, you will integrate technology and address content standards (if applicable) in your content area.

Your instructor will direct you to school district websites for guidance in finding standards and identifying/writing objectives. Refer to Table 1: Using Technology to Enhance Teaching/Learning in this chapter for ideas on how you might use various technology tools to meet your instructional objectives.

Remember, objectives are what your students will be able to do as a result of your instruction. You should also refer to Table 2: Teaching Strategies, for ideas on how you will structure your lesson.

✓ You will design and write this lesson, share it with a classmate, ask for feedback, and then make any changes or corrections.

1. Sign in to your Google account and access the **Documents** link at the upper left side of your Gmail account.
2. Then, select **Create new>From Template** and do a search for **Simple Lesson Plan** using the **public templates**.[*]

3. Click **Search Templates** and use the **Simple Lesson Plan** template by Google. Click **Use this template**, and the template will be ready in your Google Docs window for editing.

---

[*] This information was correct at the time of publication. However, Google Docs is constantly changing, so this information could be out-of-date. If that is the case, your teacher will direct you to another lesson plan template suitable for this activity.

69

4. Before you start editing, make sure you rename the file, calling it **YourLastName_lessonplan**. To do this, click the name of your lesson plan at the top left of your document (it will be named "Copy of Simple Lesson plan."

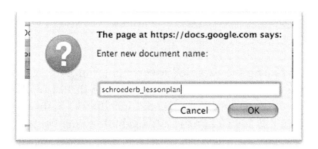

5. Share your lesson plan with your instructor and a classmate with by clicking the share drop-down box at the upper-right and selecting **Share.**

6. Enter the email address (it should be a Google account) and then click **Share.**

7. After you invite your collaborator, you can send them an email, which will provide them with a link to your document. You are now ready to start working on your lesson plan!

8. Begin to enter information and complete your lesson plan.

Technology-Supported Lesson Plan Requirements

1. One relevant Clip Art or other image
2. Name of Lesson: (Make this a catchy title!)
3. Grade Level:
4. Subject:
5. Prepared by:
6. Overview and Purpose: Brief description of what the lesson plan is about and its purpose.
7. Educational Standards: Obtain these from your school district's website or national standards, whatever your instructor advises.
8. Objectives: Specify what students will be able to do, using verbs from Bloom's Taxonomy for the Cognitive Domain or language directly from your school district's performance standards.
9. Materials Needed: Really think about all that you will need. You don't want to arrive at class missing an important material.
10. Other Resources: (websites, videos, books, etc.)
11. Information: This would be an outline/steps/description of your lesson plan, with enough detailed information that it could be taught by a substitute teacher.
12. Verification: Provide assessment/procedure to check for student understanding.
13. Activity: Describe activity that students will complete to practice/reinforce the lesson.
14. Notes (Optional)

✓ As with all artifacts you complete for your Technology Teaching Portfolio, make sure that your lesson plan has no spelling/punctuation/grammatical errors, and is professional and attractive.

How to Publish Your Google Doc

You can publish your Google Docs lesson plan so that you can easily insert it into your Technology Teaching Portfolio. To publish your document, follow these steps:

1. Open the document you'd like to publish, and click the **Share** drop-down in the upper-right corner of the screen.

2. Choose the **Publish as web page** option.

3. On the following page, click **Publish document**.

Once you do this, a URL appears. Simply distribute this link to anyone you'd like to access the presentation.

Your presentation will be accessible from this URL until you either delete it, or elect to stop publishing. To stop publishing, simply click **Stop publishing** from the **Publish** tab. After this is done, anyone accessing the presentation from the published URL will no longer have access.

*Required artifact for Standard 2.

Summary

The next section of your textbook will introduce you to spreadsheet software, a technology tool that can enable higher-order learning and help with numerical calculations, asking "what if" questions and improving teacher and student productivity.

You will learn how to use and manipulate a spreadsheet, first creating a sample student gradebook and then moving on to other exercises, which you can add to your Technology Teaching Portfolio.

This technology skills section and spreadsheet exercises were adapted from *Educating Teachers* (2007) – Pollard, C., VanDehey, T., and Pollard, R.

The spreadsheet can be one of the most versatile and useful tools in a teacher's repertoire. On the surface, a spreadsheet is a tool for organizing information concisely, in rows and columns, and graphically, in bar graphs, line charts, pie charts, etc. It is the computer equivalent of a paper ledger sheet consisting of a grid made from columns and rows. Once entered, however, the information can be used for performing calculations, making predictions and showing patterns, changing dynamically as new data replace old.

In the classroom, spreadsheets offer concrete ways to explore abstract concepts not only in mathematics but also in other subjects. Using spreadsheets promotes higher order thinking by assisting students in the development of problem solving skills. Students feel the power of spreadsheets as they use formulas to determine the answer to "what if" type questions. They are able to easily manipulate and analyze as well as visually organize information through the use of charts and graphs.

As a teacher productivity tool, spreadsheets can be used to determine grades, maintain classroom and extracurricular budgets and to even create interactive review exercises. Mastering the spreadsheet provides another tool at your disposal for teaching and learning.

 Spreadsheets: Microsoft Excel 2011 for Mac (Appendix F)

Spreadsheets: Microsoft Excel 2007 for Windows

In this section, you will explore the many uses of *Microsoft Excel 2007* to organize, calculate and analyze data by building a worksheet from start to finish. A worksheet consists of rows designated by numbers and columns designated by letters. The intersection of a row and a column is called a cell; in the example below, the cell **A1** is

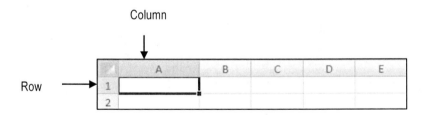

the active cell. A worksheet contains 65,536 rows and 256 columns. A collection of worksheets is called a workbook. When you open *Excel 2007* to begin a spreadsheet, you are presented with a three-sheet workbook by default. You can add as many worksheets as you want in a workbook, limited only by your computer's available memory. Although there are many times in the classroom that your students will only use a single worksheet in a workbook, multiple worksheets allow you to keep related worksheets in one file and even allow you to perform calculations and use the information among the worksheets.

When *Excel* first opens, it displays a new, empty workbook containing three worksheets. There are many of the common window elements for *Office 2007* applications: Microsoft Office button, Quick Access toolbar, mini toolbar, ribbon with application-specific command tabs, and a status bar. After working with *Word 2007*, you are already familiar with many of the commands available on the Home,

Insert, Page Layout, Review, and View tabs; however, the commands on the Formulas and Data tabs are specific to the use of spreadsheets. There are also two new elements in the *Excel* window, a **formula bar** and a **name box**. The name box displays the cell **A1,** which is the name of the currently selected cell. Cell names are also called **cell addresses** or **cell references**.

The tabs at the bottom of the workbook window are labeled **Sheet1**, **Sheet2**, and **Sheet3**; they allow you to move easily among the worksheets. Additionally, you are able to name your worksheets, add or delete worksheets and move the position of the worksheets within the workbook. Navigating in the worksheet can be accomplished by clicking in a specific cell, hitting the enter key, using the tab key, and/or using the arrow keys. To return to cell **A1**, the very first cell in your worksheet, hold down the control key and the home key at the same time (**Ctrl + Home**).

Types of Data

The three basic types of data that can be entered into a worksheet cell are labels, values, and dates/times.

1. **Labels:** text entries that do not have a value associated with them. Text is left aligned in the cell.

2. **Values**: numeric entries that can be used in calculations. Values are right aligned.

3. **Dates/Times**: either a time (11:20 AM) or a date (1/1/2003). Dates/times are right aligned.

You are also able to include recorded sounds, graphics and hyperlinks within your worksheets.

Designing A Spreadsheet

The time you take in designing your spreadsheet is well spent. The first step is to determine the information you need and the calculations to be performed. You must decide how to arrange data to determine the appropriate formulas for data analysis. Finally, you will want to use formatting features to make the spreadsheet easier to read and more visually appealing.

The exercise you will complete in this section leads you through the design and development of a class gradebook that will look similar to the one on the next page. In this gradebook, you will learn how to enter values (text, numbers, and formulas), how to format cells, how to add WordArt and Clip Art to customize your spreadsheet, and most importantly, how to use the power of a spreadsheet to make instant calculations and conduct analysis.

	A	B	C	D	E	F	G	H	I	J	K	L	M
1					**English 9**								
2	Student Names	HW-1	HW-2	HW-3	Homework	P-1	P-2	Projects	E1	E2	Exams	Final	Score
3	Possible Points	15	12	17	44	25	35	60.00	55	25	80.00		
4													
5	Engle, Mary	10	7	15	0.73	20	21	0.68	52	24	0.95	0.80	B
6	Garcia, Jose	13	10	10	0.75	23	31	0.90	53	22	0.94	0.89	B
7	Jones, Sally	15	12	17	1.00	25	34	0.98	45	20	0.81	0.92	A
8	Little, Ian	5	5	5	0.34	15	15	0.50	25	13	0.48	0.46	F
9	Smith, John	7	8	11	0.59	18	28	0.77	50	20	0.88	0.78	C
10	Sully, Todd	11	6	9	0.59	18	21	0.65	49	21	0.88	0.73	C
11	Average Scores	10	8	11	0.67	20	25	0.75	46	20	0.82	0.76	
12	Highest Scores	15	12	17	1.00	25	34	0.98	53	24	0.95	0.92	
13	Lowest Scores	5	5	5	0.34	15	15	0.50	25	13	0.48	0.46	

For your class gradebook, you determine that the following elements will need to be included:

1. Class title
2. Student names
3. Class assignments (by category)
    a. Homework
    b. Projects
    c. Quizzes/Exams
4. Student performance in each of the assignment categories
5. Student performance for the grading period
6. Each student's final grade
7. Class average for each assignment
8. Highest grade for each assignment
9. Lowest grade for each assignment

There is another decision for you to make before you begin the gradebook design for your class. You must decide how important each of the assignment categories is in determining your students' overall performance. The actual number of points that you give for any assignment can vary, but you must ask yourself, "How much weight should each assignment category carry in determining a student's final grade?" In this way, you are able to better assess a student's performance and not have to worry about counting total points for a grading period before you are even sure about the number of assignments your students will be able to complete.

For this gradebook, you decide that homework will be worth 20% of the final grade, quizzes/exams account for 40%, and that projects will constitute 40%.

Now that you have determined all of the elements necessary for the gradebook, you will need to plan the layout of the spreadsheet and think about the formulas you will need to use. Your gradebook will require formulas for determining homework, projects, and exam scores, the average class score, lowest and highest scores, weighted scores, and the final scores for the grading period with the letter grade the student earned.

Beginning Your Spreadsheet

Starting Excel

1. Click the **Start** button on the task bar in the lower left corner of your screen.
2. Move the mouse pointer to **All Programs** to display the submenu.
3. Click *Microsoft Office,* and then Click the program you want to access, in this case, *Microsoft Office Excel 2007*.

      The first step, as you always remind your students, is to save your newly opened workbook on a flash drive, class network drive or on your hard drive (just make sure that you know where you can locate it at a future time). If you do not name your workbook, *Excel* will save it with the title, Book1.

Save As

1. Click the Microsoft Office button .

2. Click . You now need to choose the file format for the saved file. If you do not make a choice, the default is *Excel 2007*. That means that the file will be saved as an *Excel 2007* file and can easily be opened in *Excel 2007*; however there may be compatibility issues with earlier versions of *Excel*. For most users of this text, saving the document i the *Excel* Workbook format (the 2007 default) will be the chosen option.

3. Once you have decided on the format in which to save your workbook, make sure that you are saving it in the right location. If you do not choose a location, your workbook would be saved with the title of Book1 in the Documents directory on the hard drive of the computer you are currently using. As you want to be able to easily locate this in the future, you decide the drive, folder and subfolder in which to save the gradebook spreadsheet.

4. Click your chosen file format and hit enter. The **Save As** window becomes available.

5. Create a new folder by clicking on the New Folder icon .

6. Name the New Folder **Spreadsheet Exercises**. You can save all of your spreadsheet exercises from this book in your folder.

7. Click the **File name** box, and type **YourLastName gradebook**.

8. Click [Save] in the lower right hand corner.

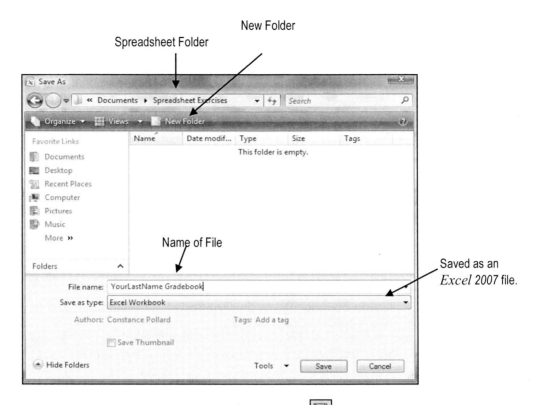

New Folder

Spreadsheet Folder

Name of File

Saved as an *Excel 2007* file.

Now you can save frequently by clicking the save icon ![save icon] on the **Quick Access** bar and know exactly where your workbook is located. Also note that the title of your workbook **YourLastName gradebook**, is now displayed in the *Excel* title bar.

Although there is more than one way that a gradebook may be designed, this gradebook will feature the student names in the rows with the assignments, scores, and grades in the columns. With your workbook open, you begin your class gradebook.

Entering Labels

Active Cell

Formula Bar

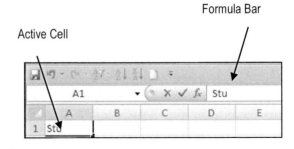

1. Click cell A1 and enter **Student Names**. As you type, note that the entry appears both in the formula bar and in the active cell (**A1**). When you are finished, lock in the entry by pressing **Enter**.

2. To make the cell wide enough to view the full text, put your cursor at the intersection of columns A and B. Hold down the left mouse button as you drag the column to the desired width. (You can also double-click the same intersection and the width will adjust to the student names text).

3. Continue by entering labels for the assignments (Homework – HW, Projects – P, and Exams – E) labels.

4. Click cell **A2** and enter **Possible Points**, to reflect the total number of points for each of the assignments. Include the total point values for each of the assignments in the corresponding columns.

5.   Enter the student names on each of the rows below the **Possible Points** row, along with the values for their assignments. Your spreadsheet will contain the following values:

◇	A	B	C	D	E	F	G	H	I	J	K	L	M
1	Student Names	HW-1	HW-2	HW-3	Homework	P-1	P-2	Projects	E1	E2	Exams	Final	Score
2	Possible Points	15	12	17		25	35		55	25			
3	Smith, John	7	8	11		18	28		50	20			
4	Engle, Mary	10	7	15		20	21		52	24			
5	Garcia, Jose	13	10	10		23	31		53	22			
6	Little, Ian	5	5	5		15	15		25	13			
7	Jones, Sally	15	12	17		25	34		45	20			
8	Sully, Todd	11	6	9		18	21		49	21			
9	Average Scores												
10	Highest Scores												
11	Lowest Scores												

If you make an error, cell contents are edited by first selecting the cell and making corrections or by selecting the cell and clicking in the formula bar to make your changes. When the correct data have been entered, either click the **Enter** button ☑ on the formula bar or hit the **Enter** key on the keyboard.

Now that you have entered the student names and assignments, it's time to determine their grades. Remember, by weighting the scores, you are able to give any number of assignments and to allocate any number of points to an assignment. Although your imaginary students have three homework assignments and only two projects and exams, the homework will only be worth up to 20% of their final class grade.

Entering Formulas in a Spreadsheet

Once the scores are filled in for each student, you will enter the formulas to determine your students' and the total class performance in each of the assignment. *Excel* uses the following arithmetic operators and comparison operators.

Arithmetic Operators		Comparison Operators	
Addition	+ (plus sign)	Equals	=
Subtraction	- (minus sign)	Greater than	>
Multiplication	* (asterisk)	Less than	<
Division	/ (forward slash)	Greater than or equal to	>=
Exponentiation	^ (caret)	Less than or equal to	<=
		Not equal to	<>

When determining formulas for use in *Excel*, be aware that the following **order of operations** will be performed:

Parenthesis
Exponentiation
Multiplication
Division
Addition
Subtraction

> Memorizing this phrase may help your students to remember the order of operations:
> **P**lease
> **E**xcuse
> **M**y **D**ear
> **A**unt **S**ally

You will use formulas, functions, and the fill handle to copy formulas to other cells. First, you will learn how to use the SUM function to add a range of cells.

Using the SUM Function to Total Scores

In Row 2, you have the total possible points for each of the assignments. You will want *Excel* to automatically calculate the totals for each of the assignments. The formula, therefore, will calculate new totals should you decide to change or add assignments in a new class, for instance.

1. Select cell **E2** and start with the = sign (indicates you want *Excel* to perform a calculation). Enter **=SUM**
2. Enter an opening parenthesis after the word **SUM** to include the range of cells to include in the function, **=SUM(**
3. Point to cell **B2** and drag your mouse across cells **B2** to **D2** ending with a closing parenthesis.
4. Then click the enter key or checkmark at the end of the formula bar. The formula will look like this: **=SUM(B2:D2)**

(The colon between the cells indicates a range of cells that are included in the calculation. The parentheses indicate this is an *Excel* function. You are telling *Excel* to calculate the sum (addition) of the values in cells **B2**, **C2**, and **D2**.)

You should see the total of 44 in cell **E2**.

◇	A	B	C	D	E	F	G	H	I	J	K	L	M
1	Student Names	HW-1	HW-2	HW-3	Homework	P-1	P-2	Projects	E1	E2	Exams	Final	Score
2	Possible Points	15	12	17	=sum(B2:D2)		35		55	25			
3	Smith, John	7	8	11		18	28		50	20			
4	Engle, Mary	10	7	15		20	21		52	24			
5	Garcia, Jose	13	10	10		23	31		53	22			
6	Little, Ian	5	5	5		15	15		25	13			
7	Jones, Sally	15	12	17		25	34		45	20			
8	Sully, Todd	11	6	9		18	21		49	21			
9	Average Scores												
10	Highest Scores												
11	Lowest Scores												

Do the same procedure for each of the other assignments, the **Projects** and **Exams**. You should have a total for each of the assignment categories in Row 2.

Writing a Formula to Calculate Homework Score

You will write a formula to calculate the number of points for the homework assignments divided by the total points for the assignment. The total homework assignment points possible are calculated in cell **E3** for John Smith, which will include the sum of **B3**, **C3**, and **D3**. The sum function provides an easy way to add up these cells, adding the range of cells, from **B3** to **D3**, indicated in *Excel* by the colon (**B3:D3**).

1. Select cell **E3** (this is where you will enter your formula). You want *Excel* to add each of the possible homework points and then divide by the total number of points possible (the calculation you have already done in cell **E2**), so your final formula will be: **=SUM(B3:D3)/$E$2**

(The reason for including the dollar signs is to indicate you want the calculation to ALWAYS use the value in cell **E2**, since you will be copying this formula down the column.)

2. To enter the formula, first type an equal sign = (typing an equal sign tells *Excel* that you are about to enter a formula) and then SUM (since you want to use the SUM function) and an opening parenthesis **=SUM(**

3. Instead of typing in each of the cell letters, you will use the **pointing** technique and watch as *Excel* inserts that cell reference in the formula. Point to cell **B3**. You point by clicking in the **B3** cell. Once you click **B3**, you will notice that the formula bar now shows **=SUM(B3**

4. Continue dragging your mouse across the cells you want to include in the sum **(B3:D3)**

5. Next you need to tell *Excel* you want to divide by the total number of points for the homework category. The divide symbol is the forward slash: /

Since you will always want to divide by **the value in cell E2**, you will use an **absolute cell reference** for the row and column, putting dollar signs in front of each to indicate this: **$E$2**

Your final formula in cell **E3** should look like this: **=SUM(B3:D3)/$E$2**

(Remember, when entering formulas you can always point to the cell instead of entering the letters and numbers. The toggle for absolute cell reference on Windows is **F4** and for a Mac is **Apple Command + T**).

◇	A	B	C	D	E	F	G	H	I	J	K	L	M
1	Student Names	HW-1	HW-2	HW-3	Homework	P-1	P-2	Projects	E1	E2	Exams	Final	Score
2	Possible Points	15	12	17	44	25	35	60	55	25	80		
3	Smith, John	7	8	11	0.590909	18	28		50	20			
4	Engle, Mary	10	7	15		20	21		52	24			
5	Garcia, Jose	13	10	10		23	31		53	22			
6	Little, Ian	5	5	5		15	15		25	13			
7	Jones, Sally	15	12	17	1	25	34		45	20			
8	Sully, Todd	11	6	9		18	21		49	21			
9	Average Scores												
10	Highest Scores												
11	Lowest Scores												

The default number format for *Excel* is the General number format, so you see that John Smith earned a 0.590909. The amount of numbers you see will be dependent upon how wide your column is.

Using the Fill Handle to Copy Formulas

The formula you entered in cell **E3** will be the same for the rest of the students in the column. Since *Excel* uses by default a relative cell reference, it knows when you copy a formula to adjacent cells to adjust the cell references. The reason you used an absolute cell reference for the total homework possible points (cell **E2**) is to override the default relative cell reference setting. If this still does not make sense, it will as you continue to work with spreadsheets!

Next, you will be copying the formula you just entered in cell **E3** to the rest of the cells in the column.

1. Click cell **E3** and hold your mouse over the lower right corner. You will see a crosshatch symbol, which is called the fill handle.
2. Click your mouse on this fill handle and **carefully** drag the handle down the column until you reach the last student's name.
3. The formula you created in cell **E3** will be copied down the column, automatically calculating each student's score.

	A	B	C	D	E	F	G	H	I	J	K	L	M
1	Student Names	HW-1	HW-2	HW-3	Homework	P-1	P-2	Projects	E1	E2	Exams	Final	Score
2	Possible Points	15	12	17	44	25	35	60	55	25	80		
3	Smith, John	7	8	11	0.590909	18	28		50	20			
4	Engle, Mary	10	7	15	0.727273	20	21		52	24			
5	Garcia, Jose	13	10	10	0.75	23	31		53	22			
6	Little, Ian	5	5	5	0.340909	15	15		25	13			
7	Jones, Sally	15	12	17	1	25	34		45	20			
8	Sully, Todd	11	6	9	0.590909	18	21		49	21			
9	Average Scores												
10	Highest Scores												
11	Lowest Scores												

Now, go through the same steps and enter the formulas in John Smith's record for the **Projects** and **Exams** scores. Remember to use the dollar signs (to indicate an absolute cell reference) when you select the cell to divide by the total points for each of the remaining two assignments (cells **H2** and **K2**).

After you calculate John Smith's scores for the Projects and Exams, position your cursor on the fill handle and drag down to copy the formula to the other students.

Next, you will use *Excel* to help you weight the individual assignments, to create a final score.

Calculating the Final Weighted Score (Column L)

You will calculate the final scores using the weighted score for each of the assignments areas (homework @ 20%, projects @ 40%, and exams @ 40%). The weighted score in each of the areas will be calculated to determine the student's final grade.

1. Select cell **L3** (this is where you will type your formula). Notice **L3** shows in your formula bar in blue lettering and the **L3** cell in your spreadsheet is shown as active.
2. You will begin with an equal sign to indicate your want *Excel* to make calculations. You will use the **pointing** technique and watch as *Excel* inserts that cell reference in the formula.
3. Enter the following in the formula bar: **=E3*.2** (Homework is worth 20% or .2)
4. Type a plus sign + so that you can add the next two parts of the formula (projects and exams).
5. Click **H3** (the project score) and then enter ***.4** (projects were 40% of the total grade).

6. Type a plus sign + and click **K3**. Enter ***.4** (exams were 40%). The formula bar should look like this **=E3*.2+H3*.4+K3*.4**

7. Click the **Enter** button ☑ to enter your formula.

8. John Smith's score should be .77

Remember, since this formula will be the same for all of the rest of the students, you will simply need to select the fill handle at the lower right of cell **L3** and drag it down to copy to the rest of the students' final scores. Do this now.

Calculating the Letter Score (Column M)

John Smith's final score is a .77, but you still need to determine his letter grade for this grading period by using an **IF** formula. Your school's grading scale is as follows:

90% – 100% = A
80% - 90% = B
70% - 80% = C
60% - 70% = D
Under 60 = F

Your **IF** formula will tell *Excel* to give a student an A if he scores greater than or equal to .9, a B if he above or equal to .8, a C if he scores above or equal to .7, a D if he scores above or equal to .6, and an F for any other scores. Each IF statement stipulates a condition.

Type the following IF formula followed by the enter key in the cell **M3** to determine your student's letter grade:

=IF(L3>=.9,"A", IF(L3>=.8,"B", IF(L3>=.7,"C", IF(L3>=.6,"D","F"))))

The formula must be entered exactly with close attention to punctuation marks and spacing. Note that there are four closing parentheses **))))** to correspond with the four opening parentheses for the four IF statements.

If your formula does not work, check it carefully as quotation marks and commas must be correctly placed in the formula.

You have included all the formulas you need to determine a student's assignment area score, final score and letter grade. Only one student's grade has been calculated, but you will not have to enter new formulas for each student; you can use the fill handle and easily copy the formulas to adjacent cells. The cell references, called *relative cell references*, automatically reflect the row or column to which they have been copied. Use the fill handle now to copy the letter score formula to the cells below.

◇	A	B	C	D	E	F	G	H	I	J	K	L	M
1	Student Names	HW-1	HW-2	HW-3	Homework	P-1	P-2	Projects	E1	E2	Exams	Final	Score
2	Possible Points	15	12	17	44	25	35	60	55	25	80		
3	Smith, John	7	8	11	0.590909091	18	28	0.766666667	50	20	0.875	0.77484848	C
4	Engle, Mary	10	7	15	0.727272727	20	21	0.683333333	52	24	0.95	0.79878788	C
5	Garcia, Jose	13	10	10	0.75	23	31	0.9	53	22	0.9375	0.885	B
6	Little, Ian	5	5	5	0.340909091	15	15	0.5	25	13	0.475	0.45818182	F
7	Jones, Sally	15	12	17	1	25	34	0.983333333	45	20	0.8125	0.91833333	A
8	Sully, Todd	11	6	9	0.590909091	18	21	0.65	49	21	0.875	0.72818182	C
9	Average Scores												
10	Highest Scores												
11	Lowest Scores												

Using the ROUNDUP Function

One of the most important things you should remember about spreadsheets is that you must review them. It is very easy to accept their results as correct, but sometimes you make a mistake in a formula, copying cells, or any number of errors. That is why it's important to double-check your work.

Take a look at the letter scores in your spreadsheet. Mary Engle has a final letter score of C, but if her final number percentage were rounded up to the nearest two decimal points, for instance, she would receive a B. Mary would probably want to receive a B rather than a C.

You will need to tell *Excel* that you want to round up the scores in the final column so that your letter score calculations are accurate. Therefore, you will use the ROUNDUP function in *Excel* to do this, adjusting your formula in column L. Here's how you do this.

1. Click cell **L3** and change your formula to the following:
   =ROUNDUP(E3*0.2+H3*0.4+K3*0.4,2)
2. Click **Enter** or the check mark.
3. You are telling *Excel* to round up the calculation of the weighted scores to two decimal points (the number 2 after the comma at the end of the formula).
4. Now, drag the fill handle to the bottom of the student final scores. See how Mary's score has changed from a C to a B?

Using the AVERAGE Function

1. Click cell **B9** to insert the **AVERAGE** function.

2. Type an equal sign. Click the **Insert Function** icon [fx] next to the formula bar.

Average →

3. Select **AVERAGE** from the list of available functions and click **OK**.

4. The **Function Arguments** screen appears listing the cells containing numbers that directly adjoin **B8**; in this case, **B3:B8**. These are the cells that you want included.

5. Click **OK**

Now the formula bar displays the **AVERAGE** function and you see that the class average for the first homework assignment was 10.167. There were 15 points possible so as a teacher you may want to review that assignment to determine if it was clear enough to your students and if they had the prerequisite skills to complete it accurately. Use the Fill handle to copy the average formula in cells **C8** to **L8** to see the class average for each assignment area as well as the class average score.

You can also use functions to calculate the highest score on an assignment (**MAX**) and the lowest score on an assignment (**MIN**).

Using the MAX And MIN Functions

1. Click cell **B10** to insert the **MAX** function and type an equal sign.
2. Enter **=MAX(**
3. Point to the first cell you want to include and then drag across the other cells. In this case, it would be cells **B3:B8**.
4. Here is your function formula you will enter in **B10**: **=MAX(B3:B8)**
5. Click Enter or the checkmark and your average highest score will appear.
6. Select the fill handle and drag this formula across the row, through Row **L**.
7. Click cell **B11** and use the **MIN** function to determine the lowest scores for each assignment which will be **=MIN(B3:B8)**
8. Be sure to select the correct cells for the **MIN** calculation (**B3:B8**) and use the fill handle to copy them across your spreadsheet. Your spreadsheet should look like the following:

◇	A	B	C	D	E	F	G	H	I	J	K	L	M
1	Student Names	HW-1	HW-2	HW-3	Homework	P-1	P-2	Projects	E1	E2	Exams	Final	Score
2	Possible Points	15	12	17	44	25	35	60	55	25	80		
3	Smith, John	7	8	11	0.590909091	18	28	0.766666667	50	20	0.875	0.78	C
4	Engle, Mary	10	7	15	0.727272727	20	21	0.683333333	52	24	0.95	0.8	B
5	Garcia, Jose	13	10	10	0.75	23	31	0.9	53	22	0.9375	0.89	B
6	Little, Ian	5	5	5	0.340909091	15	15	0.5	25	13	0.475	0.46	F
7	Jones, Sally	15	12	17	1	25	34	0.983333333	45	20	0.8125	0.92	A
8	Sully, Todd	11	6	9	0.590909091	18	21	0.65	49	21	0.875	0.73	C
9	Average Scores	10.2	8	11.2	0.666666667	20	25	0.747222222	46	20	0.8208	0.7633	
10	Highest Scores	15	12	17	1	25	34	0.983333333	53	24	0.95	0.92	
11	Lowest Scores	5	5	5	0.340909091	15	15	0.5	25	13	0.475	0.46	

You have designed your spreadsheet, entered labels, values and formulas; now, you will learn how to use *Excel's* formatting features to format cells, and add color and graphics to your gradebook spreadsheet.

Formatting Spreadsheets

Excel features many formatting commands including the ability to add graphics, sounds, and comments as well as change fonts and use fill colors. You can also modify the size and alignment of cells, insert rows and columns, and add borders. Many of these tools are located on the mini toolbar which can be accessed by a right-click of your mouse. Of course, many more commands are available on the ribbon tabs.

With your class gradebook open, let's begin by naming the sheets in your workbook so that there will be a grade sheet for each of the high school English classes you teach. You will then place the students in alphabetical order by doing a **Sort**.

Renaming Worksheets

1. Right-click the **Sheet1** tab at the bottom of the window.
2. Click **Rename**. The Sheet1 tab is highlighted. Type **English 9** in the highlighted tab area. Hit Enter on the keyboard.
3. Right-click the **Sheet2** tab and rename it as **English 10**.

Now, you are ready to modify your gradebook by inserting rows, WordArt, a graphic and a comment. You will format cells so that the text is wrapped and vertically aligned.

Make sure that your English 9 worksheet is open by clicking the tab at the bottom of the *Excel* window. You will be using many of the tools available in *Excel* to make adjustments and enhancements to your workbook. You're already familiar with the Clipboard and Font commands that are also available in *Word*. Other commands you'll find useful in *Excel* include commands for working with numbers and cells.

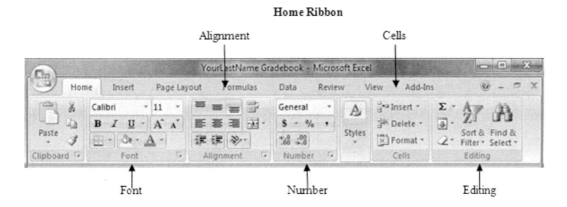

Formatting Numbers

Unless you format a cell to display numbers in a particular format, numbers will be displayed in a general format, which is *Excel's* default setting. For your gradebook scores, you will format the cells so that they display only 2 decimal places.

1. Select Colum E and locate the **General** icon `General ▾` in the **Number** section of the **Home** ribbon.

2. Click the drop down arrow at the end of the box. You are presented with a list of formatting choices including currency, date, time, percentages, etc.

3. Click **Number**.

4. Complete this for any of the columns in which you want to display 2 decimal places.

5. An example of how you might want to format your numbers and decimal points follows:

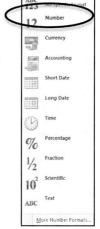

◇	A	B	C	D	E	F	G	H	I	J	K	L	M
1	Student Names	HW-1	HW-2	HW-3	Homework	P-1	P-2	Projects	E1	E2	Exams	Final	Score
2	Possible Points	15	12	17	44	25	35	60	55	25	80		
3	Smith, John	7	8	11	0.59	18	28	0.77	50	20	0.88	0.78	C
4	Engle, Mary	10	7	15	0.73	20	21	0.68	52	24	0.95	0.80	B
5	Garcia, Jose	13	10	10	0.75	23	31	0.90	53	22	0.94	0.89	B
6	Little, Ian	5	5	5	0.34	15	15	0.50	25	13	0.48	0.46	F
7	Jones, Sally	15	12	17	1.00	25	34	0.98	45	20	0.81	0.92	A
8	Sully, Todd	11	6	9	0.59	18	21	0.65	49	21	0.88	0.73	C
9	Average Scores	10.2	8	11.2	0.67	20	25	0.75	46	20	0.82	0.76	
10	Highest Scores	15	12	17	1.00	25	34	0.98	53	24	0.95	0.92	
11	Lowest Scores	5	5	5	0.34	15	15	0.50	25	13	0.48	0.46	

Now you will insert rows to your gradebook by using commands located on the **Home** ribbon.

Inserting Rows or Columns

To make your spreadsheet easier to read and more visually appealing, you will be inserting two rows – one above your student names and one below the total **Possible Points**.

1. With your cursor on any cell in Row 1, click the **Insert** command  located in the **Cells** section of the **Home** ribbon.

2. Click the drop down arrow at the end of the box.

3. Click **Insert Sheet Rows**

4. Click a cell in **Row 4** and insert a row. Now you have a blank row between your column labels and your first row of students and scores.

Now that you have inserted two rows, you will be merging the cells in those rows, resizing them and filling them with color.

Merging Cells

You will be merging the cells in the first and fourth rows of your spreadsheet.

1. To merge the cells in **Row 1**, select cells **A1** to **M1**.
2. Click the **Merge and Center** Icon 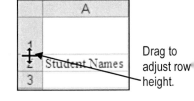 located in the **Alignment** section of the **Home** ribbon.
3. Merge **Row 4.**

You now have an area for your class banner (**Row 1**), but it is too narrow for a banner of any size. You want to insert a WordArt title and a graphic for your English 9 and will need more space.

Resizing Rows

1. Place your cursor on the intersection line between Row 1 and 2 (the cursor becomes a solid cross).
2. Hold down the left mouse button and drag the boundary below the row heading until the row is the height you want.

Drag to adjust row height.

You can easily readjust your row size if it isn't large enough once you insert your WordArt title and graphic. You should also adjust your columns so there is no wasted room on the spreadsheet.

Inserting WordArt and Other Graphics

The procedure to insert WordArt is the same in each of the *Microsoft Office 2007* applications; however, styles vary.

1. Click the **Insert** tab.

2. Click the **WordArt** command

3. Choose a design from the WordArt Gallery by clicking your choice.

4. Type **English 9** and click **OK**.

5. Click your English 9 WordArt graphic, hold down the left mouse button, and drag it to **Row 1**. (If your row is not large enough, adjust either the WordArt graphic or the row).

6. Click the **Clip Art** command 🔎 Clip Art on the **Insert** ribbon. The Clip Art task pane opens allowing you to search for Clip Art, photographs, movies and sound and even providing a link to Clips Online.

7. In the **Search text: box**, enter a search item that would be appropriate for your class.

8. When you locate a graphic you want in your class banner, click it to insert it into the spreadsheet.

9. Click the graphic image and resize if necessary by positioning the mouse pointer over one of the handles and dragging the mouse away from or (enlarge) toward the center (reduce).

10. Drag the image and place it in Row 1 next to your class title.

Now that you have a class banner, you can customize your spreadsheet even more by filling cells with color.

Filling Cells with Color

1. Click **Row 1**.

2. Click the down arrow on the **Fill Color** 🎨▾ located in the **Font** section of the **Home** ribbon.

3. Click any color of your choice.

Use the **Fill Color** feature in other places in your class spreadsheet to create boundaries between categories or make certain rows or columns more visible. You can also change the font of any cell text by selecting the cell(s) and then selecting the font type and size. You can center cell contents by selecting the

cell and clicking the center icon ▤ on the Home ribbon.

Since the column labels on this spreadsheet are fairly long (homework) and the contents of the cells in the assignment rows short (2 - 3 decimal places would be sufficient), change the orientation of Row 2 so that the cell contents are at a 90-degree angle.

Cell Alignment and Orientation

1. Select **Row 2**.

2. Click the icon at the end of the **Alignment** command Alignment located on the **Home** ribbon.
   (Notice that your text orientation is currently at 0 degrees.)

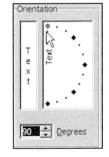

3. Position your cursor on the Text bar in the **Text Orientation** box.

4. Hold down the left mouse button and move the bar to the **90-degree** position.

5. In the **Text control** area of this menu select **Wrap text**.

6. Click **OK**

Sorting Ascending Order

Your class gradebook is looking better, but you notice that student names are not listed alphabetically. *Excel* allows you to sort cells in ascending (A-Z alphabetic or 1-10 numeric) or descending (Z-A or 10-1) order.

1. Select the student names.
2. Click the **Sort and Filter** command on the **Home** ribbon.

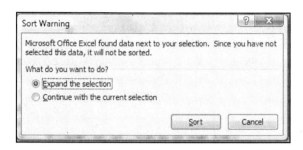

3. Select **Sort A-Z**
4. Make sure that **Expand the selection is** checked.
5. Click **Sort**.

Another *Excel* feature that you will find extremely useful as a teacher is the ability to insert comments into your spreadsheet. In the gradebook spreadsheet, for example, you might want to add a comment in a cell containing a student's score to remember that he/she is planning to resubmit a revised assignment.

Inserting Comments

1. Click cell **J9**.

2. Click **Review** tab.|

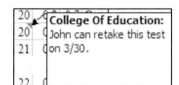

3. Click the **New Comment** command. In the text box, type, **John can retake this test on 3/30**.

4. A red triangle appears on the box and the comment becomes visible when you run your cursor over it.

5. To remove a comment, right-click the cell and click **Delete Comment**.

Check your final calculations with the spreadsheet example on the following page:

◇	A	B	C	D	E	F	G	H	I	J	K	L	M
1			English 9										
2	Student Names	HW-1	HW-2	HW-3	Homework	P-1	P-2	Projects	E1	E2	Exams	Final	Score
3	Possible Points	15	12	17	44	25	35	60.00	55	25	80.00		
4													
5	Engle, Mary	10	7	15	0.73	20	21	0.68	52	24	0.95	0.80	B
6	Garcia, Jose	13	10	10	0.75	23	31	0.90	53	22	0.94	0.89	B
7	Jones, Sally	15	12	17	1.00	25	34	0.98	45	20	0.81	0.92	A
8	Little, Ian	5	5	5	0.34	15	15	0.50	25	13	0.48	0.46	F
9	Smith, John	7	8	11	0.59	18	28	0.77	50	20	0.88	0.78	C
10	Sully, Todd	11	6	9	0.59	18	21	0.65	49	21	0.88	0.73	C
11	Average Scores	10	8	11	0.67	20	25	0.75	46	20	0.82	0.76	
12	Highest Scores	15	12	17	1.00	25	34	0.98	53	24	0.95	0.92	
13	Lowest Scores	5	5	5	0.34	15	15	0.50	25	13	0.48	0.46	

Creating Charts

A very powerful feature of *Excel* is the ability to create **charts**, which are visual representations of your data. A chart, also referred to as a **graph**, is linked to the worksheet data and is updated automatically when you change the worksheet data. A chart can enhance and simplify your students' understanding of the data. Students are able to see comparisons, patterns, and trends in data.

Using the Chart Wizard in *Excel* makes it easy to construct pie, column, bar, and line charts. Common chart elements include the following:

Title – overall description of the data charted
Labels – specific descriptions of data
Series – set of related data placed in the chart
Legend – contains the labels and identifies the data series

In determining which kind of chart to use to plot your worksheet data, keep in mind that a pie chart can include only one series of data. Each slice of the pie represents only one value from a series. If you were to design a pie chart to give your students a visual representation of the composition of their final grade in your class, it would look like the chart below.

The **pie chart** visually emphasizes the importance of each of the English 9 assignment areas.

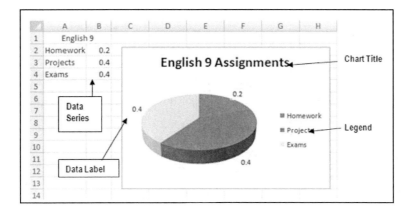

A **bar chart** is useful in visually comparing the differences between values since it can include several series of data. For example, you might use a bar chart to plot the high and low homework scores from your gradebook.

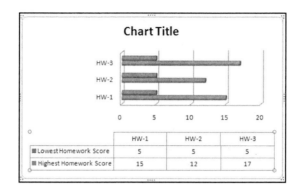

In this chart, two series of data are represented: high and low class homework scores.

Excel can also create a bar chart with vertical bars, which is called a **column chart**. A column chart can include more than one series of data and is useful in comparing differences.

A **line chart** can contain more than one series of data with each line of the chart representing a series. The values in the series are represented by points on a line. An examination of your class performance line chart shows you that your students perform better on exams and in their project activities than on the homework assignments.

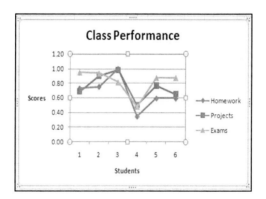

In the rest of this section, you will learn how to create charts from the data in your English 9 gradebook using *Excel's* chart tools. You will need your gradebook open to complete the following practice exercise.

Creating a Pie Chart

1. With your mouse, select the cell containing the data label HW-1. Then, while holding down the **Ctrl key, individually** click cells containing the data labels HW–2 and HW–3.
2. Keep holding down the **Ctrl key,** and click **individually** in each of the data series cells containing the highest homework scores (which were also the total points available for each assignment).
3. Click the **Insert** tab.
4. Click **Pie** in the **Charts** section.

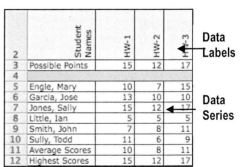

You can choose the style of pie chart you want or click **All Chart Types** and have the opportunity to view other chart types.

As you run your cursor over each pie chart, a text box explains the chart and describes its use.

5. Click an appropriate chart. If your pie chart is not correct, check your data range; also, make sure that you click each of the cells individually.

Now that your chart has been created, the **Chart Tools** tab is available with a number of tools at your disposal to design and format your chart. The **Chart Styles** area provides a gallery of styles easily viewed by clicking each one.

Chart Layouts

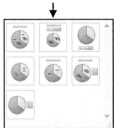

6. Click **Quick Layout in the Design Tab** and choose a predesigned layout.
7. Title your pie chart **Highest Homework Scores**

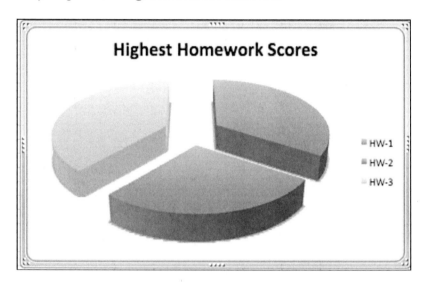

You are able to move your chart by clicking in the chart, holding down your left mouse button and dragging it to a desired location. To size the chart, grab the handles and move your mouse toward the center of the graph (reduce) or away from the center (enlarge). By right-clicking in the chart area, you can access other commands, such as **cut**, **copy**, and **chart options**. To delete the chart, select the chart by clicking in the chart area, and hitting the **delete** key on your keyboard. Now, you will use *Excel's* Chart tools to create a bar chart.

Creating a Bar Chart

1. Hold down the **Ctrl Key** while you select Data Labels – Homework, Projects, and Exams.

2. Keep holding down the **Ctrl key** select the **Data Series – Class average scores** for Homework (.67), Projects (.75) and Exams (.82).

3. Click the **Insert** tab and then on **Bar.**

4. Choose an appropriate bar chart type.

Data Labels
Assignment
Areas

Data Series
Assignment
Averages

Homework	P-1	P-2	Projects	E1	E2	Exams
44	25	35	60.00	55	25	80.00
0.73	20	21	0.68	52	24	0.95
0.75	23	31	0.90	53	22	0.94
1.00	25	34	0.98	45	20	0.81
0.34	15	15	0.50	25	13	0.48
0.59	18	28	0.77	50	20	0.88
0.59	18	21	0.65	49	21	0.88
0.67	20	25	0.75	46	20	0.82

Designing your chart layout and formatting it is easily accomplished using the chart tools that are available when your chart is selected.

Try customizing your chart, giving it different colors and changing the layout by selecting the chart and having the Design tab selected.

Charts can provide compelling arguments by their design and enable quick visualization of data.

Following is a chart representing the data selected from your gradebook spreadsheet:

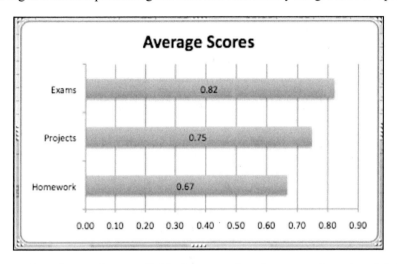

Check out the other options available for your chart layout such as data labels, legends and gridlines. Then, go to the **Format** tab and try out some of the style, fill, and shape effects.

Creating a Line Chart

1. Hold down the **Ctrl Key.**

2. Select the **Data Labels – Homework, Projects** and **Exams** (be certain no additional cells are selected).

3. Keep holding down the **Ctrl Key** and select the **Data Series – Ian Little's final score** in Homework (**.34**), Projects (**.50**) and Exams (**.48**).

Data Labels

	Student Names	HW-1	HW-2	HW-3	Homework	P-1	P-2	Projects	E1	E2	Exams
3	Possible Points	15	12	17	44	25	35	60.00	55	25	80.00
4											
5	Engle, Mary	10	7	15	0.73	20	21	0.68	52	24	0.95
6	Garcia, Jose	13	10	10	0.75	23	31	0.90	53	22	0.94
7	Jones, Sally	15	12	17	1.00	25	34	0.98	45	20	0.81
8	Little, Ian	5	5	5	0.34	15	15	0.50	25	13	0.48

Data Series

4. Make a chart title and call it **Ian Little's Scores.**

5. Provide appropriate names for the horizontal and vertical axes.

6. Provide formatting of your choice.

Take some time to modify the three charts you have created today and become familiar with the design, formatting and layout options available for charts. Change the data within your spreadsheet and view how those data change on the corresponding chart. Just think of the possibilities of using this technique with your students for a class demonstration some time. Now that you have completed your spreadsheet, create a header so that when you print it, pertinent information will be at the top of the spreadsheet.

Creating a Header

1. Click the **Insert** tab.
2. Click the **Header and Footer** 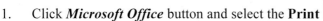 command.
3. Notice that a text box, titled header, is now at the top of your spreadsheet ready for you to type your name.
4. Click the **Current Date**  command.

Notice that there is now a code for the current date. When you check print preview, you will see the current date in the header. Other options, such as page number, current time, and number of pages can also be inserted in your header or footer.

Printing

If your worksheet and charts are too large to print on a single page, you will need to adjust the page setup before printing. *Excel* also provides options for you to print one or all of the worksheets in a workbook or just a selected area of a worksheet. A recommended practice is to always preview before printing.

1. Click *Microsoft Office* button and select the **Print** command.

2. Select **Print Preview**. If you want gridlines on your printed copy (typically this makes it easier to read), then Click **Page Setup**, the **Sheet** tab, and select **Gridlines**.)

If your worksheet contains too many columns of data, you can change the page orientation to landscape.

You then need to decide the number of copies to print, what you want to print and the print range. You can print the entire workbook, a selected area (one you have highlighted on the spreadsheet, or only the active sheet. Always remind your students to use print preview and select only the page(s) or area(s) that they want to print.

Summary

In this technology tools section of the textbook you have become familiar with some of the features of *Excel 2007* that you can use to become a more productive teacher. The gradebook you completed can be used as an artifact for ISTE NETS-T Standard 2.

In Exercise 1, you will learn how to use absolute cell references; Exercise 2 helps you to discover other useful spreadsheet features. In Exercise 3, you will learn how to design interactive learning spreadsheets to help reinforce curricular concepts and skills. More exercises are provided to help you discover ideas for using the spreadsheet as a curricular tool.

Exercise 1: Absolute Cell References

You have already practiced using absolute cell references in the gradebook activity. In this practice exercise you will construct a worksheet using an absolute cell reference in the formula. By default, *Excel* automatically calculates values using relative cell references, which automatically reflect the row or column to which they have been copied. However, there will be times when you want the cell reference to remain the same, as is the case in this practice exercise.

✓ Always begin your spreadsheet by saving it in the appropriate directory and folder.

1. Title this workbook, **YourLastName Spreadsheet Exercises**. You will be saving all of the spreadsheet exercises you complete from this text in this workbook. Each exercise will be placed on a separate named sheet.

2. Title Sheet 1, **Book Orders**. (Select Sheet 1 tab, right-click>Rename).

Your students want to order books from the Youth Books Company, which requires the price of the book plus $1.45 in shipping charges per pound. You construct a worksheet to determine the exact cost for each student's order as shown on the next page:

	A	B	C	D	E
1		Youth Books Order			
2	Order Due Date	30-Nov			
3	Shipping (per lb)	$1.45			
4					
5	Book Title	Book Price	Weight (lb)	Shipping	Total per book
6	Dinosaurs	$8.75	1.4		
7	World Wonders	11.5	1.7		
8	Mammals	4.95	0.8		
9	Riddles	3.95	0.5		
10	War Stories	7	1		
11					
12				TOTAL	

In cell **D6**, you will write the formula to determine the shipping charges for the first book, Dinosaurs. The shipping rate is located in cell B3, so your formula would be =**C6*B3**. However, if you were to copy that formula from C6 through C10, B3 would become B4, B5, B6 and so on. To prevent this from happening, you will enter the formula in cell **D6** as =**C6*$B$3** and **copy it from C6 through C10**.

Complete this exercise by totaling the price per book and then determine the total order amount. Compare with your classmates to see if your answers are the same. By now you should be able to define an absolute cell reference and when you would need to use one.

Exercise 2: CHOOSE, VLOOKUP, COUNTIF

This practice exercise provides instruction in other *Excel* features that you will find useful in working with spreadsheets. In the gradebook exercise, you learned how to use the AVERAGE, MAX, and MIN functions. By completing this exercise, you will have practice in using the COUNTIF, CHOOSE, and VLOOKUP functions.

✓ Save this spreadsheet exercise in **YourLastName Spreadsheet Exercises** workbook.
✓ Title this sheet **CHOOSE**

Using CHOOSE

The CHOOSE function is designed to return a value from a list of values and is written as follows;

$$=CHOOSE(<choice>, <option_1>, <option_2>, ..., <option_N>)$$

The CHOOSE function returns the value in a list of arguments <options> that correspond to <choice>. For this exercise, students are assigned extra credit points based on the projects that they complete. Each project is worth a given number of points with Project 1 receiving 100 points, Project 2 receiving 70, Project 3 receiving 50, and Project 4 receiving 40 points. Given the choice (Project #), a corresponding number of points will be awarded.

1. Construct the following spreadsheet listing the students' names and the projects they have completed:

	A	B	C	D
1	Student	Project	Extra Credit	
2	John Lopez	2		
3	Maryah Anders	3		
4	Cecile Bonavieux	1		
5	Richard Jones	4		
6				

2. Write the following function in cell C2 **=CHOOSE(B2, 100, 70, 50, 40)**
3. Use the fill handle to copy the function from C2 to C5.

Using VLOOKUP

The VLOOKUP function is used to return a value from a table of values stored in the spreadsheet and is written as follows:

$$=VLOOKUP(<value>, <range>, <column>)$$

For this exercise, the teacher has told her students that their extra credit work will count no more than 100 points in the final grade. She has set up a scale assigning final grade points to correspond to the extra credit points earned (Cells D7 – E16). Column D contains the extra credit points, and Column E the corresponding points earned toward the final grade.

✓ Rename the sheet as **LOOKUP** in **YourLastName Spreadsheet Exercises** workbook.

1.   Construct the following spreadsheet:

	A	B	C	D	E
1	Student	Points Received	Final Grade Points Earned		
2	John Lopez	130			
3	Maryah Anders	300			
4	Cecile Bonavieux	95			
5	Richard Jones	175			
6				Final Points	
7				0	0
8				75	25
9				100	35
10				125	45
11				150	55
12				175	65
13				200	75
14				225	85
15				250	95
16				300	100

2.   Write the following function in cell C2 **=VLOOKUP(B2, $D$7:$E$16, 2)**
3.   Use the fill handle to copy the function from C2 to C5.

Using COUNTIF

The COUNTIF function is used to determine how many cells meet a certain condition and is written as follows:
=COUNTIF(Range, "Criteria")

For this exercise, you will determine how many of your students passed the math exam. To pass the exam, a student must receive a grade of 70 or above.
✓   Rename a sheet as **COUNTIF** in **YourLastName Spreadsheet** Exercises workbook.
✓   Construct the following spreadsheet:

	A	B
1	Student	Math Exam
2	Alice Hall	87
3	Kim Chung	70
4	Dan Nichols	56
5	Esther Williams	38
6	Edward Ramirez	98
7	Colt Warden	25
8	Emily Meadows	13
9	Jon VanDal	73
10		
11	Passing Scores	

✓   Write the following function in cell B11 **=COUNTIF(B2:B9,">=70")**

In this exercise, you have learned three additional *Excel* functions that will prove useful for you and your students. Of course, there are many more functions available and worthwhile for your independent investigation.

Exercise 3: Technology Review, Interactive Spreadsheet

NETS-T Standard 1

This practice exercise teaches you how to use *Excel* to construct a spreadsheet activity that provides immediate feedback to your students. Students simply type a response in a cell and view the feedback in an adjoining cell.

An activity of this nature can be designed for any grade level and content area. Interactive learning spreadsheets allow a means for teachers to develop activities to reinforce curricular concepts.

✓ Save this spreadsheet exercise in **YourLastName Spreadsheet Exercises** workbook.

✓ Title this sheet **YourLastName Technology Review**

Planning the Spreadsheet Activity

In developing an interactive learning spreadsheet, you will be using the IF formula, hiding formulas (so students cannot locate the answers on the spreadsheet itself), and protecting your worksheet (so students cannot accidentally delete formulas).

You will need to give some thought as to the placement of items (text or graphics) on the worksheet, response cells and feedback cells.

Also, you will need to write very clear directions for your activity so that students can complete it on their own and even take it home with them.

The technology spreadsheet you are developing for this exercise will contain only ten items: eight pieces of hardware that the student will identify as **input** or **output** devices and two common technology terms to define.

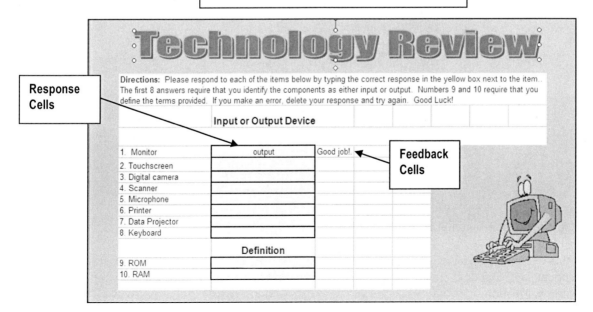

Designing the Physical Layout

For aesthetic purposes, you will create a frame surrounding the activity and fill it with a light color.

1. Select cells **A1 – A 17** and merge/center the cells.

2. Select cells **J1 – J17** and merge/center the cells.

3. Using the same procedure, merge cells **B1 – I1** and cells **B17 – I17**.

Now that the cells are merged, you will use the **Fill Color** icon color the merged areas.

4. Click inside the merged cells on each side and fill with a light color.

5. Enlarge your merged areas by holding down your left mouse button on the boundaries and dragging.

    Hold down the left
    mouse button and drag.

6. Insert WordArt, titling it **Technology Review**.

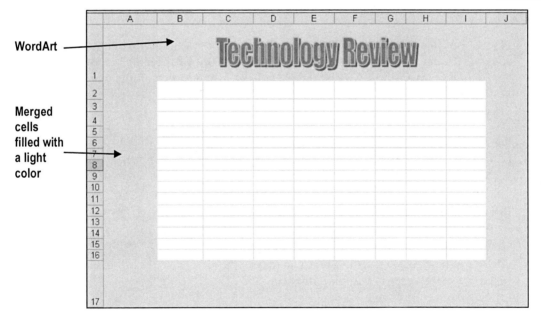

WordArt

Merged
cells
filled with
a light
color

With the worksheet framed and your title in place, you are ready to write the directions for the activity. This requires an area large enough to display the directions so you will need to merge cells and then format them so that the text (which is several lines long) will wrap.

Activity Directions

1. Select and merge cells **B2 – I2**.

2. Wrap the text in this merged cell.

3. Type the following directions:

Directions: Please respond to each of the items below by typing the correct response in the yellow box next to the item. The first 8 answers require that you identify the components as either input or output. Numbers 9 and 10 require that you define the terms provided. If you make an error, delete your response and try again. Good Luck!

4. Adjust Row 2 so that all of the directions can be viewed.

5. Merge cells **B3 – I3** (see illustration on the next page) and fill with color so that your directions are framed and emphasized.

Technology Terms and Column Titles

You will enter the technology terms that you want identified as input or output in Column B starting in cell B5. Students will identify each term as an input or output device by typing their response in the adjoining Column C. The feedback will be displayed in Column D.

1. Type **Monitor** in **B5**. Continue typing the remaining 9 technology terms (**Touchscreen, Digital Camera, Scanner, Microphone, Printer, Data Projector**, and **Keyboard**) in Column B. Leave cell B13 blank (adjust column width so that all the words are visible).

2. Type **ROM** in **B14** and **RAM** in **B15**.

Now that you have entered all of the technology terms, you can apply formatting features to enhance the appearance of the spreadsheet activity.

3. Merge cells **B4 – E4**.

4. Using bold format, enter **Input or Output Device** in the merged cells B4-E4 (You may need to use the space key to place the text directly above the column).

5. Using bold format, type **Definition** in cell **C13** (enlarge Row 13).

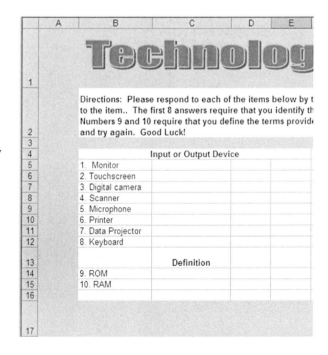

Formatting the Response Cells

Students will be typing their responses in Column C. In order to make it easier for them to know where to type, you will fill the cells with a light yellow color and then place a black border around each cell.

1. Select cells **C5 – C12** and fill with a light yellow color. (Remember the directions told students to write their responses in the yellow boxes).

2. Fill cells **C14** and **C15** with the same yellow color.

3. With **C5** selected, put outside borders around the cell.

4. Repeat the process in each cell so that every response cell is yellow and surrounded by a border.

Adding a Graphic

Inserting graphics and/or pictures to your spreadsheet learning activities enhances visual appeal.

1. Select and merge cells **G5 – I16**.

2. Fill with the color you used for your spreadsheet frame.

3. Insert an appropriate graphic in the colored area depicting one or more of the technology terms included in the spreadsheet.

Creating the Feedback Cells

When students enter a response, they will receive immediate feedback on whether it is correct, incorrect, or perhaps a clue as to the correct response.

The cells containing the feedback for student responses need to be located adjacent (or as near as possible) to the response cells.

The **If formula** used in the feedback cells basically says that if the response cell equals the correct response (located in a cell in the worksheet), then the positive feedback (located in a cell in the worksheet) is the result; however, if the response cell does not contain the correct response, then the negative feedback (located in a cell in the worksheet) is the result.

So, the first step is to write the correct response, positive feedback, and negative feedback in worksheet cells that you can point to in the formula.

1. Type **Output** in cell **E25** (this is the correct response for the first item on the worksheet – a monitor is an output device.

2. Type **Good job!** in cell **F25** for the positive feedback

3. Type **Try again** in cell **G25** for the negative feedback.

4. Continue entering the responses and feedback in the cells as illustrated in the following table:

	E	F	G
25	output	Good job!	Try again.
26	input	Good job!	Try again.
27	input	Yes!!!	Incorrect.
28	input	Correct!!	Try again.
29	input	Good job!	Try again.
30	output	You got it!	Try again.
31	output	Yes!!!	Try again.
32	input	Good job!	Try again.
33			
34	read only memory	Exactly!	Begins with "read"
35	random access memory	Yes!!!	Begins with "random"

With the correct responses and feedback available, you can now write your formula in the feedback cell. For this exercise, the feedback will appear in the cells to the right of the student's response (in column D).

Using the If Formula

1. Click in cell **D5** and type this formula:

=IF(C5<>"",IF(C5=E25,F25,G25),"")

You can see how the formula works. Basically, it says that if C5 is empty, then leave it empty; if C5 is equal to E25 (output), then F25 (Good Job!) appears; if C5 is not E25, then G25 (Try again) appears. The formula must be written **exactly**:

=   always starts a formula

IF   turns on the IF function. If is always followed by a forward parenthesis

C5   tells the computer which cell is being analyzed

<>   means the cell is empty

""   tells the computer to leave those cells empty

,   ends the first condition of the formula

Now we will add a second condition

IF   is added again followed by another forward parenthesis

C5   tells the computer which cell is being analyzed

=E25 if C5 is equal to E25 (correct answer),

,F25   then F25 (positive feedback) will be displayed in D5

,G25   if it is not equal, then G25 (negative feedback) will be displayed in D5

),"")   end of the formula – there must be a backward parenthesis for each
         forward parenthesis. There must also be equal "" and commas.

2. Use the fill handle to copy the formula from cells **D6 to D15** (you will need to delete the formula in cell D13 as that is not a feedback cell).

Try entering a response in the response cell to determine if your formula is working correctly. Remember, the formula must be entered exactly as follows:

=IF(C5<>"",IF(C5=E25,F25,G25),"")

Once your formula is working correctly, change the font in the answer and feedback cells to white so that your students cannot see the answers.

3. Select cells **E25 – G35**. Make the font white.

Locking and Hiding the Formula

You will want to lock the cells containing the formula so that they cannot be changed and unlock the cells for student answers (as you want students to be able to enter these cells).

You will also want to hide the formula so that your students cannot locate the answers.

1. Select the feedback cells containing the If formula – cells **D5 – D16**.

2. Right-click the cell and select **Format Cells**.

3. Click the **Protection** tab.

4. Make sure that the <u>L</u>ocked and <u>Hi</u>dden boxes are checked for these formula cells **D5 – D16**.

Although you want the formula cells locked when the worksheet is protected, you will want to make sure that the cells where students write responses are unlocked so that responses can be entered in those cells.

5. Select cells **C5 – C16** (the response cells)

6. Right click and select **Format Cells**.

7. Click the **Protection** tab.

8. Neither the locked or hidden box should be checked.

> Make sure the boxes are **NOT** checked for C5 – C16 where students type in answers.

Now you are ready to protect the worksheet so that no changes can be made except by you. The only cells that can be changed are the unlocked response cells where your students will be typing their answers.

Protecting the Worksheet

1. Click **Format** in the **Cells** section of the **Home** ribbon.

    (**Tools>Protections>Protect Sheet** for Mac OS X)

2. Click  **Protect Sheet.**

3. You can password protect your sheet so that no one can unprotect it without the password. **Be sure to use a password that you will not forget.**

4. Enter a password if you choose to password protect your spreadsheet. If you don't enter a password, it is still protected but can be unprotected by anyone who knows how to unprotect spreadsheets.

5. Click **OK.**

You want your students to only be able to select the cells, but not to change any of the worksheets.

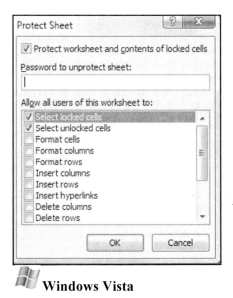

Windows Vista

Mac OS

✓ If you want to make any changes, you will need to unprotect the worksheet by going through the same steps, only this time select "Unprotect Sheet."

✓ If you have assigned a password, you will be asked for this before unprotecting the sheet.

*Could be used as an artifact for Standard 1.

Blog Reflection

Interactive learning spreadsheets allow you to customize activities for your students. These activities are excellent for reviewing concepts and providing enrichment exercises. How might you use this activity to design learning in your own classroom? Could students create interactive learning spreadsheets to demonstrate learning, for instance? Use these exercises as time to reflect upon how you might use technology in your classroom and post to your blog.

Exercise 4: M & M Spreadsheet Activity

ISTE NETS-T Standard 3

This exercise is one that has been popular with educators for some time and variations on the exercise can be located on the Internet. It is an entertaining way for your students to learn math concepts as well as spreadsheet functions. It requires that you have at least three bags of M&Ms (or Skittles, jelly beans, etc.) to supply the data for your spreadsheet (if you are in a class situation, three or more students, each with a bag of M&Ms, can work together).

Optional Collaborative Activity: Use Google Docs Spreadsheet and work with a partner or small group, experimenting with the features. You will find this tool very similar to Microsoft *Excel*.

✓ Save the file as **YourLastName Spreadsheet Exercises**.
✓ Name the sheet **YourLastName M&M Exercise.**
✓ Construct a spreadsheet using *Excel* functions that enable you to answer the following questions:

1. How many M&Ms of each color are contained in each bag?
2. How many total M&Ms of each color are there?
3. How many total M&Ms are there?
4. What is the average number of each color of M&Ms?
5. What is the average number of M&Ms in each bag?
6. What is the maximum number of M&Ms?
7. What is the maximum number of each color of M&Ms?
8. What is the minimum number of M&Ms?
9. What is the minimum number of each color of M&Ms?
10. How many M&Ms would be contained in a pound of M&Ms?

The spreadsheet design can vary, but must have a pleasing appearance and include the following components:

1. Group members' names (or M&M bag identification numbers, i.e., M&M1, M&M2, etc.)

2. Colors of the M&Ms

3. *Excel* functions – sum, average, maximum and minimum functions

4. 2 fonts and/or font sizes

5. Color

6. 1 graphic

7. Header with your name and date

*Could be used as an artifact for Standard 3.

Exercise 5: M & M Spreadsheet Charts

ISTE NETS-T Standards 1 & 3

This exercise requires that you present your M&M findings visually through the use of charts. (If you used Google Docs Spreadsheet for the previous exercise, try out the charts and see how they differ from those in *Excel*.) If you worked with a partner or small group in the previous exercise, then continue using Google Docs Spreadsheet and create charts using the Google Docs Spreadsheet chart wizard or investigate inserting a chart gadget.

✓ Open your file **YourLastName M&M Exercise**

✓ Create at least 3 different charts to illustrate your findings in the M&M Spreadsheet Exercise. Your charts must include the following components:

    1. Each of the 3 charts must be of a different chart type (pie, column, bar or line).
    2. Title
    3. Labels
    4. Legend
    5. Chart elements should correspond to M&M colors being illustrated (i.e., a pie chart illustrating the composition of a bag of M&Ms should have pie slices that correspond to the M&M color they are labeled)

*Could be used as an artifact for Standards 1 and 3.

Exercise 6: Curricular Interactive Spreadsheet

ISTE NETS-T Standard 1

In this exercise, you will design an interactive spreadsheet activity using Microsoft *Excel* that will help your students reach curricular goals. The spreadsheet could be used as a group or individual activity to reinforce concepts and/or to provide for a test review. Make sure that you have worked your way through the Exercise 3 (Interactive Learning Spreadsheet, pg. 102) before you begin this exercise.

✓ Save the spreadsheet activity as **YourLastName Interactive Activity** in an appropriate folder.

✓ Create an interactive learning spreadsheet that addresses concepts in your curricular area and grade level. The spreadsheet activity should be visually appealing and contain the following elements:

    1. Appropriate Learning Activity Title
    2. Grade Level
    3. Curricular Area
    4. Standards – (review state and/or national standards to determine concepts and skills for each curricular area and grade level). Remember, each school district curriculum is based on the state's standards and are more specific in nature than the standards. Locate a school district curriculum on the Internet and go to the grade level and/or subject area you plan to teach. In this way, you will be able to see the specific content and skills your students will be learning.

5. Clear directions for student use

6. Spreadsheet elements to be included:

- Merged cells

- 2 fonts and/or font sizes

- Color

- Graphic

- Pleasing appearance and arrangement of items

- Minimum of 15 student choices

- Appropriate IF formula, locked and hidden cells, and protected worksheet.

*Could be used as an artifact for Standard 1.

Exercise 7: Problem Solving with Spreadsheets
ISTE NETS-T Standard 2

This exercise presents an example of a way that spreadsheets can be used to answer a "What if" question. Students are asked to determine their household's electrical use and compute the cost of operating individual appliances. What if they were to run the dishwasher only once a day? How much could they save in energy (and money) by turning off TVs, computers, etc.?

✓ Save the spreadsheet as **YourLastName Electrical Usage** in **YourLastName Spreadsheet Exercises** workbook.

✓ Design a spreadsheet to illustrate the cost of operating common appliances based on the rate of kilowatt use per hour and the cost per kilowatt. You have a list of common appliances from which to choose, the kilowatt use per hour and the cost per kilowatt (students could use their parents' electrical bills to determine the cost per kilowatt, but an example is provided for this exercise).

✓ Your spreadsheet should be designed to answer the following questions:

1. What appliances are used during a typical month?

2. How many hours per day are they used?

3. How many days during the month is the appliance in use?

4. What is the total cost of operating an individual appliance each month?

5. What would my total electric bill be for the month?

Common Appliances	
Item	Kilowatt (KWH) use per hour
Electric blanket	0.075
Coffee pot	0.12
Hair Dryer	1.3
Iron	1
Microwave	1
Oven	1.3
Computer	0.075
Clock radio	0.02

Burner	1.2
TV	0.23
Vacuum	0.75
VCR	0.025
Electric razor	0.035
Refrigerator	1.25
Washer	1
Dryer	5
Dishwasher	1

Cost of 1 kilowatt:
0.0915

✓ Your spreadsheet should contain the following components:

1. Merged cells containing the title of your spreadsheet

2. Column headings with appropriate labels

3. Header with your name and date

4. Formula(s) to determine the monthly total cost of electricity for each appliance based on the number of hours used each day and the number of days used during the month. Include a formula for the total monthly cost for all appliances.

Once you have completed the spreadsheet, try variations on the number of hours used each day or the number of days used the appliance is used during the month. As you change amounts, the cost for operating the appliance changes as well as the total cost of electricity.

*Could be used as an artifact for Standard 2.

> **Exercise 8: The Field Trip**
>
> ISTE NETS-T Standard 4

There will be many opportunities for you and your students to use spreadsheets. This collaborative exercise presents a common school scenario that lends itself well to a curricular spreadsheet lesson.

✓ Use either Microsoft *Excel* or Google Docs Spreadsheet for this exercise, collaborating with a partner or small group.

✓ Save the spreadsheet as **YourLastName Field Trip.**

Scenario: Your sixth grade class wants to raise money for a field trip. They are examining a number of fundraising activities and need to decide which one(s) would be the best choice(s) and how much they need to sell of each item to earn the estimated total cost of the field trip ($585). The fundraising opportunities you have chosen are as follows:

Candy – a box of 10 candy bars will cost $4.00 and can be sold for $6.75
Cards – a box of 15 cards will cost $10.00 and can be sold for $15.00
Car Wash – cleaning materials will cost $.50 a wash and each car could be charged $3.00

✓ Develop a spreadsheet with the following components:

    1. Merged cells containing the title of your spreadsheet
    2. Column headings with appropriate labels
    3. Formula(s) to determine the amount students will make for a single item sold, the total amount estimated to be made from each fundraiser, the difference between the amounts raised (individually and collectively) and the total $585 goal
    4. Chart that illustrates the goal for each fundraising activity
    5. Any other elements that would add to understanding and visual appeal

As the teacher, you can choose to distribute the fundraising activities based on your opinion of how successful each will be and how much money might be raised. Once you have determined the goals for each fundraiser, create a chart to illustrate those goals for your students.

With the spreadsheet, you can easily illustrate the possibilities (what if questions). *What if we wash 80 cars, how much will we make? How much do we still need to earn as we complete each fundraiser?* The answers to these questions will help in decision-making. Additionally, as your students complete their fundraising activities, they can enter in the exact amounts earned and be able to tell how much more money must be raised to reach the $585.00 goal.

*Could be used as an artifact for Standard 4.

Exercise 9: Curricular Spreadsheet Lesson
Required: ISTE NETS-T Standard 3

You have seen the many possibilities presented for using spreadsheets. For this two-part exercise, you will design a problem scenario for your students requiring that they create a spreadsheet (**Spreadsheet Exercise 7 *Problem Solving*** as a model). Then you will actually construct the spreadsheet that the problem requires.

This exercise can be completed with a partner or small group, since you will be using Google Docs and Google Docs Spreadsheet.

Part 1 – Spreadsheet Problem Lesson

For Part 1 of this exercise, you will create a Google Docs document presenting a scenario/problem and directions for your students. Your directions should be clear and include the components you expect your students to include in their spreadsheets.

✓ Save your Google Docs document describing the Part 1 spreadsheet lesson as **YourLastName Spreadsheet Problem**

✓ Create a spreadsheet problem that addresses concepts in your curricular area (review state and/or national standards to determine concepts and skills for each curricular area and grade level). Use the headings below and address each of the areas:

1. **Grade Level** (grade level for which your spreadsheet problem is designed)
2. **Curricular Area** (curricular area to be addressed)
3. **Standards** – (review state and/or national standards to determine concepts and skills for each curricular area and grade level). Remember, each school district curriculum is based on the state's standards and are more specific in nature than the standards. Locate a school district curriculum on the Internet, go to the grade level and/or subject area you plan to teach. In this way, you will be able to see the specific content and skills your students will be learning.
4. **Scenario/Problem** (the actual scenario/problem that you will give your students)
5. **Guidelines/Directions** (your expectations for the spreadsheet that your students create – what do they need to include?)

Part 2 - Spreadsheet

For Part 2 of this exercise, create the spreadsheet that you expect your students will be constructing to answer the problem. Use Google Docs spreadsheet for this part of the exercise. The spreadsheet will contain the components that you have given in your Guidelines/Directions above.

Your Google Docs spreadsheet could be shared with your students AFTER they complete this activity, for comparison and self-assessment.

*A required artifact for Standard 3.

Exercise 10: Team Story Problem
ISTE NETS-T Standard 4

Although story problems are an effective way to teach math and reasoning skills, they present a challenge for most students. By designing a spreadsheet to complete the calculations and present findings through graphs, students can hone their problem solving skills. Your instructor will assign you to a team. Each team will have a unique name.

✓ Work with your team to complete this exercise, which requires that you create a word problem that can be solved using a spreadsheet.

1. Working with the members of your team, think of a problem that requires at least 2 steps to solve and involves at least 3 basic math operations.
2. Now, create a story/scenario (at least a paragraph in length) to go with the problem.
3. Use Google Docs to write your story and **share** your document with your team members, who can edit the document at the same time. Remember to name your file (click the file name at the upper-left corner) and name your file **YourTeamName Story Problem** (Include the grade level for which your spreadsheet problem is designed.)
4. Create the solution spreadsheet in a Google Docs Spreadsheet and insert a graph (experiment with the various graph gadgets in Google Docs Spreadsheet) that would help with understanding the solution.
5. Now, share both your story problem Google Doc and your solution Google Docs Spreadsheet with another team and see if they can solve the problem and create the spreadsheets and graphs required.
6. **Publish** your spreadsheet and lesson plan and insert on a new page on your Technology Teaching Portfolio.

*Could be used as an artifact for Standard 4.

Exercise 11: Verifying and Analyzing Data Using Google Squared
ISTE NETS-T Standard 4

Google Squared is a search tool that helps you quickly build a collection of facts from the Internet on any topic you specify.

✓ For this exercise, you will create a Google Squared spreadsheet for students to verify and analyze information.
1. Navigate to http://www.google.com/squared and select one of the squares already made or make one of your own. (How about roller coasters?)
2. Create a lesson plan in Google Docs and include detailed instructions for students. For instance, you might want them to sort and analyze data in columns and ask more questions, coming up with assumptions or predictions.
3. Insert your Google Squared Spreadsheet and Docs lesson plan on a new page on your Technology Teaching Portfolio. (Make sure you **publish** both files, so they will be visible to anyone.)

*Could be used as an artifact for Standard 4.

How might you evaluate and assess student learning in your classroom using technology? ISTE NETS-T Standard 2 states: "Teachers design, develop, and evaluate authentic learning experiences and assessment incorporating contemporary tools and resources to maximize content learning in context and to develop the knowledge, skills, and attitudes identified in the National Educational Technology Standards for Students (NETS-S)."

The standard states that use of these tools is not exclusive to the teacher. Digital Age assessment tools are effective, if not essential, in the hands of students to allow for self-evaluation. With students as active participants in developing their own educational goals, effective Digital Age teachers can "develop technology-enriched learning environments that enable all students to pursue their individual curiosities and become active participants in . . . managing their own learning and assessing their own progress."

Effective teachers who have identified their students' unique and diverse learning styles can effectively "customize and personalize learning activities." Through using multiple assessment and evaluation tools, including those that leverage technology, teachers can modify activities, work strategies, cognitive load, modality of delivery (i.e., visual, auditory, kinesthetic), and other critical components that impact student learning and engagement.

Finally, as effective Digital Age teachers actively design and develop learning experiences and assessments, they "provide students multiple and varied formative and summative assessments." These tools, aligned with content and technology standards, can use those data to continually inform learning and modify instruction.

This chapter will help you, the teacher, better understand the role of assessment and evaluation, introduce you to various assessment strategies, direct you to web-based tools for creating assessments, and guide you through the development of your own authentic artifacts. You will also be guided through the rudimentary use of *Microsoft Excel* 2007 (for PC) and Google spreadsheets (all platforms).

What is assessment?

The assessment of student learning plays a critical role in teaching. Through the assessment process, you are able to understand what students are learning, provide feedback, and ultimately improve student learning. The information you gather about student achievement can be used to help you to make instructional decisions and enhance learning. An integral part of that information gathering includes the use of summative and formative assessments.

Formative assessment takes place as students are in the process of learning and can help you adjust instruction and meet student needs. The ways in which you can gain this information include something as basic as asking question to see if students understand the lesson and then clarifying any misconceptions or a more structured assessment, such as administering a quiz. This type of assessment is intended to help identify material which needs to be clarified or re-taught and can assist in determining whether curriculum or learning activities need to be modified. Fundamental to formative assessment is the need to use the information obtained to ensure student learning. With that in mind, providing descriptive feedback to students is also a crucial part of the formative assessment process.

Summative assessment, on the other hand, is more cumulative in nature and is administered after the instructional process is completed. This is the measure of student learning at the end of a unit of instruction. Often the results of these assessments provide the primary basis for assigning students' grades and for reporting to parents and school officials. Summative assessments include such items as end-of-unit or chapter tests, end-of-term or semester exams, district assessments and state/national standardized tests.

There are a great many assessment strategies for collecting information about student achievement such as **traditional assessments,** in which students *choose* a response from a given list, such as multiple-choice, true/false, or matching. In the past, teachers relied almost solely on traditional assessments, and, of course, standardized tests are still a primary measure of student achievement.

However, as part of the school restructuring movement, alternative assessment strategies were adopted by teachers as effective ways to assess student learning. **Alternative assessment** is any type of assessment that requires students to create a response to a question or task instead of merely choosing the correct response and include a variety of strategies. Authentic and performance assessments are considered alternatives to traditional assessment as well, and these terms are often used interchangeably although some experts believe that there are slight differences among the three.

The key to **authentic assessment** is to provide real-world (authentic) tasks for students that require they apply the knowledge and skills they have learned. Students learn and practice the application of important knowledge and skills for authentic purposes. In authentic assessment, students actually conduct experiments and research, solve math problems involving real-world applications, analyze a political cartoon or a social problem and prepare a persuasive essay in response, create a portfolio, etc. Presenting a "real-world" challenge to students and requiring that they respond to that challenge truly represents their ability to apply what they have learned and develop a deeper understanding:

> When teachers effectively design an engaging, authentic task that is appropriately aligned with a learning standard, students will discover multiple entry points to the material which allows and encourages them to connect prior knowledge and experience to the new material in meaningful ways. As a result, students can begin constructing their own meaning to develop deep and substantial understanding of concepts or skills. (Mueller, 2005, p. 5)

Typically, a **rubric** is used in evaluating student performance in authentic assessment.

Performance assessment is a term often used in combination with authentic assessment. Performance assessment requires students to demonstrate their knowledge, skills, and strategies by creating a response or a product. You can see that the definitions are quite similar, but here is an example that might help clarify the differences between the two assessment strategies:

> Some performance tasks are designed to have students demonstrate their understanding by applying their knowledge to a particular situation. For example, students might be given a current political map of Africa showing the names and locations of countries and a similar map from 1945 and be asked to identify and explain differences and similarities. To be more authentic (more like what someone might be expected to do in the adult world), the task might be to prepare a newspaper article explaining the changes. (McBrien & Brandt, 2007, p. 77-78)

Tasks used in performance-based assessment include essays, oral presentations, open-ended problems, hands-on problems, and real-world simulations. Again, many educators use the terms alternative, authentic and performance assessment interchangeably given the similarities in definition. Regardless of the assessment strategy chosen, however, teachers can employ technology in support of the assessment task and in evaluating student performance.

Assessment and Technology

An obvious use of technology in the assessment process is to use it as the tool for students to create required projects and products. Using Internet resources, word processing, spreadsheets, and presentation software to do research and prepare products is common in the "real-world." These tools provide an "authentic" means of creating responses/products for students and of demonstrating their knowledge and skills.

For the classroom teacher, there are other uses of technology to employ in the assessment process to provide formative and summative information. Designing assessment instruments, whether traditional or alternative, is greatly facilitated with technology. Many textbooks provide electronic test banks, and there is a proliferation of online test and survey tools free of charge that greatly expedite the test creation process. For the development of rubrics, you will find many websites with examples as well as rubric generators to assist you in developing customized rubrics.

Formative assessment can be more easily included in daily classroom activities, through handheld student response devices and other mobile tools. As a teacher, you should plan on assessing students' current knowledge before beginning an instructional unit. If your students already possess those skills, then you might want to skip that section and move on. Or, you may discover some students can act as individual tutors for other students, allowing you to free up your time to help individual students or prepare other instruction.

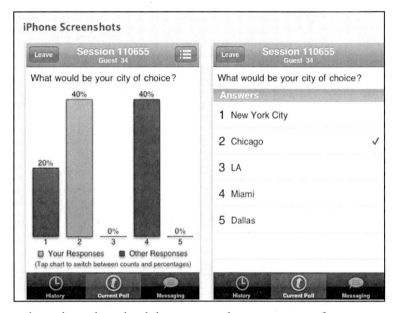

Your job as a teacher will be more like a mentor and coach, helping students progress at their own speed and level. By incorporating formative assessments throughout the school day, you can be more aware of current student progress and be more efficient at planning instruction. You should be very knowledgeable of student response systems in your school and integrate them throughout your school day.

Another role technology plays in the assessment process is in providing timely data to inform instruction. Administering a test electronically with the ability to obtain instantaneous scores is not only a real time saver for teachers, but also helps students who are not performing well is timely as well. Some websites provide the ability to create and automatically grade tests online, but may charge a fee to do so. Using electronic tools for communicating student progress with students and parents is another way technology is employed in the assessment process.

Assessment Resources

Turning Technologies: Student Response Systems
http://www.turningtechnologies.com/studentresponsesystem

ResponseWare for iPod, iPhone, iPad
http://itunes.apple.com/us/app/responseware/id300028504?mt=8

Poll Everywhere: Audience Response Systems
http://www.polleverywhere.com

Google Forms: Create Online Surveys and Quizzes
http://docs.google.com/support/bin/answer.py?answer=87809

Survey Monkey: Create Online Surveys
http://surveymonkey.com

The Concept of Formative Assessment
http://www.vtaide.com/png/ERIC/Formative-Assessment.htm

Authentic Assessment Toolbox
http://jfmueller.faculty.noctrl.edu/toolbox

Office of Research Performance Assessment
http://www.ed.gov/pubs/OR/ConsumerGuides/perfasse.html

Assessment, Assessment Rubrics and Evaluation Guidelines
http://www.techlearning.com/article/4668

Critical Issues in Assessment North Central Regional Ed. Laboratory
http://www.ncrel.org/sdrs/areas/as0cont.htm

Easy TestMaker (free for basic program – charge for plus program)
http://www.easytestmaker.com/default.aspx

RubiStar (free)
http://rubistar.4teachers.org/index.php

QuizStar (charge – includes student accounts)
http://quizstar.4teachers.org/

References

McBrien, J. L., & Brandt, R. S. (1997). *The language of learning: A guide to education terms.* Association for Supervision and Curriculum Development.

Mueller, J. (2005). The Authentic assessment toolbox: Enhancing student learning through online faculty development. *Journal of Online Teaching and Learning, (1)*, 1.

Assessment Exercises

Exercise 1: Creating a Test and Answer Sheet

ISTE NETS-T Standard 2

For this exercise, you will use an online test generator to develop a 20-question test for your students. The directions feature the use of EasyTestMaker (http://easytestmaker.com), which provides a free online test generator. If this website is down or removed, locate another test generator online to complete the exercise.

Registering is easy and the website promises not to sell your information. Once you have registered, login using your selected username and password. You will see that you can save your tests and create a new test. The online directions are easy to follow. Your task is to create a 20 item test using 4 test question types from the following: multiple choice, fill in the blank, matching, short answer or true and false.

✓ Requirements for the exercise include:

- Title should reflect the curricular area and/or topic

- Divide the test into at least 2 sections with appropriate headings

- 20 questions and correct answers using 4 test question types

- Save the file as **YourLastName Test**

Saving Test/Answer Sheet

When you have finished creating your test, click the preview and print test/answer sheet link at the top of the page, which will bring you to the screen below. Note that you can

only download the test if you are a plus member, which requires a subscription fee. However, you can still have a copy of the test for free.

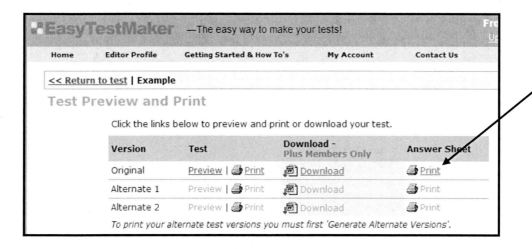

1.   Click the **Print** command (located in the Answer Sheet column).

2.   Select and copy the entire answer sheet (which also contains the questions).

3.   Open a *Word* document (or a Google Doc)

4.   Paste the answer sheet into the *Word* document (or Google Doc)

5.   You may need to reformat to improve appearance after pasting the contents.

6.   Save the document as **YourLastName Test**

*Could be used as an artifact for Standard 2.

Exercise 2: Creating a Rubric

ISTE NETS-T Standard 2

For this exercise you will use RubiStar at http://rubistar.4teachers.org to create a rubric for a class project that you have planned for your students.

✓ Provide the following information on the same page as the rubric:

- **Grade Level** (grade level for which your spreadsheet problem is designed)

- **Curricular Area** (curricular area to be addressed)

- **Standards** – (review state and/or national standards to determine concepts and skills for each curricular area and grade level). Remember, each school district curriculum is based on the state's standards and are more specific in nature than the standards. Locate a school district curriculum on the Internet, go to the grade level and/or subject area you plan to teach. In this way, you will be able to see the specific content and skills your students will be learning.

- **Assignment Description** – provide a brief description of the assignment you have given your students, and for which you are developing a rubric.

✓ Create a rubric with the following specifications:

- **Title** – should reflect the assignment

- **Categories** – minimum of five

- **Descriptors** – clearly identify expected student performance

*Required artifact for Standard 2.

Exercise 3: Providing Parent Feedback: Mail Merge

ISTE NETS-T Standard 5

Technology provides an efficient way for you to communicate with parents. This exercise requires that you prepare a class spreadsheet (one you might prepare to keep track of your students' skill levels) with performance indicators for each of your students. Open an *Excel* workbook and title it **YourLastName Student Information.**

✓ Create a spreadsheet with the following student information:

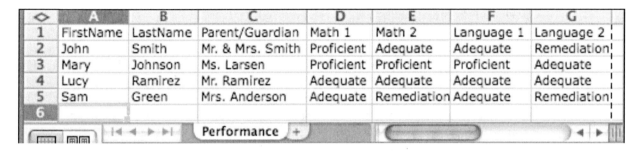

	A	B	C	D	E	F	G
1	FirstName	LastName	Parent/Guardian	Math 1	Math 2	Language 1	Language 2
2	John	Smith	Mr. & Mrs. Smith	Proficient	Adequate	Adequate	Remediation
3	Mary	Johnson	Ms. Larsen	Proficient	Proficient	Proficient	Adequate
4	Lucy	Ramirez	Mr. Ramirez	Adequate	Adequate	Adequate	Adequate
5	Sam	Green	Mrs. Anderson	Adequate	Remediation	Adequate	Remediation
6							

Performance

✓ Name the worksheet **Performance.** (By default there are 3 sheets in *Excel* for Windows, but only one in *Excel* for Mac.) Now you will prepare a letter for your parents and use mail merge to quickly generate a customized report for each parent or guardian.

✓ Follow the directions for creating a mail merge document as follows:

1. Open *Microsoft Word*

2. Save the document as **YourLastName Parent Letters** in an appropriate folder.

3. Click the **Mailings** tab to access the mailings ribbon and the **Start Mail Merge** command.
    In *Word* for Mac 2011, click **Tools>Mail Merge Manager**.

4. Click the **Start Mail Merge** and select the **Step by Step Mail Merge Wizard**

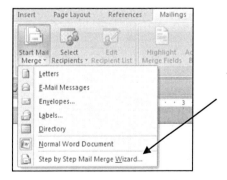

You will go through 6 steps listed at the bottom of the mail merge task pane.

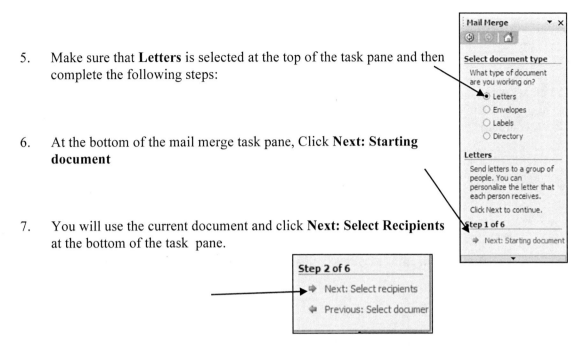

5. Make sure that **Letters** is selected at the top of the task pane and then complete the following steps:

6. At the bottom of the mail merge task pane, Click **Next: Starting document**

7. You will use the current document and click **Next: Select Recipients** at the bottom of the task pane.

Make sure that **Use an existing list** is selected at the top of the mail merge task pane, and then Click **Browse** to locate the YourLastName Student Information workbook and then select the **Performance** worksheet.

The Mail Merge Recipients screen appears. All of your students are selected as recipients, and since you are sending a letter to every parent, you can Click the **OK** button. Note that you have options to sort and filter the informaton as well.

8. Click **OK**

9. Click Next: **Write your letter** at the bottom of the mail merge task pane.

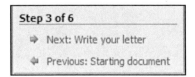

10. Begin typing your letter to the parents with the salutation:

Dear

As you are using mail merge, you would not enter the actual parent or guardian's name. Instead you would insert the cosde for Parent/Guardian.

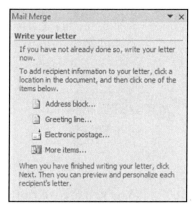

11. Click the **More items . . .** command in the Mail Merge task pane.

12. Select the **Parent/Guardian** field and click the Insert button at the bottom.

The **<<ParentGuardian>>** code is now inserted in your document and you can continue typing and inserting fields in your letter where indicated. Fields in the example on the next page have been highlighted (remember you need to insert these from the **More items** command.

Your letter should look like the one on the next page with the codes entered for those fields in which mail merge will insert the appropriate information for each student.

13. Click **Next: Preview your letters**. (*Note*: After viewing your letter, you may need to make changes or adjustments. Simply Click **Previous: Write your letter** to make those changes.)

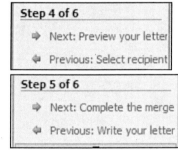

Dear «ParentGuardian»:

Your child, **«FirstName» «LastName»**, recently completed the assessments for the State Math Standards and State Language Standards. Your child's skill levels are listed below:

Math Standard 1 - **«Math_1»**

Math Standard 2 - **«Math__2»**

Language Standard 1 - **«Language_1»**

Language Standard 2 - **«Language_2»**

Please call me at your earliest convenience to discuss **«FirstName»'s** performance on these skill assessments.

14.   Once you have made any necessary corrections, Click **Next: Complete the merge.**

You are given the choice of completing the merge by printing all 4 letters or editing the letters by clicking **Edit individual letters…** to make sure they were merged properly. There is no need to print the letters for this exercise so you will save the letters electronically.

15.   Click **Edit individual letters . . .**

16.   Click **OK** to merge all of the records to a new document.

17.   Save the merged letters (a 4 page document) as **YourLastName Parent Letters** in an appropriate folder.

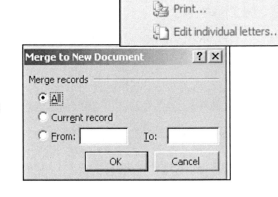

*Could be used as an artifact for Standard 5.

Exercise 4: Online Surveys: Google Forms

ISTE NETS-T Standard 5

Online survey tools provide free and easy ways to obtain parent information and other data. In this exercise, you will use a Google Forms template to collect parent information.

1. Navigate to your Google Docs and click **Create new>From template.**
2. Narrow your type by clicking Forms
3. Click the Public Templates tab.
4. In the Search Templates box, enter "Parent Information."
5. Preview some of the templates and select "Use this template" for the one you want to try.
6. Edit some of the fields as needed.

If you cannot find a template that works for you, create your own form.

7. View the published form and enter information.
8. Then, view your spreadsheet associated with the form and see how the data is presented. How might you better organize the survey to present data that can be easily sorted?
9. Create a new page on your Technology Teaching Portfolio and insert (embed) your form. Include a reflection on this exercise and other ways you might use this powerful tool.

Think of ways you might use Google Forms in your classroom. How about student surveys, quizzes, instant classroom polls? How about using Google Forms on a mobile device, to enter data from any location?

Need more help? Do a search for Google Forms and view Docs Help for Forms:
http://docs.google.com/support/bin/answer.py?answer=87809

View "Using Forms in Google Docs" YouTube video:
http://www.youtube.com/watch?v=IzgaUOW6GIs

*Could be used as an artifact for Standard 5.

NETS-T Standard 3 requires that teachers "exhibit knowledge, skills, and work processes representative of an innovative professional in a global and digital society." Standard 1 likewise encourages teachers to "promote, support, and model creative and innovative thinking and inventiveness" and "engage students in exploring real-world issues and solving authentic problems using digital tools and resources" (ISTE, 2008). Teachers need to know about tools that will enable collaboration, for instance, and how to model the use of those tools to students, parents, and peers. Instead of focusing on students memorizing information, we need to show them how to access information, how to manipulate it, and how to use higher-order thinking to evaluate that information.

Bloom's Taxonomy

Remember Bloom's taxonomy (classification) of how we learn? It starts at the bottom with lower-level knowledge and then builds from there to higher-level ways of thinking.

In 2001, Anderson and Krathwohl revised Bloom's original taxonomy by combining both how we think and know. Bloom's taxonomy is most commonly used to help teachers write learning objectives. This taxonomy can also help teachers set up appropriate learning activities for students to locate and research online resources, construct knowledge, and apply higher-order processes of analysis, evaluation, and creation.

Andrew Churches (2008) extends this taxonomy to include digital terminology, which can further help teachers when planning instruction with technology. For instance, when conducting Boolean searches, Churches proposes that this activity would fall under the category, "understanding," a lower-level thinking process. After locating resources on the Internet, students might then proceed to higher-order processes, such as "applying," which might include sharing those resources with others, "evaluating," or reading discussion forum posts, and finally "creating," or writing a blog post about the topic.

Searching the Internet

Your students might be familiar with many features of the Internet, but do they know how to perform effective online searches? You may find you need to teach them how to locate information and then how to critically evaluate that information.

The typical starting place is a search engine, which is an online database of Internet files or pages. A search engine is specialized software, which searches web pages for keywords and returns the list of links matching the search criteria. Therefore, it is essential that a student's search criteria be constructed correctly. Each search engine has its own criteria and different ways of categorizing content. There are many specialized search engines available for a variety of purposes, so don't feel like you are limited to one. For this textbook, however, we will focus on the most used and popular search engine, Google (http://google.com).

> Although most people use the terms Internet and World Wide Web (Web) interchangeably, the Web is actually a subset of the Internet. The Web is a web browser, invented in 1989 by Sir Tim Berners-Lee and made available to the public in 1990. The Web enabled a much easier use of the Internet, and thus made this tool available to the general public.

Google Search

Some search engines use Boolean searching (using operators such as and, or, and not) to refine the scope of the search, but Google makes searching easier. Of course, choosing the right search term is the key to locating the right information. Listed below are the essentials of a Google search presented at the Google Web Search Help Center:

1. Searches are NOT case sensitive.
2. There is no need to include Boolean operators as Google returns only pages that include all of your search terms.
3. The order in which terms are entered will affect the search results with the first term being the most important.
4. To refine the scope of the search, just include more terms.
5. Common words and characters, such as "where" and "how" and single digits and letters are not included as search criteria unless you put a + sign in front of it (be sure to include a space before the + sign).
6. Putting quotation marks around two or more words ensures that all common words, single digits and single letters are included as search terms.
7. Google will search for words that are similar to some or all of you search terms and highlight the variants of your terms.
8. If your search term has more than one meaning, use a minus (-) in front of words related to the meaning you want to avoid (again, be sure to include a space before the minus sign).
9. Clicking the **I'm Feeling Lucky** button will bypass the search results page and take you directly to the first link on the search results page.
10. Use the Advanced Search Page to search for specific file types (Word, PDF, *PowerPoint*) and also to search for images labeled for reuse. This is especially important when inserting images into any of your work.

Google uses a patented technology called **PageRank** that basically ranks the results of your searches based on the number of pages linked and lists those results in ranked order. Google has an added search capability called, **Google Scholar** (http://scholar.google.com) to help in searching for scholarly literature. Another specialized Google search engine is called **Google Insights for Search**, http://www.google.com/insights/search/#, where you can compare search volume patterns across specific regions, categories, time frames, and properties. Try this search engine and think about how you might use it in the classroom.

Evaluating Internet Sites

Once your students know how to locate information on the Internet, they will need to know how to evaluate those resources for credibility. Before accepting the credibility of a site, they will need to determine the purpose and author of that site. You can help your students quickly identify credibility of a source by telling them to look at the domain extension. Common domains are listed in the following table.

Domain	Source	Credibility
.edu	School or University	Credible
.gov	Federal, state or local government agency	Credible
.mil	U.S. Military	Credible
.net	Anyone	May or may not be credible
.com	Generally a business	May or may not be credible
.org	Generally a nonprofit organization	May or may not be credible

Although the domain name can give you basic information about the source, there are other guidelines to use in determining credibility. Some basic indicators of poor website credibility include no author listed, no way to contact the author, bad grammar or misspelled words, confusing site to navigate, and/or a general lack of quality control.

Evaluation guidelines can be used to determine not only the credibility of the site but the appropriateness and accuracy of the information presented. University of California at Berkeley (http://www.lib.berkeley.edu/TeachingLib/Guides/Internet/Evaluate.html) provides an online tutorial focusing on five criteria for evaluating Internet sources:

1. Accuracy
2. Authority
3. Objectivity
4. Currency
5. Coverage

There is a wealth of relevant, credible information on the Internet so taking the time to evaluate a website is well worth the effort. One way to make sure your students are accessing relevant sites appropriate for their grade level and curricular goals is to design Internet instruction using websites you have evaluated in advance. Not only will you be sure that the site is appropriate, but your students' time will be spent in actually working with the information and not in searching.

Encouraging Inquiry: WebQuests

WebQuests (http://webquest.org) are online lessons in which most or all of the information/sources from which students work are located on the Internet. Typically they are group-oriented with the division of labor specified in the WebQuest; students are assigned roles within the group. One of the key concepts of the WebQuest is that students use their time in actually interacting with the information and not searching for it.

There are thousands of WebQuests of varying quality available on the Internet spanning all grade levels and discipline areas. These online lessons were tailored to curricular goals and objectives that may be similar to the ones you will be teaching some day. As a teacher, you will want to design your own WebQuest tailored to your school's curricular needs and your students' needs. This is easily accomplished as the essential parts of a WebQuest are clearly labeled and explained by the originators, Bernie Dodge and Tom March (San Diego State University, 2008). WebQuests feature the critical components listed below:

1. **Introduction:** The introduction must relate to your students' interests and should be motivational in nature. Your goal is to make the activity fun and/or interesting to your students. For example, you might begin with, "*You are a journalist covering the Civil War*", "*You are a scientist who has been asked to find an alternative fuel source*", or for a first grade class, "*I wonder why frogs like the water so much– can you help me find out why.*"
2. **Task**: This is a description of what the students will have accomplished by the end of the WebQuest. Such as, "*Your task will be to become an expert on frogs and to design a poster of the life cycle of a frog to show to the class.*"
3. **Process**: A step-by-step description of what students should do to successfully complete the project. If individual roles are to be given to group members, the titles and responsibilities of each role should be clearly defined here.

4. **Resources**: These are the links to the relevant websites for the information required to complete the WebQuest. Other resources (such as books, models, etc.) can also be used, but most or all of the information is typically located online.
5. **Evaluation:** A rubric should be provided to evaluate students' work. The rubric should set clear guidelines for what will be considered "excellent" work and what is considered the minimum accepted.
6. **Conclusion**: This section describes what was learned through the WebQuest, a way of concluding the lesson and summarizing.
7. **Teacher Directions**: Although this section is not always a WebQuest component, it assists other teachers in using your WebQuest by providing helpful information such as the time it may take to complete the exercise, any special considerations (i.e. students need to know how to create presentations or graphs), and background information students may need to know before beginning the WebQuest. Be sure to list the standard(s) and/or curricular area goals/objectives addressed by the WebQuest.

As mentioned previously, there are many WebQuests online, so take an opportunity to examine these and get a better feel for what components constitute an effective WebQuest.

Internet Scavenger Hunt

Another popular Internet-based teaching activity is the Internet scavenger hunt. They are easy to create and can be geared to any curriculum area and grade level. Additionally, they can be used as a whole class activity, group activity or for individual students. Typically, students are presented with a list of questions with an Internet source to assist in answering that question. For example, here are some questions from an Internet scavenger hunt on ants, featured in Education World (http://www.education-world.com/a_lesson/lesson087.shtml):

THE "STUD-ANTS" GO MARCHING... HURRAH! HURRAH!

1. Name three parts of an insect's body.
   Source: Entomology for Beginners

2. What are the three main jobs of worker ants?
   Source: Life and Habits of Ants

3. About how many different kinds (or species) of ants can be found in the world? Choose the correct answer: 80, 800, or 8,000.
   Source: Anteater: Digging Up Ants and Termites

Although Internet scavenger hunts do not require that the Internet link be included, it is highly recommended that you do so in the interest of making the best use of your students' learning time. Also, check links to make sure they are working before giving them to students. There are many other Internet-related teaching activities, many of which utilize emerging social media platforms.

Web 2.0 and Instructional Context

The term Web 2.0 originated in late 2004 (O'Reilly, 2005) and quickly became the "buzzword" that best portrayed the evolution of the web from its original, more static nature (Web 1.0) to a more dynamic, participatory environment (Web 2.0). This second generation of Internet-based services has transformed the web from a collection of websites to an infrastructure supporting user participation, social interaction and collaboration. The paradigm shift to Web 2.0 has been a dramatic one featuring an emphasis on sharing and creating content and a move away from simply retrieving constant, unchanging content. Today's Internet users are not satisfied with merely viewing web pages; with Web 2.0 tools, they are able to actually create content and interact with the web and their peers.

One of the defining features of the Web 2.0 movement is the development of service-oriented architectures (SOA). In previous generations of Internet technology, files remained on servers as independent resources of information. As a user, we would navigate to a specific URL or web address and investigate the text, hypertext, images, and media posted in that location. If the information were to change, it required effort on the part of the author or hosting agent to change the data being stored at that web address. For example, a company called "Ali's Glass Blowing" might publish a webpage containing the stories, pictures, and links to relevant information for that boutique. Any new media or information would have to be uploaded and republished by the owner or developer, and the visitor would have to go to the site again to see if anything on the site had been updated.

This process was incredibly cumbersome and restrictive. However, SOA allows webpages to share information openly with any resource interested in capturing it. We can now allow our webpage to subscribe to feeds from another webpage, bringing other people's thoughts, ideas, and media into a place where we can make good use of it. Likewise, others can construct their webpages, mobile applications, or even e-mail to "listen" for changes, updates, or new publications from webpages and content we develop. This concept capitalizes on a simple technology known as RSS (or Real Simple Syndication).

This functionality creates a different kind of Internet. Through the eyes of a teacher, it allows our students to capture meaningful ideas and media to reuse or remix into our own artifacts. It makes possible and encourages inclusion of the content of others in our own artifacts in a free and unrestricted way.

Internet Teaching Resources

Google Scholar
http://scholar.google.com

Evaluating Web Pages
http://www.lib.berkeley.edu/TeachingLib/Guides/Internet/Evaluate.html

WebQuests, San Diego State
http://webquest.org/index.php

Rubric for Evaluating Webquests
http://webquest.sdsu.edu/webquestrubric.html

Internet Scavenger Hunts, Education World
http://www.education-world.com/a_lesson/archives/hunt.shtml

Facebook
http://facebook.com

Educational Uses of Web 2.0

Of course, with the advent of each new social media tool comes the subsequent discussion of how that tool can be used in education. Lauded as a new wave of innovation for educators, Web 2.0 applications are being used in a variety of ways (Boulos, Maramba, & Wheeler, 2006; Williams & Jacobs, 2004). This section provides an overview of educational uses of Web 2.0 programs that transform the classroom into a virtual e-learning workspace.

Social Software

In the broadest sense, social software includes all Web-based programs that facilitate interaction among users allowing them to work together and share data with others. These programs promote social human contact through computer-mediated communication and include such web based communication tools as weblogs, wikis, instant messaging, chat, social bookmarking, social networks and virtual worlds.

A national research study (National School Boards Association, 2007) reported that, "Nine- to 17-year-olds report spending almost as much time using social networking services and Web sites as they spend watching television. Among teens, that amounts to about 9 hours a week on social networking activities, compared to about 10 hours a week watching TV." The most common activities included posting messages, downloading and uploading music and videos, and updating online profiles and websites. Less popular activities included blogging, creating and sharing virtual objects, and participating in collaborative projects.

Growing in popularity are social networking sites that allow users to build online profiles and share information. A majority of online users, especially younger ones, are members and users of one, two or more social networking sites with Facebook (http://facebook.com) being one of the most widely used.

There are other social networks that might be helpful for educators. Ning (http://www.ning.com/) is a social network that offers a multitude of communities to join, based upon your interests. The home page provides a sampling of social networks you can join, or you can search for networks by using keywords. A popular and growing social network for educators in Ning is called Classroom 2.0, aimed toward educators interested in using Web 2.0 tools and collaborative technologies in their classrooms (http://www.classroom20.com/).

You might consider using a social network as a classroom webpage, since they are simple to set up, students can easily join, you can make them private or public, and they can provide timely, relevant content. Teachers have used social networking sites as a place to post homework assignments on their students' walls, post educational videos, and educational websites. Additionally, social networks can be used to stimulate conversation, discussion or debate among students or to invite experts to share their thoughts or ideas.

Social bookmarking is another type of social software tool that can facilitate learning. Instead of bookmarking individual websites to one computer, you can create an account with delicious.com (http://delicious.com) and bookmark relevant websites. You can then access these bookmarks from any computer with an Internet connection. Think of ways you might use delicious.com in your classroom. You can create a class delicious.com bookmark to keep track of online resources for a group research project, for instance. Delicious works by allowing you to assign tags (keywords) to your websites. You should tag your websites on delicious.com with keywords that you will remember. You can also include notes about the website and make your bookmarks private or viewable to the world. Go to delicious.com, create an account, and see how this tool works.

Social software can be used in a variety of ways to enhance community in your classroom and beyond. Remember, many of the sites can be private, so that only members can access and view the site. This might be a necessary option when creating an online community for younger students.

Blogs and Microblogging

Blogs have been around as early as 1997 and quickly gained in popularity in the educational community (Williams & Jacobs, 2004). The online equivalent of a personal journal, the blog provides a web based mechanism for teachers to post class assignments and course materials as well as a way to structure class discussions. Students can use blogs to collaborate with students and teachers from any location. Through the medium of this user-friendly technology, student work is showcased and communication and reflection are supported.

What is a blog? Blog is the shortened word for weblog, which is a form of micropublishing. Blogs consists of posts, published in reverse-chronological order. That means that the newest post shows at the top of your blog. Blog posts can also include the ability for readers to comment, which can create an online conversation on a certain topic. You can insert video, audio, images, and other multimedia within your blog post. Blogs can also include the ability to make pages, which makes a blog look even more like a web page. And blogs are RSS-feed enabled, which means your readers can subscribe to your blog, with your posts being sent to their feed reader or aggregator of their choice. You may be surprised to see how easy it is to create a very attractive and professional-looking blog and begin writing.

And how have instructors used blogs as an instructional strategy? One of the most common educational uses of blogs is to replace a class web page in which the instructor can post assignments and pertinent links. Some teachers have utilized blogs to establish a community of learners encouraging their students to post their reflections on class discussions or read material and then to comment on peer postings. The blog then becomes a mechanism for promoting discussion and debate, and often is motivational for students who might not otherwise participate in the traditional classroom.

Blogs can also be used to stimulate discussion by having students post questions and inviting an expert to respond to those questions as one instructor (Olwell, 2008) did to teach about the use of oral history in historical research. Students were required to read a book about the Vietnam War and then post their questions to a class blog. The author of the text then responded to the questions over a period of a couple of weeks.

Blogs can be authored singly or also by groups of authors. You can make blogs public or private, something that might be important to younger students. Blogs support constructivist epistemologies by offering ways to communicate, organize, reflect, create, and collaborate (Schroeder, 2006).

Microblogging is a subset of blogging, useful for posting small snippets of news and information. A popular and growing microblogging service is Twitter, which provides an easy way to send messages and follow other peoples' tweets. Twitter posts are limited to 140 characters.

Web-Based Blogging Software	
Blogger	http://blogger.com
WordPress	http://wordpress.com
Bloglines	http://bloglines.com
Edublogs	http://edublogs.org

Wikis

Wikis also provide a user-friendly web-based environment, but offer more versatility than a blog. Unlike the blog, which features a more chronological listing of posts and responses, a wiki is a non-linear workspace for students allowing for multiple contributors. A wiki is quick and easy to set up and start creating content. Typically authored and edited by a number of people, the wiki is the ideal tool for encouraging collaboration and showcasing student work. Wikis do not require knowledge of HTML and now include many visual editing tools that simplify the process of editing and creating content.

> Wiki wiki means "quick" in Hawaiian. Ward Cunningham created the first wiki in 1995.

Your students are probably very familiar with wikis, but may not know it! For instance, a very popular (and sometimes controversial with educators) is Wikipedia (http://en.wikipedia.org). Wikipedia can be a very useful source of information, but again, must be approached and analyzed for credibility when citing any of its information.

As an alternative to Wikipedia, you should be aware of the "Wikipedia Selection for Schools" (http://schools-wikipedia.org/), an online encyclopedia targeted around the UK National Curriculum and useful for much of the English speaking world. It has about 5500 articles (as much as can be fitted on a DVD with good size images) and is about the size of a twenty-volume encyclopedia (34,000 images and 20 million words). You can download the entire encyclopedia on a DVD, which can then be distributed to your students, especially useful for those who do not have Internet access at home.

The Center for Scholarly Technology (CST) at USC identified some general approaches for how wikis could be implemented (Higdon, 2005):

1. student journaling – demonstrate writing proficiency, understanding of conceptual knowledge and reflection
4. personal portfolios – make connections among artifacts including documents, images, web resources, audio/video files, and presentations
5. collaborative knowledge base - create a shared knowledge base of information particularly as a group project
6. research coordination and collaboration – using the wiki as a collective digital space for ideas, drafts, timelines, and study results

Wikis can enhance the learning experience by providing a rich digital environment in which learners are directly engaged and able to interact with others. Wikis, as social software, can involve learners in the construction of knowledge and the ability to collaboratively engage in dialogue (Parker & Chao, 2007; Schroeder, 2009).

Web-Based Wiki Software	
Google Sites	http://sites.google.com
Wikispaces	http://wikispaces.com

Podcasting

Podcasts are audio or video files you can subscribe to, like other RSS-enabled technologies. This makes them very convenient to receive updates, since all new episodes are automatically added to your podcast aggregator (such as iTunes). To get started with podcasts, begin by going on a "podcast spree" http://www.apple.com/itunes/podcasts. We suggest you subscribe to podcasts related to teaching and technology. An excellent weekly podcast produced by two of this book's authors is available through the iTunes store. Do a search for "Cool Teacher Podcast" and subscribe or go to their website http://coolteachers.org.

Virtual Worlds

Some instructors have taken advantage of another social software program that provides a virtual world environment ripe for learner interaction and collaboration. A virtual world is a computer-based simulated environment in which interaction is accomplished through the use of avatars. These three-dimensional graphical representations are able to communicate through text and/or sound.

The most popular of the virtual worlds, Second Life, has quickly become the top choice of educators and researchers with over 200 established educational campuses . Educators currently teaching in Second Life cite similar benefits attributed to wikis and blogs, namely that it is a mechanism for enhancing student learning, promoting collaboration, and building student and faculty communities. However, the ability to create objects and actually have a classroom experience with students in a virtual environment makes Second Life a unique web-based learning environment. Moreover, instructors are able to build three-dimensional, interactive lessons that grab students' attention much the same as popular computer games. The educational uses for virtual worlds are growing and include such things as: role playing, scavenger hunts, simulations, experiencing a historical period first hand, building objects, synchronous lectures and discussions.

To get started with Second Life, you need to download the software, located at http://secondlife.com and then create an account. There are several websites devoted to exploring the educational uses of Second Life, which can help you decide if Second Life might be suitable for your teaching environment. Do a search using the terms "Second Life in education," and you will find several resources.

School Blocking of Websites

You may find that your school district blocks some social software tools and websites, such as YouTube, wikis, Google Apps, and other helpful tools for both you and your students. While there is not one solution to suggest for this issue, you can make a big difference in accessibility to all technology tools for you and your students. The more you know about how technology can be used effectively to enhance student learning, the lesson plans you create that use these tools, and your ability to educate all stakeholders are all part of a strategy to effect change in your school and our educational environment. Many times it just involves educating others, to show them how these tools can engage learners and enhance learning.

The social software tools discussed thus far in this section provide web-based environments ripe for teaching and learning. Educators and researchers have developed innovative uses for these tools in an attempt to enhance the learning environment and expand opportunities for student creativity and critical thinking. More links are provided next for you to investigate some of these social tools.

Social Media Tools		
Communicating	Twitter Gmail Voice & Video Meebo Instant Messaging VoiceThread Delicious Skype	http://twitter.com http://mail.google.com/videochat http://meebo.com http://voicethread.com http://delicious.com http://skype.com
Slide Sharing	AuthorStream Slideboom Slideshare	http://authorstream.com http://slideboom.com http://slideshare.net
Photo Sharing	Flickr Picasa	http://flickr.com http://picasa.com
Video Sharing/Broadcasting	YouTube Google Video Vimeo ustream	http://youtube.com http://video.google.com http://vimeo.com http://ustream.tv
Multimedia	Blip TV	http://blip.tv
Online Notetaking	Evernote	http://evernote.com
Online Forums	Google Groups	http://groups.google.com
Project Management	Zoho Projects	http://projects.zoho.com
Online Meetings	Dimdim WizIQ	http://dimdim.com http://wiziq.com
Diagram Tools	Gliffy online	http://www.gliffy.com
Timelines	xtimeline	http://www.xtimeline.com
Online Bibliographic Managers	Zotero	http://zotero.org
Online Resource Management	CiteULike	http://www.citeulike.org
Synchronized File Storage/Sharing	Dropbox	https://www.dropbox.com

Online Application/Collaboration Tools

Anyone with an Internet access has a profusion of online tools available that once were only available when installed on a computer. These tools make it possible to create documents, spreadsheets, databases and presentations. Additionally, it is possible to store and share files online.

On the surface, these tools provide access to students to complete assignments that require specific applications, but the added ability to share makes it possible for students to collaborate on projects – actually sharing files and editing them. Of course, the sharing capability can extend to include all students, even students who are geographically located at great distances. And these programs only scratch the surface of the Web 2.0 tools available for enhancing instruction. There are a number of sites offering the free use of online application tools, but this article will focus on the *Google* applications, as they are very versatile and especially popular in the educational community.

Google Docs

Establishing a Google (http://gmail.com) account is a relatively easy task requiring only a few minutes of your time. A Google account allows you to create, edit and upload documents spreadsheets and presentations or to create new ones from scratch. Files are stored online and can be easily accessed from anywhere as long as you have a Web browser and Internet access. Additionally, you can invite people to share your documents and make changes. The programs have many of the formatting capabilities already familiar such as toolbar buttons to bold, underline, etc. The possibilities for students using Google Docs range from assignments that require specific programs to complete (i.e. spreadsheet for a math assignment) to more collaborative, group assignments featuring group presentations and/or reports. Google Docs allows multiple users to co-write articles and collaborate on all kinds of projects.

A presentation can be shared in real-time or be available whenever needed by students so anyone around the globe can virtually attend. Presentations can be more interactive as during an online presentation, those attending can participate in a chat room to the right side of the presentation slides. Multiple users can view or edit a presentation online, and are able to embed a presentation in a web page or blog so that it can be readily accessed.

Of course, educators have discovered many uses for Google Docs, one of those is to use it as a platform for collaboration on research projects. A recent report (Dekeyser & Watson, 2007) recommends Google Docs, citing the online editing features, support of multiple authors, and extremely rare update conflicts as ideal components for collaborative research.

Google Sites

Another online application program provided free of charge is Google Sites which allows you to create web pages in your browser and easily publish them on the Google server. This textbook includes detailed information on how to set up a Google Site for your Technology Teaching Portfolio in Appendix A. More information along with website links about Google applications can be found on our companion website, http://dats.boisestate.edu.

Dropbox

Google Docs offers easy and convenient ways to share, collaborate, edit, and publish documents, accessing them from any computer. But what if you want to work on a file on your local computer and be able to access that file's latest version on another computer? When you are teaching, you may be working on a *Word* document, for instance, at your school, and then need to continue working on that document from home. How can you access that document, make sure it is the most recent version, save it, and then access it from any computer?

New tools now allow you to easily do this, and one tool you should try out is Dropbox: https://www.dropbox.com. This tool allows you to save a file in your Dropbox public folder, work on it, and then access the same document on other computers. All you need to do is create an account on dropbox.com, install the software on your computers, and then place your files into your public dropbox folder on one computer. Whenever you work on a document in your dropbox file on one of your computers and save it (**Ctrl + S**), it is automatically saved to all of your computers. This tool will help you avoid unnecessary mistakes in using the wrong version of a file and simplify the saving and accessing of files across multiple computers

Creating and Connecting: Research and guidelines on online social and educational networking (PDF Format)
http:// www.nsba.org/site/docs/41400/41340.pdf

4Teachers.Org
http://www.4teachers.org

Online Education Database: 101 Web 2.0 Teaching Tools
http://oedb.org/library/features/101-web-20-teaching-tools

Encyclopedia of Educational Technology (San Diego State University wiki)
http://eet.sdsu.edu/eetwiki/index.php/Main_Page

Technology Teacher Blog (Dr. Barbara Schroeder)
http://itcboisestate.wordpress.com

References

Alexander, B. (2006). A new wave of innovation for teaching and learning. *Educause Review*, 41 (2).

Boulos, M. N., Maramba, I., & Wheeler, S. (2006). Wikis, blogs and podcasts: a new generation of Web-based tools for virtual collaborative clinical practice and education. *BX Medical Education*, 6 (41).

Dekeyser, S., & Watson, R. (2007). Extending Google Docs to collaborate on research papers. Queeensland, Australia: University of Southern Queensland.

Ferris, S. P., & Wilder, H. (2006). Uses and potentials of wikis in the classroom. *Journal of Online Education, 2*(5).

Google. (n.d.). Web Search Help Center. Retrieved from http://www.google.com/support/bin/static.py?page=searchguides.html&ctx=basics&hl=en

Higdon, J. (2005). Teaching, learning, and other uses for wikis in academia. *Campus Technology*.

Anderson, L. W., & Krathwohl, D. R. (2001). A taxonomy for learning, teaching, and assessing: A revision of Bloom's taxonomy of educational objectives. Longman: New York.

Mengel, M. A., Simonds, R., & Houck, R. (n.d.). Educational uses of second life. Retrieved from http://www.youtube.com/watch?v=qOFU9oUF2HA.

National School Boards Association, N. S. (2007). Creating and connecting: Research and guidelines on online social and educational networking. Grunwald Associates, LLC.

Olwell, R. (2008, January). Taking history personally: How blogs connect students outside the classroom. *Perspectives on History*.

O'Reilly, T. (2005). *What is Web 2.0*. Retrieved from http://www.oreillynet.com/pub/a/oreilly/tim/news/2005/09/30/what-is-web-20.html

Parker, K. R., & Chao, J. T. (2007). Wiki as a teaching tool. *Interdisciplinary Journal of knowledge and learning Objects, 3*.

San Diego State University. (2008). Webquest.Org. Retrieved from http://webquest.org/index.php

Schroeder, B. (2006). Ready, set, start blogging! [Electronic Version]. *Learning Technology, 8,* 30. Retrieved from http://lttf.ieee.org/issues/october2006/index.html#_Toc148658494

Schroeder, B. (2009). Within the wiki: Best practices for educators. *AACE Journal, 17*(3), 181-197. Retrieved from http://www.editlib.org/p/28183

Villano, M. (2008, January 1). 13 tips for virtual world teaching. *Campus Technology*, 1-5.

Williams, J. B., & Jacobs, J. (2004). Exploring the use of blogs as learning spaces in the higher education sector. *Australian Journal of Educational Technology, 20*(2), 232-247.

Digital Age Work and Learning Exercises

Exercise 1: Creating a WebQuest

Required: NETS-T Standards 1

Collaboration Option: Partner with a classmate or work with a small group on this WebQuest, using Google Docs as your collaborative tool. Publish your WebQuest in Google Docs when you are done and then insert it on a new page on your Technology Teaching Portfolio.

✓ Review the information on WebQuests included in this section and on the Internet (http://webquest.org) to make sure that you understand the purpose and necessary components. Next, decide the curricular area and grade level that you would like to teach. Then visit a school district website to determine the specific concepts and skills to be taught. These will serve as your guide in creating a WebQuest.

✓ Create a WebQuest that addresses concepts in your curricular area. Be sure to include major WebQuest components:

1. Introduction
2. Task
3. Process
4. Resources
5. *Evaluation (see instructions below on developing a rubric)
6. Conclusion
7. Teacher Directions (include standards and/or curricular goals/objectives)

✓ Your WebQuest must be visually appealing and:

- be easy to read and understand;
- contain no errors (grammatical, spelling, typing, and/or conceptual errors);
- include a minimum of 2 graphics;
- include links to a minimum of 5 relevant, grade appropriate websites; and
- essential WebQuest components (Introduction, Task, Process, Resources, Evaluation, Conclusion, Teacher Directions) hyperlinked within the WebQuest so that the user can Click the component title (usually located at the top) and go directly to the WebQuest component.

*Evaluation

For this part of your WebQuest Exercise, you will develop a very basic rubric using an online rubric generator.

1. Go to the 4teachers.org website – http://4teachers.org
2. Click the Rubistar option listed on the homepage.

Notice the rubric template areas available:

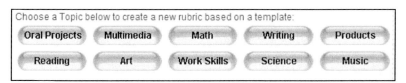

Although it is a free service, allowing you can to save and edit rubrics online, you will want to register to save your rubrics.

Now, you are ready to create a new rubric. Given the primary rubric categories listed, choose the one that corresponds to your WebQuest. For example, if you were evaluating collaborative work skills, you would click that link and be taken to a screen.

Your WebQuest Topic

1. Name your rubric and begin the creation of your rubric at the bottom of the page.

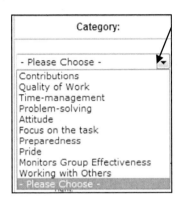

2. Click the dropdown arrow to see the categories that might be included in an evaluation of your topic area (in this example, Collaborative Work Skills.)

3. Click one that you would want to evaluate and then note that descriptors are provided to help assess the students' performance in that area. Of course, you are able to customize the descriptors and/or write your own. The number of categories you wish to include in the rubric would vary and depends on your instructional goals.

4. Continue choosing categories until you complete the rubric and then click **submit**.

5. Select the rubric and copy and paste it into your document.

6. You can modify the rubric and/or save it to the 4teachers.org database to view/modify later. You can also make it available online.

✓ For purposes of the WebQuest assignment, it would be preferable to have the rubric actually in the body of the WebQuest.

✓ If you used Google Docs, insert your file on a new page on your Technology Teaching Portfolio. If you used *Word*, upload your file to your File Cabinet page and link to that file.

*A required artifact for Standard 1.

Exercise 2: Internet Scavenger Hunt

ISTE NETS-T Standard 1

Review the information on Internet Scavenger Hunts included in this section and on the Internet to make sure that you understand the purpose and format. Next, decide the curricular area and grade level that you would like to teach. Then visit a school district website to determine the specific concepts and skills to be taught. These will serve as your guide in creating an Internet scavenger hunt.

Collaboration: Work with a partner or small group and create your Scavenger Hunt together. You could use Google Docs, share the document with each other, publish, and insert on a page on your Technology Teaching Portfolio. Or, you could create a new page on your Technology Teaching Portfolio and post directly on that page.

✓ Create an Internet scavenger hunt with the following specifications:

1. Minimum of 10 items
2. Links to relevant, grade appropriate websites for students to locate answers
3. Easy to read and understand
4. Contain no errors (grammatical, spelling, typing, and/or conceptual errors)
5. Answers provided

*Could be used as an artifact for Standard 1.

Exercise 3: Creating an Internet Search Activity

ISTE ISTE NETS-T Standard 1

In this exercise, you will design an Internet search activity for your students requiring them to evaluate websites on the following components: accuracy, authority, objectivity, currency, and coverage.

Collaboration: Work with a partner or small group and create your Internet Search Activity together. You could use Google Docs, share the document with each other, publish, and insert on a page on your Technology Teaching Portfolio.

✓ Create an Internet search activity for your students and include:

1. Clear directions – is this an individual or group activity?
2. Links to at least 4 websites for students to evaluate
3. A table or form for them to complete in evaluating the websites (use Google Forms for this if desired.)
4. Provide a completed table or form (If using Google Forms, then results will automatically populate a spreadsheet.)

*Could be used as an artifact for Standard 1.

Exercise 4: Assistive Technologies Website

Required: ISTE NETS-T Standard 4

Previously in this text you have located assistive technology websites that will be useful in your teaching. Create a **List** page on your Technology Teaching Portfolio, include at least 10 of these sites with a short description of each, and the website URL of each website/resource.

✓ List at least 10 preferred Assistive Technology websites and include the following information:

      1.   Name of Organization sponsoring the website
      2.   Website name
      3.   Website address
      4.   Description of website
      5.   Reason for choosing this website in your assistive technology website collection

*Required artifact for Standard 4.

Exercise 5: Create a Class Blog

Required: ISTE NETS-T Standard 3

 For this exercise, you will create a blog, then add members, and finally post to this class blog.

Preplanning Note: One person will need to create the blog, and this person will add the class members to the blog. Your teacher may want to do this or assign a specific person or group to take on this task. Give your blog a catchy title, something related to technology and education.

*Team members can either be administrators or not. Administrators can edit all posts (not just their own), add and remove team members (and grant admin access), and modify the blog's settings and template. Non-administrators can only create and edit their own posts.

NOTE: For this class blog, the team members will NOT be administrators.

First, you will need to create your blog.

Steps to Creating a New Blog in Blogger
(For detailed instructions on how to set up a blog using Blogger, you can also visit http://www.blogger.com/features. This website provides all of the information you need to get started with your personal blog.)

How to delete a Blogger blog
Click the **Settings>Basic** tab and select the **Delete blog**. You will be asked to confirm this again.

      1.   Login to your Gmail (Google) account.

      2.   Go to http://blogger.com

      3.   On the upper-right, use your Gmail password to sign in to Blogger.

      4.   Enter your display name, click **I accept terms of service** and **Continue**.

      5.   Next, you will provide a title for your blog. You should name it something that indicates it is a class blog for a certain class, such as your class name and number and maybe semester. You can use upper case and spaces, as this will NOT be the URL of your blog, but the title that appears at the top of your blog site.

6. Select a short, but easy to remember URL for your blog. You can click **Check availability** to see if this name is available. When you have decided upon a name, click **Next**.

7. You can select from many professional templates. You can always change your mind once you've set up your blog, so don't take too much time here. Keep clicking the **Next** button to proceed to the next screen.

8. You will arrive at the final screen that your blog has been created and you can start blogging.

9. From here, you will be sent to a screen where you can write your first post.

10. Explore Blogger and add gadgets and customize your settings.

11. To find out more about Blogger, visit this excellent site that tells you about blogs and how to get started using Blogger: http://www.blogger.com/tour_start.g

Now, turn the blog you just created into a class blog!

How to Create a Class Blog

1. After you have created your blog, go to **Settings | Permissions**:

2. Then click **Add Authors**.

3. Next, type the email addresses of the people you're inviting to the blog, separating each address with a comma. (Use your classmates' Gmail accounts they are using for assignments throughout this textbook.) They'll receive an email with a confirmation link soon.

4. When you're ready to send the invitations, click **Invite**.

✓ After you have joined this class blog, please create a new post and include the following:

1. Tell us about yourself, what you want to teach and how you plan to use technology in your classroom.
2. Write about one new tool you have learned about and are using. Rate the tool or provide additional information that might help the reader decide if the tool would be worthwhile to use.
3. Comment to at least one other post.
4. Reflect upon blogs and how you might use them in your classroom.
5. Insert a movie file, audio file, and experiment with various types of posts.
6. Go back to this blog in a few days and view how the blog has developed. Make more comments as needed.

*Required artifact for Standard 3.

Exercise 6: Teaching with Technology Blog

Required: ISTE NETS-T Standard 5

Now that you've experienced working with a group in a team blog, create your own blog and set it up the way you want it to look. For this exercise you will create a Teaching with Technology blog and be able to customize it as you wish.

✓ Create a blog, giving it the title your **Firstname Lastname: Teaching with Technology**. This blog should focus on teaching with technology, what you are learning, and how you might use technology in the classroom.
✓ Post at least 5 times to the blog. Make sure you check for spelling and grammar. You should get in the habit of writing in a style that will be appropriate for your students and parents.

*Required artifact for Standard 5.

Exercise 7: Working with Images: Digital Story

Required: ISTE NETS-T Standard 5

You will work a lot with images in the classroom, such as taking student pictures, finding and collecting appropriate images on the Internet, creating photo slideshows, and numerous other ways to present visual content. In this exercise you will create a digital story, a collection of still images along with narration that tells a compelling short story. You will need to have access to a good microphone (sometimes the built-in ones are pretty good) and if you want to use your own images, a camera and/or scanner.

What is a digital story? You can find many good digital stories online to view. Here are some resources you can start with:

- Digitales, http://www.digitales.us/gallery/index.php
- Bringing Digital Stories to the Classroom, http://www.mcli.dist.maricopa.edu/learnshops/digital/examples.php

- Educational Uses of Digital Storytelling: University of Houston, http://digitalstorytelling.coe.uh.edu

In this exercise you will use VoiceThread, a free multimedia online tool that allows you to record and manipulate image slideshows. This tool not only allows you to create a great looking multimedia presentation, but it allows others to visit your story and also comment on it, either by directly narrating or recording a video.

View some of the examples on the VoiceThread site (http://voicethread.com) and then sign up for an account. If you need help using VoiceThread, visit their support page: http://voicethread.com/support/faq

Begin the process by answering the following questions:

1. Who is the audience for my story?
2. What is my dramatic question?

Then, write your script (what you will read and what your viewers will hear). You could use Google Docs for this if you want to share your ideas with a classmate for feedback and review. You might also begin with a collection of images and then write your story.

✓ Include the following in your VoiceThread Digital Story:

1. An interesting story title along with your name.
2. Each narration should last nor more than about 20 seconds.
3. Keep the length of your digital story at about 2 minutes, and no more than 20 images.
4. The story should begin with a dramatic question or issue.
5. Images should be clear.
6. Narration should be clear and easy to understand.

✓ When you are finished, embed your VoiceThread on your Technology Teaching Portfolio and also on your blog: http://voicethread.com/about/embedding
✓ Reflect upon what you learned in this activity and how you might incorporate VoiceThread in your future classroom.
✓ Share your VoiceThread with other classmates and view at least 3 of your classmates' VoiceThreads.

*Required artifact for Standard 5.

Exercise 8: Creating an Annotated Video Playlist

Required: ISTE NETS-T Standard 5

In this exercise you will create a custom video playlist using YouTube. Please work through Appendix H, starting on page 311 to create your playlist. Please include the following:

1. Embed your video playlist on your Technology Teaching Portfolio
2. Include a one-paragraph reflection on what you learned and how you might integrate this activity in your future classroom.

*Required artifact for Standard 5.

This chapter focuses on ISTE NETS-T Standard 4, which states that teachers should "promote and model digital citizenship and responsibility and apply those principles in practice." Included in this standard is the need for teachers to assist in providing technology resources for all students, teach ethical use of technology, and promote the safe use of technology.

Digital Divide/Digital Inequality

The digital divide is defined as the gap between those who have access to digital technology and those who do not. This disparity has been the subject of much research and debate over the last dozen or more years. Although over the last decade there has been increased use of computer technology, there are groups of the population who have not kept up with the changes. This is often referred to as digital inequality. The 2004 U.S. Department of Commerce report "Entering the Broadband Age" states that even as record numbers of people own computers and go online, the gap may be growing due largely to ethnic, geographic, societal, and economic factors. A U.S. Department of Education press release (2003) discussed the results of two government reports:

> The pace of technological change is truly astounding and has left no area of our lives untouched, including schools, These reports are good news and show how much progress has been made in connecting nearly every school in the nation to the Internet. But there are still big differences in home computer use that need to be addressed before we can declare the digital divide closed. We need to address the limited access to technology that many students have outside of school. There is much more we can do. Closing the digital divide will also help close the achievement gap that exists within our schools.

In 2010, the Federal Communications Commission (FCC) developed and released the National Broadband Plan to ensure every American has broadband access. You can read more about this plan on the FCC http://broadband.gov website.

Addressing issues of digital inequality is one of the leading challenges to education. Student computer and Internet availability will vary depending upon the school resources and the socioeconomic makeup of the community. Teachers must be aware of these limitations particularly when assigning work to be completed outside of the classroom. You will have students who do not have a computer and/or Internet access at home.

Copyright and Plagiarism

Copyright refers to the right to copy an author's work under certain conditions until that time in which the work actually enters the public domain. Copyright law is addressed in Title 17 of the United States Code (and covers everything from literary and musical works to motion pictures and computer programs). In general, copyright protection includes the following (United States Copyright Office, 2008):

- literary works;
- musical works, including any accompanying words;
- dramatic works, including any accompanying music;
- pantomimes and choreographic works;
- pictorial, graphic, and sculptural works;

- motion pictures and other audiovisual works;
- sound recordings; and
- architectural works.

Although the holder of the copyright does own his/her work, the doctrine of fair use allows limited use of a work in some cases such as for teaching and research. There are limitations to this use, which are outlined in sections 107 through 118 of the Copyright Act (United States Copyright Office, 2008). Section 107 also sets out four factors to be considered in determining whether or not a particular use is fair:
- the purpose and character of the use, including whether such use is of commercial nature or is for nonprofit educational purposes;
- the nature of the copyrighted work;
- amount and substantiality of the portion used in relation to the copyrighted work as a whole; and
- the effect of the use upon the potential market for or value of the copyrighted work.

Fair Use Guidelines: Educational Purposes

Text - print and/or multimedia: Poem (under 250 words) Articles, stories, or essays (under 2,500 words) Excerpt from a longer work (10% of work or 1,000 words, whichever is less Single copy: chart, picture, diagram, graph, cartoon or picture per book or per periodical issue
Video Videotapes, DVDs, and Laser Discs (Purchased or rented) – shown in entirety if legally acquired Portions of lawfully acquired copyrighted video works (10% or three minutes (whichever is less) of "motion media")
Graphics, Illustrations, and Photographs Single graphic, illustration and/or photograph (no more than 5 images by an artist or photographer) Collection of graphics, illustrations and/or photographs (no more than 15 images or 10%, whichever is less)
Music Musical composition in a multimedia project (10% maximum)
Computer Software Must be legally acquired, but an archival copy may be made
InternetImages (may be downloaded with restrictions as noted above) Music (may be downloaded with restrictions as noted above)
Television Broadcasts Live broadcasts (no restrictions) Tapes made from broadcasts (minimum rights allowed for 10 school days)

As you can see, it is still not completely clear as to what can or cannot be used, and copyright laws, and interpretations of the law, are updated from time to time. Digital fair use is a newer area of copyright law and one that is constantly changing. With that in mind, be sure to keep abreast of copyright law and review guidelines if ever in doubt. The following table provides some general guidelines.

Of course, any time that you use another author's work, you must give to the author for that work. Failure to cite the source is considered plagiarism. All of the following are considered plagiarism (Turnitin, 2008):

- turning in someone else's work as your own
- copying words or ideas from someone else without giving credit
- failing to put a quotation in quotation marks
- giving incorrect information about the source of a quotation
- changing words but copying the sentence structure of a source without giving credit
- copying so many words or ideas from a source that it makes up the majority of your work, whether you give credit or not (see our section on "fair use" rules)

The Internet has made plagiarism easier than ever before and teaching your students about the necessity of fair use and citing sources must be a part of your class routine. Students are not always aware of the dangers of plagiarism and its seriousness as an offense.

Software programs designed to detect plagiarized student papers are becoming more prevalent, and course management systems, such as *Blackboard,* are including plagiarism detection services. The **Safe Assignment** option in *Blackboard,* can be used by teachers and students to check for possible plagiarized material. However, the very best approach is to help your students understand what plagiarism is and how to avoid it.

Creative Commons

Creative Commons is a licensing system that provides simple and standardized alternatives to the "all rights reserved" model of traditional copyright. It is a global, non-profit organization that promotes access, economic growth, citizen engagement, and transparency. You can easily choose a license you want for your published work through their website: http://creativecommons.org (click the "Choose License" button at the top right). For example, educators can use a Creative Commons license to share and modify work, collaboratively building textbooks, lectures, lesson plans, and other educational content. This type of licensing is helping to fuel more open-source content on the Internet and level the playing field for accessing content.

Open Source Initiative

Open source is a development model for software that allows it to be freely distributed. The benefits of open source are consumer driven, resulting in better quality, higher reliability, more flexibility, lower cost, and an end to "predatory vendor lock-in" (Open Source Initiative website, paragraph 1). As an advocate for open technology access for all students, you should be aware of open source products and applications and ways they might be used in the schools.

Cyber Citizenship

Technology has provided us with new ways to communicate, share, and illustrate ideas, but with every new technology comes new concerns. Cyber dangers, such as cyber bullying, cyber crime, online predators and child luring, have become commonplace and are of great concern for parents and educators alike. And, of course, these are not the only cyber dangers students might encounter; they could be victims of hackers, privacy invasion and identity theft, computer viruses, malware and spyware. These cyber dangers have given rise to the need to educate our youth to be responsible cyber citizens. Alerting students to the dangers of the Internet, providing Internet use guidelines and social behavior manners (netiquette), and making cyber ethics a focus in your technology lessons are the first steps in helping your students become responsible cyber citizens.

Cyber Bullying

The Stop Cyber Bullying website (http://www.stopcyberbullying.org/) defines cyber bullying as:

"Cyber bullying" is when a child, preteen or teen is tormented, threatened, harassed, humiliated, embarrassed or otherwise targeted by another child, preteen or teen using the Internet, interactive and digital technologies or mobile phones. It has to have a minor on both sides, or at least have been instigated by a minor against another minor. Once adults become involved, it is plain and simple cyber-harassment or cyber stalking. Adult cyber-harassment or cyber stalking is NEVER called cyber bullying.

The range of activities included as cyber bullying is extensive and includes such things as bashing websites, death threats, harassing text messages, and posting confidential information online. With the rise in mobile phone and Internet use, cyber bullying is occurring more often and is now a topic that is addressed in the schools.

Online Predators

The anonymity of the Internet makes children an easy target for online predators. Email, chat rooms, instant messaging, social networks and other Internet communication mechanisms allow online predators to establish contact and gradually establish a relationship with children. Although the parents' role in protecting their children from online predators is a crucial one, teachers can also play a role in prevention. Discussing the dangers of the Internet and providing Internet safety guidelines are crucial to insuring your students' safety.

Computer Viruses and Other Computer Intrusions

Other dangers encountered by Internet use include computer viruses, malware, adware and spam. Created by hackers, computer viruses are programs that infect computer systems. Although some viruses are more harmful than others, all are designed to interrupt normal computer operations. They spread from computer to computer either by way of storage devices, email attachments or downloaded software. Computer viruses that run on your computer without your knowledge are called malware (malicious software) and include such programs as worms and Trojan horses. A worm uses a network to send copies of itself to other computers on the network while Trojan horses are typically innocent-looking programs made available on the Internet or as email attachments that, if downloaded, infect your computer.

Hidden software, called spyware, gathers information about your computer use and preferences and communicates this information to advertisers. The result of the spyware application may be adware, which causes pop-up advertisements even when you are not actively surfing. And, of course, spam, unsolicited email, if unblocked, is another intrusion on your computer usage.

Students must be aware of computer viruses and other computer intrusions to protect their privacy and their computers. Again, the necessity of establishing Internet safety guidelines cannot be emphasized enough.

Cyber Crime

While not as common as some cyber dangers, the ease of obtaining hacker tools has given rise to cyber crime. Often the hacker begins his/her illegal activities as a child. The Department of Justice describes three types of computer crimes as follows:

- The computer as a target - attacking the computers of others (spreading viruses is an example).
- The computer as a weapon - using a computer to commit "traditional crime" that we see in the physical world (such as fraud or illegal gambling).
- The computer as an accessory - using a computer as a "fancy filing cabinet" to store illegal or stolen information. (The Cyber Citizen Partnership, 2008)

Students need to be aware of the seriousness of cyber crime and the consequences of those crimes.

Educational Safeguards

There are a number of ways for educators to help prevent cyber abuse. Schools have adopted acceptable use policies, which clearly outline the appropriate use of technology. These typically are contracts between the student and his/her parent and the school district requiring that the student and parent sign them. Basically, the acceptable use policy provides guidelines for appropriate technology use and stipulates the consequences of student misuse of technology. Some schools are adding a provision to include off-campus cyber bullying if it affects the student while in school.

There are also technology safeguards, such as firewalls and filtering software programs that are used in an effort to prevent inappropriate Internet use. Schools typically have network firewalls that prevent network intrusion by controlling and regulating the traffic between the school network and the Internet. Additionally, filtering software programs developed to block access to undesirable material on the Internet are commonly used by schools and parents to help ensure Internet safety.

In today's high-tech world, the need to help students become responsible cyber citizens is of paramount importance. The role of the schools is to provide Internet safety education, educate students in the dangers inherent in technology and provide them with the safeguards necessary to effectively use technology.

The following table provides more resources for you to research more on social, ethical, legal, and human issues related to digital citizenship. Following this chapter, you will find practice exercises that can be used as artifacts for ISTE NETS-T Standard 4.

The National Broadband Plan: Connecting America
http://www.broadband.gov

Digital Divide Network
http://www.digitaldivide.net/

Digital Divide Org
http://www.digitaldivide.org/dd/digitaldivide.html

Fair Use Guidelines Chart for Teachers (PDF)
http:// www.halldavidson.net/copyright_chart.pdf

Copyright Law of the United States of America and Related Laws Contained in Title 17
http://www.copyright.gov/title17/92chap1.html#10 1

Creative Commons
http://creativecommons.org

Open Source Initiative
http://www.opensource.org

Sample Acceptable Use Agreements and Policies
http://nces.ed.gov/pubs2005/tech_suite/app_a.asp

Plagiarism.org
http://www.plagiarism.org/

Stop Cyber Bullying
http://www.stopcyberbullying.org

The Cyber Citizen partnership Program
http://www.cybercitizenship.org/

Age-based guidelines for kids' Internet use
http://www.microsoft.com/protect/family/age/stages.mspx

Developing an Acceptable Use Policy, Education World
http://www.education-world.com/a_curr/curr093.shtml

The Core Rules of Netiquette
http://www.albion.com/netiquette/corerules.html

References

The Cyber Citizen Partnership. (2008). *What is cyber crime?* Retrieved from
http://www.cybercitizenship.org/crime/crime.html

The National Broadband Plan: Connecting America. (2011). Retrieved from http://www.broadband.gov

Turnitin. (2008). *Learning Center*. Retrieved from
http://www.plagiarism.org/learning_center/what_is_plagiarism.html

U. S. Department of Commerce. (2004). *A nation online: Entering the broadband age.* Washington, D.C.:
U.S. Government Printing Office.

U. S. Department of Education. (2003). *Internet access soars in schools, But "Digital Divide" still exists
at home for minority and poor students.* Washington, D.C.: U. S. Government Printing Office.

United States Copyright Office. (2008). *Copyright law of the United States of America.* Retrieved from
http://www.copyright.gov/title17/92chap1.html - 101

Digital Citizenship Exercises

Exercise 1: Addressing Digital Inequality

ISTE NETS-T Standard 4

Scenario: You discover that over half of your class does not have access to computers and/or the Internet at home. This exercise requires that you prepare a memorandum to your principal describing digital inequality and providing three specific recommendations creating equal digital opportunities for all students. You will find the Digital Equity Toolkit (scroll down to download the PDF file: http://www.edutopia.org/digital-equity) quite helpful in completing this assignment.

✓ Save the *Word* document or Google Doc as **YourLastName Digital Inequality** in an appropriate folder

✓ Write a memorandum to your principal that includes the following information:

1. **Opening paragraph(s)**: a general explanation of what the digital divide is and the effects of digital inequity

2. **Body of the Memo**: list and explain (paragraph for each) at least 3 specific recommendations for resources that might help address issues of digital inequality in your classroom, the school, or community.

3. **Closing paragraph(s)**: summarize your recommendations and offer your assistance.

*Could be used as an artifact for Standard 4.

Exercise 2: Digital Inequality Websites

ISTE NETS-T Standard 4

In doing the research for the memo you wrote above, you discovered some excellent websites with information about digital divide/digital inequality.

✓ Add a new list page to your Technology Teaching Portfolio and name it "Digital Divide/Digital Inequality Resources."

✓ List and describe at least 5 relevant websites.

*Could be used as an artifact for Standard 4.

Exercise 3: Plagiarism and the Importance of Citing

ISTE NETS-T Standard 4

In this exercise you will prepare a Google Docs presentation to present to your students the first time you assign them a project or research paper requiring Internet research. (You can create this artifact with a partner, then publish and insert on your Technology Teaching Portfolio. Make sure you share your document with your partner.)

✓ Save the presentation as **YourLastName Plagiarism**

✓ Design a presentation that includes the following information:
  ▪ Grade level (include on title slide)
  ▪ Definition of plagiarism
  ▪ Examples of plagiarism
  ▪ How to avoid plagiarism
  ▪ Include speaker notes for each of your slides (Instructions included in the sidebar to your right.)

✓ Insert your Presentation on a new page on your Technology Teaching Portfolio.

> **Adding Speaker Notes to your Google Docs Presentation**
>
> Click the **View Speaker Notes** button in the bottom right corner of the slide show screen. The speaker's notes window will open in a panel to the right of the slide.
>
> Type your notes into the speaker notes window. You can format them just like regular text with the type formatting toolbar above the slide.

Tip: After adding artifacts to your portfolio, link to your artifact file or page from the ISTE Standards page/artifact link. Include your reflection on how the artifact meets that Standard and make sure all links work.

*Required artifact for Standard 4.

Exercise 4: Age-Appropriate Internet Safety

ISTE NETS-T Standard 4

This exercise provides an opportunity for you to tailor your Internet safety guidelines to the age group/grade level that you hope to teach some day. Prepare a Google Docs presentation outlining Internet safety for your students.

✓ Save the presentation as **YourLastName Guidelines**
✓ Design an **age-appropriate, grade level** Internet safety presentation that includes the following information:

  ▪ Grade level (include on title slide)
  ▪ Cyber Dangers
  ▪ Ways to safeguard against cyber dangers
  ▪ Include speaker notes for each of your slides

*Could be used as an artifact for Standard 4

Exercise 5: Age-Appropriate Netiquette Guidelines

ISTE NETS-T Standard 4

This exercise provides an opportunity for you to tailor netiquette guidelines to the age group/grade level that you hope to teach some day. Prepare a Google Docs presentation outlining specific netiquette guidelines.

✓ Save the presentation as **YourLastName Netiquette**
✓ Design an **age-appropriate, grade level** netiquette guidelines presentation that includes the following information:
- Grade level (include on title slide)
- Rules for proper netiquette
- Include speaker notes on each of your slides

*Could be used as an artifact for Standard 4.

Exercise 6: Creating a Creative Commons License

ISTE NETS-T Standard 4

✓ Visit the Creative Commons website (http://creativecommons.org)

1. Click the **Choose License** button at the top left.
2. Decide what type of license you want to assign to your work.
3. Answer the questions and then select your license.
4. Copy and paste the embed code to the Welcome! (Home) page of your Technology Teaching Portfolio.

*Could be used as an artifact for Standard 4.

Exercise 7: Critiquing an Acceptable Use Policy

ISTE NETS-T Standard 4

One of your key roles as an instructor is to make the learning environment effective for all students.

1. Do some Internet research and locate your school district's Acceptable Use Policy for Internet use.
2. Read through this policy and compose a new post on your blog, critiquing some elements. Do you agree/disagree and why?
3. Back up your statements with relevant resources (use Google Scholar to conduct research). What changes might you recommend to your school district?

*Could be used as an artifact for Standard 4.

Chapter 7: Professional Practice, Growth, and Leadership

This chapter of the textbook addresses NETS-T Standard 5, which stipulates that, "teachers continuously improve their professional practice, model lifelong learning, and exhibit leadership in their school and professional community by promoting and demonstrating the effective use of digital tools and resources."

Effective teachers can find ways to improve student learning by participating in local and global learning communities. Technology tools for communication, collaboration, and interaction can help eliminate these physical borders and boundaries. Teachers and students can interact with their counterparts in other schools, cities, states, and even countries by leveraging Digital Age tools.

ISTE NETS-T also calls for engaged and effective teachers to actively take a leadership role. By personally demonstrating technology integration, developing of technology and leadership skills of others, and sharing decision-making and community building, strong Digital Age teachers can effectively promote appropriate technology use.

Teachers can be found demonstrating the effective use of current and emerging resources and tools to support student learning. Digital Age teachers seek out, evaluate, and call into practice current research and thinking in appropriate and effective technology integration. Keeping up on the tools, trends, and current research, as well as collaborating with innovative groups or individuals, are essential.

By being active in the global community, taking a leadership role, and staying abreast of current research and trends, Digital Age teachers "contribute to the effectiveness, vitality, and self renewal of the teaching profession and of their school and community."

Teacher Productivity

Many of the day-to-day activities fundamental to the work of a classroom teacher can be facilitated through the use of technology. In a typical school, teachers spend a considerable part of their day preparing instructional materials, distributing and collecting assignments, and grading and returning assignments to students. Preparing supplemental instructional materials for absent and learners with special needs, communicating with parents, and the posting of assignments can be added to the list of typical teacher work responsibilities.

Technology can greatly assist teachers in creating assignments customized for content, grade level, and learning objectives. There are many websites available to teachers with lesson plans, instructional aides (including audio/visual aides), specific content information, and other teacher assistance. Teachers can quickly locate instructional materials and tailor them to content standards and their students' individual needs. Additionally, teachers can communicate with their colleagues, as well as experts, in the planning of lessons, discussing classroom management issues, collaborating on instructional projects, or seeking instructional advice.

Technology can be used to expedite the performance of those activities that require a substantial amount of teacher non-instructional time and energy. As you have worked through this textbook and completed many of the technology exercises, you have seen the power of technology to assist teacher productivity. Although the use of individual software applications to assist in preparing and grading assignments, record-keeping, and communicating with students and parents does aid teacher productivity, many school districts have gone to Student Information Systems (SIS), also called student information management systems (SIMS, SIM), student records system (SRS) or student management system (SMS).

Student Information Systems

A Student Information System (SIS) is an integrated, database program designed to store and manage relevant student data including demographic information, attendance, grades, and schedules. Given the data reporting demands of *No Child Left Behind*, and the ability for web-based applications, Student Information Systems have become commonplace in schools around the nation. The benefits of an SIS extend beyond its obvious record-keeping ability as an SIS provides accessibility to parents and communication features as well. An SIS can become a true portal for student, parent, and teacher communication. The majority of SIS offerings allow teachers to enter attendance, grades, and homework assignments directly into the system from their classrooms, data that can then be accessed by parents and students via a web-based interface.

One of the first web-based SIS programs, *PowerSchool*, provides a centralized relational database of student information including grades and attendance. The benefits, however, go beyond the data to include data-driven decision making and increased parental involvement. The *PowerSchool* website (http://www.powerschool.com/product) reports the following student, parent and teacher benefits to using their system:

- **Insight-Driven Decision-Making**
  PowerSchool takes you beyond administrative reporting, enabling you to use data to increase student achievement and quickly spot trends that may affect student outcomes.

- **Turning Parent Involvement into Student Achievement**
  PowerSchool gives you the power to stay on top of student progress-with email updates, and online access to schedules, grades, homework, attendance information and teacher comments.

- **Simplifying Teacher Tasks**
  PowerTeacher simplifies the tasks teachers perform daily such as taking attendance, entering grades, initiating student and parent communication, posting assignments, and assessing student alerts and demographic information. And since PowerTeacher is web-based, teachers can work anytime...from anywhere...as long as there is an Internet connection. PowerTeacher promotes progressive grading methods, including grading student groups, easy creation of formative, summative, and diagnostic assignments, and multiple measures of central tendencies (mean, median, mode). You're able to assess student progress from many different angles in order to maximize student achievement

A Student Information System enables teachers to complete the day-to-day record-keeping tasks required by the school district as well as a means to create and analyze assessment information. And once the teacher enters information into the SIS, it is available at the administrative level as well as available to students and parents.

What is professional development?

In the broadest sense, professional development is the process of increasing the professional capabilities of teachers by providing training and educational opportunities. For many, professional development is the natural outcome of their desire for lifelong learning. The U.S. Department of Education (1996) advocates professional development as more than continuing education, but as a means to increase student achievement:

> Professional development plays an essential role in successful education reform. Professional development serves as the bridge between where prospective and experienced educators are now and where they will need to be to meet the new challenges of guiding all students in achieving to higher standards of learning and development.

To achieve this goal, the report recommends the following criteria for professional development, that it:

- focuses on teachers as central to student learning, yet includes all other members of the school community;
- focuses on individual, collegial, and organizational improvement;
- respects and nurtures the intellectual and leadership capacity of teachers, principals, and others in the school community;
- reflects best available research and practice in teaching, learning, and leadership;
- enables teachers to develop further expertise in subject content, teaching strategies, uses of technologies, and other essential elements in teaching to high standards;
- promotes continuous inquiry and improvement embedded in the daily life of schools;
- is planned collaboratively by those who will participate in and facilitate that development;
- requires substantial time and other resources;
- is driven by a coherent long-term plan;
- is evaluated ultimately on the basis of its impact on teacher effectiveness and student learning; and this assessment guides subsequent professional development efforts.

Professional development is considered a critical element in keeping teachers current and in promoting student achievement; however, providing opportunities for teacher growth and professional development is often challenging. Teachers work full-time and find it difficult to add to their workloads and travel to attend classes and/or workshops. Technology can certainly play a major role in providing access to specific professional development activities as well as to professional organizations with current research and practice-based information and instructional assistance. Professional development activities are often delivered online and include everything from a master's degree to online tutorials. Teachers can access and complete professional development activities at their own pace and time.

Professional Organizations

There are many professional organizations available for teachers, and all of the professional organizations host websites with useful information about their organization, membership requirements, and benefits of joining that organization. Organizations exist for every content area, such as the National Council of Teachers of English, National Science Teachers Association, and the National Council of Teachers of Mathematics as well as organizations for teachers in general, such as National Education Association. Joining a professional organization is the first step in professional development to stay current in the field of teaching and provide opportunities for professional development. Conferences and online activities feature more effective teaching strategies and materials, and most professional organizations have blogs allowing you to communicate with colleagues across the nation and across the world.

Teacher Productivity and Professional Practice

PowerSchool
http://www.powerschool.com

Boise State University, Educational Technology
http://edtech.boisestate.edu

Technology Teacher Blog
http://itcboisestate.wordpress.com

Cool Teacher Podcast
http://coolteachers.org

PBS TeacherLine
http://www.pbs.org/teacherline

Teachnology
http://www.teach-nology.com/tutorials

National Education Association
http://www.nea.org/index.html

Professional Productivity Tool: RSS

Although the acronym RSS can refer to Rich Site Summary or RDF Site Summary, the most common terminology associated with RSS is **Really Simple Syndication**. This technology, using a form of XML, allows the user to subscribe to content on the Web. Initially, that content consisted of online news sources that syndicated their latest published articles, making them available to subscribers. Today, the variety of organizations offering users the opportunity to subscribe has grown and is continuing to grow at a tremendous rate. A great deal of information is disseminated across the Web through the use of RSS technology providing teachers with a means of keeping up to date in their field as well as with their professional organizations.

In much the same way as you might peruse your newspaper scanning for those sections that are of most interest, RSS feeds scan the headlines from Web sources to which you subscribe. So, instead of having to go through every page of your newspaper, you can view the headlines on your computer screen, Click the headline for a synopsis of the article, and if it interests you, click to the web to access the original, full article. In this way, the content on the web to which you subscribe actually comes to you.

Using RSS allows you to organize frequently updated content so that it can easily be retrieved; and, of course, the content is not limited to news sources. One of the first uses of RSS feeds, and growing quickly in popularity, is to subscribe to weblogs. Moreover, the type of content currently being retrieved through RSS feeds is expanding and includes everything from PDF files to audio and video files.

Although RSS has been around since 1999, it wasn't until 2003, with the tremendous growth of weblogs, that more and more sites have become syndicated. And, the number of applications using feeds is increasing daily, making it a valuable technology resource for educators and students.

Benefits of RSS Feeds

An obvious benefit of subscribing to RSS feeds is the opportunity the technology presents to keep informed with the most up-to-date information available as soon as it becomes available. You no longer need to take the time to visit each of the sites you find of interest searching for new postings; you will be notified of new material, scan the headlines, read a short synopsis (sometimes this may be all the information you require), and then go onto the site containing the full posting if you need more information. The information is "delivered to your door" and you can access it, ignore it, or even delete it.

Another benefit, aligned with the one described above, is the ability for the RSS site to get its information to those most interested in it. D'Souza (2006) describes RSS as a "pulling" technology because users can subscribe to your information instead of your simply posting information on a website and broadcasting (or "pushing") it hoping that someone will attend to that information.

A search of the web discloses many websites that are encouraging visitors to subscribe to their feeds knowing that this is an excellent means of getting their message to those who are most interested. For example, the British History Online homepage (http://www.british-history.ac.uk/rss-web-feeds.asp) proclaims that RSS web feeds will keep you up-to-date without revisiting the site. The visitor is told that he/she can avoid information overload by subscribing to one of British History Online's RSS web feeds.

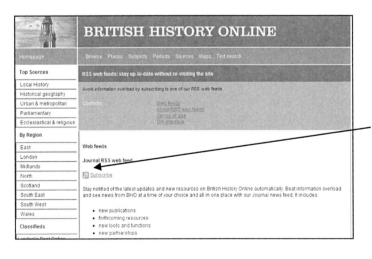

By subscribing, you are notified of the latest updates and new resources.

Gaining control over information overload is often touted as a benefit of RSS technology. Surfing the web for information is an overwhelming task for many people requiring that they scan whole sites looking for pertinent information. RSS feeds take over that task for you focusing on your particular needs and continually updating information as it becomes available.

An added advantage to subscribing to RSS feeds is the anonymity afforded to the user who does not have to disclose an email address when subscribing and is thus not increasing exposure to other dangers such as viruses or identity theft. And, finally, you do not have to formally "unsubscribe" from an RSS feed; you can easily delete the RSS feed from the aggregator. Given the varied benefits of RSS feeds, how are educators currently using this technology for teaching, learning and research?

How Do I Start Using RSS Feeds?

The idea of subscribing to RSS feeds may at first seem a little daunting, but it is a technology that is easily applied. You need only to set up an aggregator (sometimes called a news aggregator, RSS reader, feed reader, news reader, or feed aggregator) to collect the RSS feeds to which you subscribe. Basically, there are two types of aggregators: those that can be installed as software and those that are web-based. Although software aggregators may have more features, a web-based aggregator is easy to use and is free. Additionally, using a web-based aggregator allows you to view your RSS feeds at any location in which you have Internet access.

Setting up an account with an aggregator or reader takes just a few minutes of your time, and learning how to use it is relatively basic. Although there are a number of aggregators available on the web, this manual features the use of a very popular aggregator, Google Reader, located at http://www.google.com/reader.

To set up your free account at Google Reader you need only go to the site and use your Google email account and password. With Google Reader, you will be able to keep track of your favorite website, stay up to date, and simplify your reading experience. Moreover, you can access Google Reader as long as you have Internet access, even on mobile devices.

Finding and Subscribing to RSS Feeds

The opening screen of your reader provides you with the ability to locate pertinent RSS feeds that are categorized according to emphasis – news, sports, fun and more, or you can enter a search term and browse for a specific interest area.

1. Click the **Add a subscription** button and enter the keyword **teachers** in the search term box. Click **Add**.

Google Reader lists feeds that have some connection to teachers, although you will have to determine which are more pertinent to you. Click any of the links that interest you to see if you would like to subscribe to that resource.

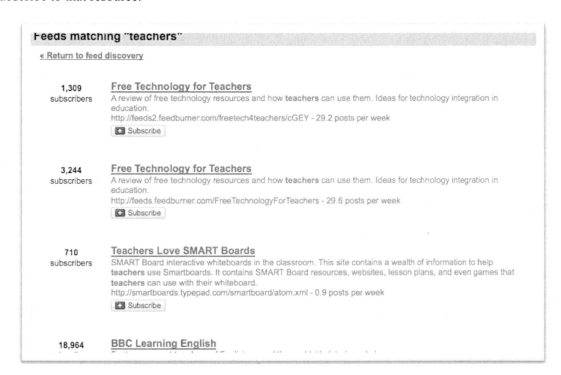

You should see a link **Surfing the Net with Kids** on this page. (Of course, this site might become unavailable, so if it does, click any of the links to view content and find one you would like to subscribe to).

2.   Click the link **Surfing the Net with Kids** to view some of the content.

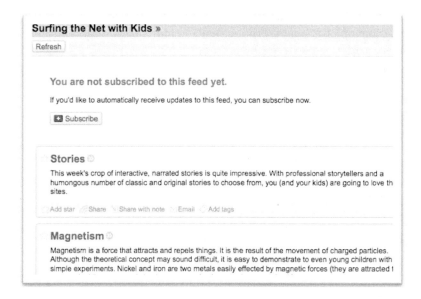

3.   You will see a notice at the top of the page that you are not yet subscribed to this feed. In order to subscribe to this feed, simply click the **Subscribe** button.

You have now subscribed to the Surfing the Net with Kids feed and will be able to access the most recent articles from this feed as well as the others in which you are interested by simply going to Google Reader. To organize your feeds, you can easily place them in pertinent folders by clicking the **Manage subscriptions** link on the bottom left-hand side of the screen.

Subscribing to Feeds through RSS links/URLs

This, of course, is not the only way for you to subscribe to a syndicated site. Although you cannot subscribe to a regular web page, you can identify those sites that provide RSS feeds as they display an RSS or XML tag or have a link for the XML version of the page.

For example, when you visit the homepage (http://nces.ed.gov/index.asp) of the U.S. Department of Education, National Center for Education Statistics, you will notice an XML/RSS tag [XML RSS] at the bottom of the page. By clicking the tag, you are taken to a page displaying two URLs, one to the **What's New** feeds at the National Center for Education Statistics and another to the **Recent Publications** feeds. The page prompts you to copy the URL into your reader; this is the most common procedure for subscribing to a feed.

4.   Click the link to the **What's New** publication. You will be directed to another page (depending upon your browser). Copy the URL (remember the shortcut, **Ctrl+C** for copy)

162

5. Open Google Reader, and click **Add subscription** button

6. Click in the search box and paste the URL (**Ctrl+V**) in the search box and click **Add**

You have now subscribed to the NCES feed **What's New** and will be able to locate the most up-to-date reports by accessing Google Reader.

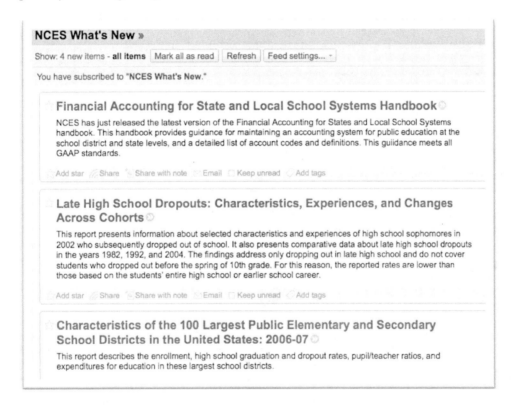

Of course, the process for subscribing may differ slightly from site to site featuring different icons and/or prompts, and may even differ because of your web browser. But, essentially it can be accomplished by copying the URL into your reader/aggregator.

Sharing and Publishing Items

A very powerful feature in Google Reader is the ability to share items that you find particularly interesting and/or relevant for class instruction or for sharing with your colleagues. Google Reader.

1.   Click the **Your shared items** link in the left side of the window.

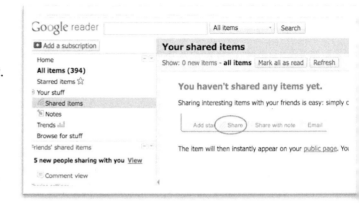

The first time you do this, you will see the prompt stating that you haven't shared any items yet. You can set up your profile and choose the background for your shared public page, a page that is available to anyone to whom you give the link.

Now that you have a shared page, you can select the articles or reports that you want to share with your students, colleagues or friends.

2.   To share an item, simply click **Share** at the bottom of the feed.

Google Reader provides a public shared page with an URL that you could provide (email or otherwise) to your students, colleagues, parents, and/or friends. The page can be easily modified at any time by clicking **Unshare** to eliminate the current item and/or by clicking **Share** to place any item on your shared page. Below is an example of a shared page:

There are many possible uses of the shared page and your students could also create a shared page as long as they have a Google account.

Creating Public Pages for Starred or Tagged Items

You can also create public pages for your starred or tagged items in Google Reader. Since these items are private by default, you'll need to make them public first. Here's how:

1. Click the **Settings** link in your Google Reader Account (upper right hand corner).
2. Another window will open. Click **Folders and Tags**.

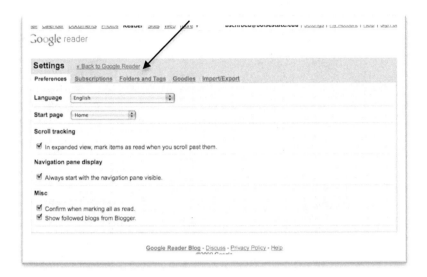

3. Use the check boxes to select the tag you want to share. There's also an option for your starred items, if you want to share those instead.
4. From the **Change Sharing** menu/drop-down box select **Public**.

Anything you've made public will now have a public page associated with it. Just click the view public page link next to any public tag to see how it looks.

Planning a Lesson Integrating RSS Feeds

For that first lesson using RSS feeds in your classroom, focus on students creating an account and subscribing to one or two feeds that you recommend. Caution them about the quality and quantity of feeds to which they subscribe and assist them in the managing of their feeds. Take time to discuss the benefits and potential drawbacks to Web feeds. Once the students feel comfortable with the technology, then consider ways that the technology can help in reaching curriculum goals.

One strategy would be concentrate on one crucial concept or issue to be covered in your course and have students search for appropriate feeds. This can be a group and/or class effort in which feeds can be recommended and shared among classmates and published on a shared page.

If your students have not already created blogs for class use, then that activity would be the logical next step. You might start with a blog that allows multiple authors to encourage a more collaborative approach. You and your students could subscribe to the blogs and know when they are updated.

References

D'Souza, Q. (2006). *RSS ideas for educators*. Retrieved from http://www.teachinghacks.com/wp-content/uploads/2006/01/RSS%20Ideas%20for%20Educators111.pdf

Haarsh, M. (2003). The next killer app for education. *The Technology Source Archives.* (July, August 2003). Retrieved from http://technologysource.org/article/rss/

Information Today Online (2004). Blogging and RSS – the 'what's it?' and 'how to' of powerful new web tools for educators. *Information Today Online.* (January, February 2004). Retrieved from http://www.infotoday.com/MMSchools/jan04/richardson.shtml

U. S. Department of Education. (1996). *Achieving the goals: Teacher professional development.* Washington, D.C.: U.S. Government

Productivity and Professional Practice Exercises

Exercise 1: Professional Websites
Required: ISTE NETS-T Standard 5

As you search the Internet, you have found many professional websites that will be useful in your teaching.

✓ Prepare a **List** page on your Technology Teaching Portfolio, listing at least 10 of these sites with a short description of each and their URL.

✓ List at least 10 preferred professional websites and include the following information:

- Name of organization sponsoring the website
- Website name
- Website address
- Description of website
- Reason for choosing this website in your professional website collection

*Required artifact for Standard 5

Exercise 2: Publishing a Shared RSS Page
Required: ISTE NETS-T Standard 1

Now that you have a Google Reader account and have subscribed to RSS feeds, publish a shared RSS page for your students or colleagues.

✓ Publish a Google Reader Shared RSS Page with the following criteria: 4 articles and/or reports
✓ Include the following on your web page:

1. Describe the intended audience for your shared page (other teachers, students, or parents)
2. Describe focus (theme) of your shared page
3. Explain how you would use the page
4. Link to your shared page

✓ Create a new page on your Technology Teaching Portfolio, describing RSS and how it might be used in your classroom.

✓ Include a link to your Shared Google Reader Page and make sure it works!

*Required artifact for Standard 1.

Chapter 8: Engagement and Creativity

Experts agree that engagement is a critical element in academic success. Learning requires a student to be an active participant. Even with an enthusiastic and energetic teacher, learners who are not actively engaged in the lesson or activity are less likely to learn or retain what is being taught. However, when students are engaged in the curriculum and classroom activities, they are often self-directed, support their classmates, are aware of their own personal progress, self-assess, actively question and inquire, interact with a community of learners, look for opportunities for leadership, are creative and innovative, and enjoy the process as well as the outcome.

Engagement in the Classroom

The effects of engagement in the classroom not only benefit the student. Teachers cite a productive, busy, and industrious classroom as a major contributor to feelings of personal enjoyment and professional success. It makes sense that lesson structure, activities, and assessments that inspire this motivated learning environment and fight apathy lead to both happy and motivated teachers. Happy teachers often result in engaged and motivated students.

If engagement is required for learning, how do teachers excite and motivate students? What tools or techniques can teachers employ to develop motivated learners?

ISTE NETS-T Standard 1 directs effective Digital Age educators to "facilitate and inspire student learning and creativity." As experts of teaching and learning, instructors can use their knowledge of their subject matter and technology to build inspiring, imaginative, and motivating learning activities, artifacts, and spaces. Using face-to-face and virtual environments, effective digital age teachers use technology "to facilitate experiences that advance student learning, creativity, and innovation."

When effective teachers promote and reward creativity, students respond by being innovative and driven. As long as they feel supported, young people will make an attempt to give their instructors what they ask for. Allow them to access their own unique skill sets, talents, and ideas in organized and well designed lessons, and they will be largely self directed, motivated, and active learners. In addition, as teachers model and identify creative behavior enthusiastically in their own work, it inspires inventive thinking in the work of their students. Rewarding creativity with acknowledgment and praise creates an environment rich with innovation. Technology can support these types of environments with myriad tools of content creation.

Lessons can be both directed and open-ended to allow students to pursue their "individual curiosities and become more active participants." Technology cannot only supply a product but the process. Allowing students to manage their time on activity, reflect against their educational goals, and assess progress against given or shared goals or expectations using these technology tools can create an environment where self-directed learner can thrive.

Each student comes with a unique set of skills, abilities, talents, and needs. Because technology can offer such unique user flexibility, effective digital age teachers can customize and personalize learning activities to address students' diverse learning styles. Whether visual, auditory or kinesthetic; unique web-based tools, desktop software, hardware peripherals and input devices, can allow students flexible ways to create and participate. They can employ these tools to modify their own personal working strategies.

Effective digital age teachers can also model the use of technology for collaboration. Learning to engage in a social context is not simply limited to the classroom. Teachers and students can share "collaborative knowledge construction" using blogs, wikis, discussion boards, mashups, video and photo content sharing, social networks, and many other Web 2.0 inspired technologies. Teachers can facilitate and inspire student learning and creativity by demonstrating scripts that model and use these tools. These collaborative tools, especially where socialization is possible, offer a high level of engagement. Collaborative web-based digital tools can be asynchronous, allowing the participants to add or adapt content whenever they choose. Synchronous tools allow them to react in real time. Virtual environments even allow students to interact with one another in a digital 3-D space.

An excellent tool for allowing students to apply and share their knowledge in a creative way is a multimedia presentation. Presentation software, also called multimedia or hypermedia software, can be an effective tool for teachers and students. For teachers, a presentation, a visual slide show, can be used for the initial teaching of ideas and concepts, practice and drill, multimedia projects, review and even tests or quizzes. For students, presentation software is a learning tool to be used in developing projects, assignments, and presentations. *Microsoft PowerPoint* allows you to not only display visual information such as graphs, tables and charts, but you can also insert sound and video clips. And, you can easily make your presentation available on the web for students who have missed class or want to review class material.

Designing Presentations

When teachers were first introduced to *PowerPoint*, they used the slides in much the same as they used overhead transparencies. Slides were crammed with lots of information, viewed in a linear arrangement, and devoid of anything but text. With the multimedia capabilities of *PowerPoint,* however, you can design effective linear and non-linear slide shows that add to your presentation and reinforce the content. Your students can interact with nonlinear presentations much the same as a website by exploring links within the presentation and to the Internet. Whether your presentation is linear or nonlinear, there are some guidelines for making effective presentations:

- Keep the presentation clean and simple so your students focus on the content of the slides and not the "gee whiz" aspects of *PowerPoint.*
- Include only the main points with each slide covering only one concept.
- Limit the information you include on each slide (6-7 words per line, and 3 to 6 lines per slide).
- Don't overcrowd your slides with graphics and/or text.
- Use no more than 3 different fonts in a single presentation or slide.
- Make sure that the text is legible to all the students in your class.
- Include a conclusion slide with a summary.

In this section of the textbook, you will be preparing a *PowerPoint* presentation for the Parent Teacher Organization (PTO) in response to parent questions about the concerns of Internet use. For purposes of this exercise, you will be preparing only seven slides to present at the meeting.

Creating a Concept Map

Your first step would be to prepare an outline or concept map of your presentation. A concept map is a way for you and your students to visualize the relationship among concepts and provides a visual map of the presentation. Below is a concept map of your Cyber Dangers presentation if you were to prepare it as a linear presentation, basically showing one slide and then the next with no interaction or linking capabilities.

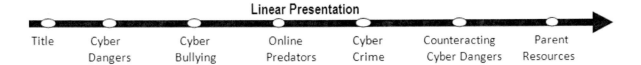

Linear Presentation

| Title | Cyber Dangers | Cyber Bullying | Online Predators | Cyber Crime | Counteracting Cyber Dangers | Parent Resources |

Although this works well for your actual presentation to the PTO since you will simply go from slide to slide, a nonlinear presentation would be better for the parents to view on their own; you could make the presentation available to the parents on the web or send it to them as an email attachment. They could move through the presentation as they wished and click the links to take them to specific slides and/or websites. A concept map of the Cyber Dangers nonlinear presentation would look like the one below:

Nonlinear Presentation

Title Slide

Cyber Dangers

Cyber Bullying   Online Predators   Cyber Crime

Counteracting Cyber Dangers

Parent Resources

In addition to a concept map, teachers will often require that their students storyboard their presentation particularly if there is limited computer access. By preparing a storyboard, the students will have every element of the presentation planned and save valuable time in front of the computer.

Preparing a Storyboard

The process of storyboarding, sketching out the elements of each slide, is also done in moviemaking. Students can conceive the presentation as a set of slides, the layout of the slides and determine graphics and/or multimedia elements to include .The *PowerPoint* program actually provides common layouts that students could use in preparing their storyboards. So, for the Cyber Dangers presentation, the first slide would be a title slide, and the *PowerPoint* title slide layout is perfect for the first slide of the storyboard and the Title and Content layout would work for the second slide.

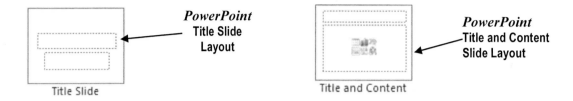

Of course, you are not limited to the layout slides available in *PowerPoint* and text and graphics may be displayed as you wish. A storyboard of the Cyber Dangers presentation could look like this:

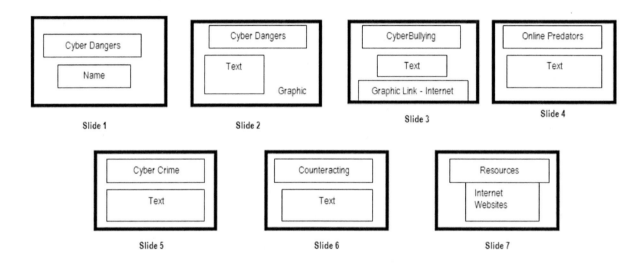

Now that you have planned your presentation and have a basic storyboard, you are ready to create the Cyber Dangers presentation for parents.

Presentation software can be a powerful tool for teachers when used judiciously and with an understanding of good multimedia learning principles. For an overview of how to create effective multimedia presentations, refer to a PDF file written by Cliff Atkinson and Richard E. Mayer, called "Five Ways to Reduce *PowerPoint* Overload" (http://www.sociablemedia.com/PDF/atkinson_mayer_PowerPoint_4_23_04.pdf). This file includes helpful hints along with sample slides to guide you in planning effective and compelling presentations.

Microsoft PowerPoint offers many advantages for teachers. Here are just a few:

1. The software is intuitive and easy to learn how to use.
2. It includes a large collection of themes.
3. Video, audio, and many forms of multimedia can be easily inserted.
4. Presentations can be reformatted to various file formats, such as movie files, PDF, and handouts.
5. It provides a great way to illustrate a visual concept.
6. By using the "Presenter" format, presenters can view their notes and slides while presenting.

The following skills section will introduce you to Microsoft *PowerPoint* 2007 for Windows, applying your skills to the creation of a "Cyber Dangers" presentation for parents.

Microsoft PowerPoint 2011 for Mac (Appendix G)

Microsoft PowerPoint 2007 for Windows

1. Click the **Start** button on the task bar in the lower left corner of your screen.
2. Move the mouse pointer to **All Programs** to display the submenu.
3. Click *Microsoft Office,* and then click the program you want to access, in this case, *Microsoft Office PowerPoint 2007*.

Although the opening screen of *PowerPoint 2007* contains many of the common ribbons and commands that you have previously used in *Word* and *Excel*, there are new elements applicable only to presentation software.

The default title is Presentation1 so you will want to save your presentation in an appropriate location and title it **YourLastName Cyber Dangers**.

Save As

1. Click the *Microsoft Office* button

2. Click [Save As ▸]. You now need to choose the file format for the saved file. If you do not make a choice, the default is *PowerPoint 2007*.

PowerPoint Presentation
Save the presentation in the default file format.

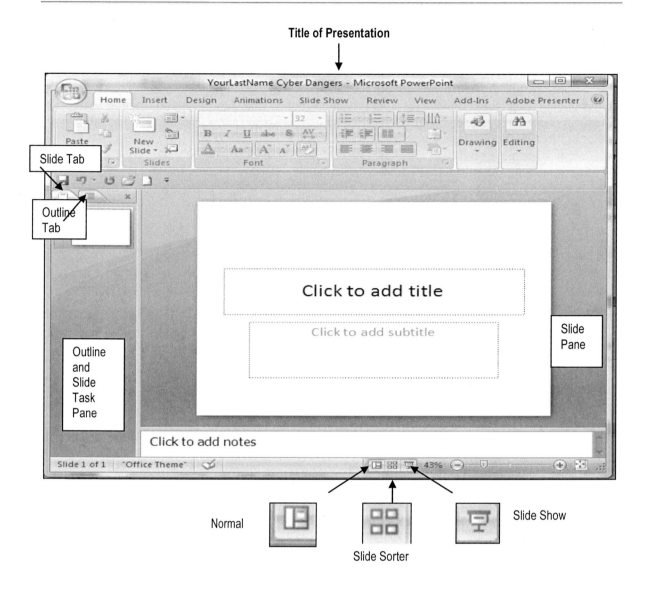

The presentation opens in **Normal** view, which is the view in which you typically create the presentation with two panes, a slide pane view and an outline and slide task pane with tabs located at the top. By clicking the outline tab, you can create a slide presentation as an outline made up of the titles and main text from each slide.

The default, however, is the slide tab view. While **Normal** view is used in creating the presentation, **Slide Sorter** view is used to determine the final arrangement of the slides in the presentation. In this view, you are able to easily reorder slides.

Clicking the **Slide Show** view displays your slides as they would actually be displayed for your audience.

The Title Slide

Notice that your opening screen presents the first slide with layout for providing a title and subtitle. Although you could change the layout, starting a slide show with a title slide is customary.

1. Click in the area **Click to add title** and enter the title of your presentation: **Cyber Dangers**.

2. Click in the **subtitle** textbox and enter **YourLastName** and **School**

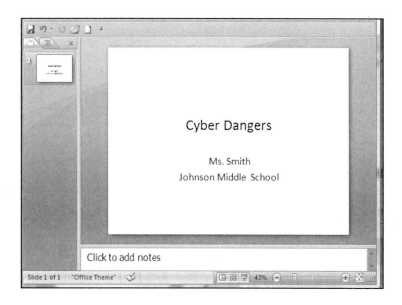

Adding New Slides

1. Click the **New Slide** icon located in the Home ribbon to add a slide. If you click the bottom of the icon, you are presented with a number of slide layouts from which to choose. If you just click the icon (top half), the default Title and Content slide layout will be inserted.

Click the arrow to choose a layout slide.

2. Click the **Title and Content** slide layout.

For the second slide you will choose the Title and Content slide layout.

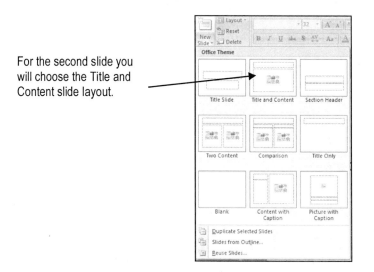

Type the title and bulleted list as shown in the slide below. You can choose the bullet style you wish for the slide.

Slide 2 – Normal View

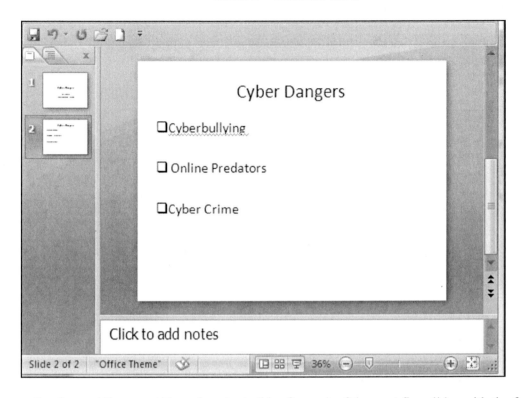

Continue adding new title and content slides for each of the next five slides with the following information on each slide:

Slide 3 – Normal View

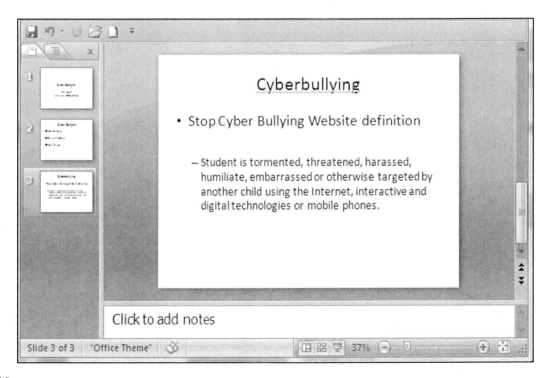

Slide 4 – Normal View

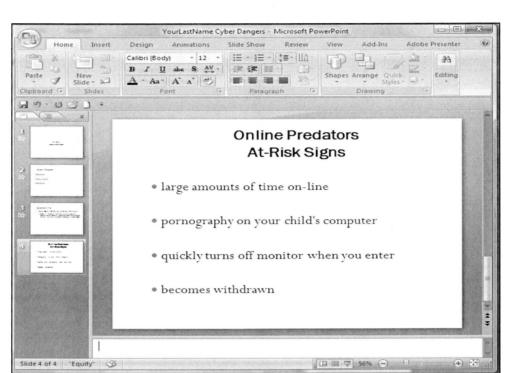

Slide 5 – Normal View

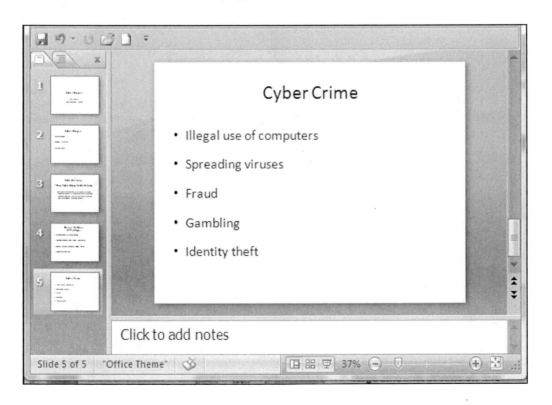

Slide 6 – Normal View

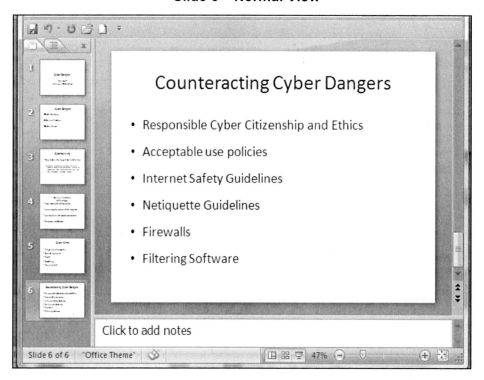

Slide 7 – Normal View

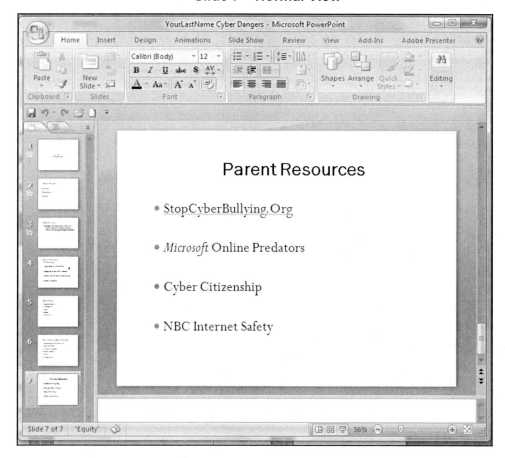

You now have a 7 slides slide show and are ready to add other elements such as graphics, background, fonts, and hyperlinks. Click the Slide Sorter icon located at the bottom of the screen to view all 7 slides and to easily rearrange your presentation.

Slide Sorter View

Inserting Graphics from Clip Art

Adding graphics to your presentation involves the same process as used in *Microsoft Word.*

1. In **Normal** view, select Slide 2.

2. Click the **Insert** tab to access the **Clip Art** command on the Insert ribbon.

    Clip Art Task Pane

3. Click the **Clip Art** icon and the Clip Art task pane opens allowing you to search for a graphic.

4. Enter **computer** in the search box.

5. Double-click your chosen graphic and it will be inserted in the slide.

6. Move the graphic to a desired location on the slide.

Inserting Graphics from Other Sources

Inserting graphics you have saved is also easily accomplished. Navigate to the Textbook Data Files link on our companion website (http://dats.boisestate.edu) to locate the required files or locate and save an image file of your choosing to a location on your computer.

1. In **Normal** view, select Slide 3.

2. Click the **Insert** tab to access the **Picture** command on the Insert ribbon.

3. Click the **Picture** icon and locate the **Stop Bullying** file in the Textbook Data Files link on our companion website or an image you have located.

4. Right-click the graphic and add a border around the graphic so that it is easier to see and arrange it on the slide. Your slide would look similar to the one below:

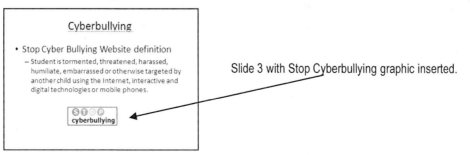

Slide 3 with Stop Cyberbullying graphic inserted.

Applying Themes and Backgrounds

Applying a theme to your Cyber Dangers presentation is easy with plenty of pre-existing themes readily available in *PowerPoint 2007*.

1.   In **Normal** view, select any slide.

2.   Click the **Design** tab to access the **theme** command on the Design ribbon.

Dropdown Gallery of Themes

Change colors   Change background

3.   There is a dropdown gallery of themes available in the **Themes** area.

4.   Hover your mouse cursor over any of the thumbnails to see a live preview of the theme.

5.   To apply the theme, click the thumbnail.

6.   You can change the theme colors by clicking the **Colors** option.

7.   If you prefer a different background than the ones offered in the themes gallery, you can set a background style or locate a theme you like on the Internet.

Take a few minutes to try some of the themes offered in *PowerPoint 2007* and a color, background and font change to determine your preferred presentation design. Next, you will learn how to add movement to your slide show. Slide transitions refer to movement from one slide to the next while animation refers to the movement of the elements on the slide.

Applying Animations

Animations are visual effects that are applied to the individual items on your slide. Animating text, graphics, diagrams, charts and other objects on your slides can help you to focus on important points, control the flow of your presentation and add interest. Again, be aware that if not used effectively, animations can distract from your presentation.

1.   Click the **Animations** tab and locate the **Custom Animation** command.

2. Select the text or object that you want to animate. In this example, the title **Cyber Dangers** has been selected

3. Click **Custom Animation** .

4. Click **Add Effect** and choose whether the animation will be an entrance, emphasis, exit or motion path effect. The example below shows the entrance effects.

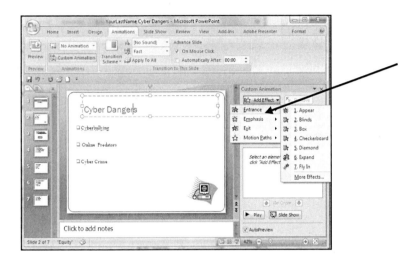

5. Click one of the effects presented or on the **More Effects** option for even more animation effects.

6. Once you choose an animation, you can see that animation applied on the slide, and the custom animation task pane now presents options for you to start the animation on a click of the mouse or automatically, the direction of the animation and the speed. You can set these as you desire.

The sequence of animations is presented in the bottom half of the custom animation task pane. In this example, only one animation has been applied and it will occur first. You can apply animations to every element in a slide and then order the sequence of their presentation. Try animating some of the elements in your Cyber Dangers slide show.

Inserting Slide Transitions

There are a variety of slide transitions available in *PowerPoint 2007* that can be quickly applied to either single slides or to the entire presentation. There are fade and dissolve transitions, wipes, push and cover, stripes and bars, and even random transitions. Determining the transitions you want to use will depend on the presentation and your audience.

1. Click the **Animations** tab and locate the **Transition to This Slide** category.

Transitions to this Slide

8. Move your mouse over the each transition for a live preview of that transition.

9. Click the transition that you want applied to the slide.

10. If you choose a transition, and then decide against it, it is easy to change by simply clicking the **No Transition** icon or an alternate icon.

11. On the **Design** ribbon, you also have the option of setting the transition speed (slow, medium and fast) as well as the ability to add a sound to the transition.

12. To add a sound, Click the Transition Sound command and choose from the dropdown list of sounds.

13. These are the transition sound options available in *PowerPoint*. If you wish to apply a sound to your transition, simply click your selected sound in the dropdown list.

14. If you have an audio file that you would like to apply as a sound transition, click the **Other Sound** option and browse your files to locate the sound file.

Try some of the sounds and determine if you want any included in your presentation. Do keep in mind that you do not want the sound to detract from your message for your audience.

PowerPoint also provides you with the ability to advance through each slide on a mouse click or to time your slide show automatically by clicking the option and then setting the desire time. Try out this feature as well.

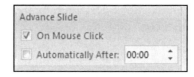

Inserting Sound and Video

You are also able to insert sounds and video into your presentations. These can be sounds from the clip organizer; from files you browse to, from CD audio tracts and from recordings. The ability to record in each slide enables you to record your presentations and make them available to students/parents who were not able to attend your class or presentation.

To record your voice, make sure you have a microphone available and select the slide in which you would like to add a recording.

1. Click the **Insert** tab and locate the **Sound** command.

2. Click **Record Sound.**

3. Click the record button and speak into your microphone.

4. When finished, Click the stop button and then **OK** if you are satisfied with the recording.

If you do not have a microphone, try inserting files from the clip organizer or from sound files you have saved.

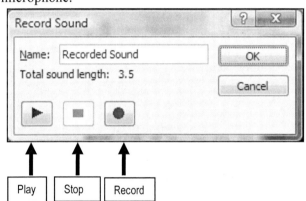

The image to the right displays the sound files that can be inserted into *PowerPoint* presentations:

In order to make your presentation nonlinear and more interactive, you are able to link within a presentation, link to other files and to the Internet. For the last part of this exercise, you will link slides within your presentation and to the Internet.

Creating Hyperlinks Within a Presentation

1. In **Normal** view, select Slide 2, Cyber Dangers, which lists the 3 dangers to be explored in the presentation. You will be using slide 2 as a table of contents, linking the 3 dangers to the individual slides that discuss each of them.

2. Select (highlight) the word that will be used as a link. For this slide, Cyberbullying, will be the link. Parents need only Click Cyberbullying and be taken to the slide that defines the term.

3. With the word **Cyberbullying** selected, Click the **Insert** tab and then on the **Hyperlink** command.

The **Insert Hyperlink** window opens displaying the slides by title and presenting a slide preview.

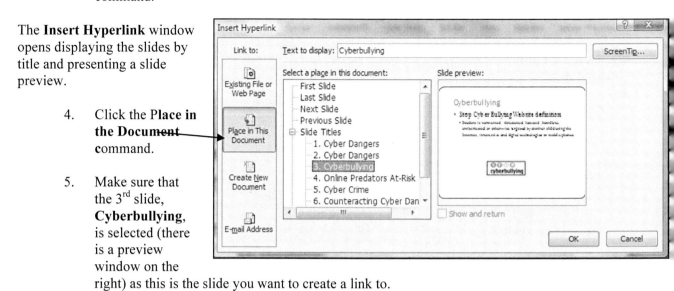

4. Click the **Place in the Document** command.

5. Make sure that the 3rd slide, **Cyberbullying**, is selected (there is a preview window on the right) as this is the slide you want to create a link to.

6. Click **OK.**

When you return to Normal view, you see that the word, Cyberbullying is now a hyperlink, but to actually use it as a hyperlink, you must be in **Slide Show** view.

7. Click **Slide Show** view icon located at the bottom of the *PowerPoint* window to try out your hyperlinks.

8. Continue linking the next 2 dangers to their corresponding slides following the directions above.

When you return to **Slide Show** view and click the hyperlinks, you discover that you now need a link to come back to Slide 2. Let's insert an **Action Button**, which works as a navigational hyperlink.

Inserting Action Buttons

As you want to be able to go back to Slide 2, which lists the 3 main presentation topics, you will add navigational action buttons to the three slides that you hyperlinked to earlier.

1. Select Slide 3, **Cyberbullying**, for the first slide to have an action button.

2. Click the **Insert** tab to access the Insert commands and click the **Shapes** icon.

3. Go to the bottom of the box to find the **Action Buttons**.

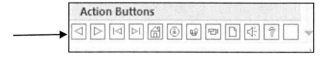

4. Click the **Back or Previous** Action Button.

Notice a box appears in which you have options to link to slides including the **Slide** options, which (if chosen) actually lists each slide by title.

5. Click **Slide 2** as you want to be able to link back to this slide.

6. Click **OK**. Drag the button to a desired location (lower left of slide).

As with your previous hyperlink, you will need to click the **Slide Show** view to see that the Previous Action Button will take you back to Slide 2.

Now that you have an action button that takes you to Slide 2, you can copy and paste that button on any slide.

7. Copy and paste the action button on slides 4 and 5 so that it is easy to return to the main contents slide (Slide 2).

Inserting More Hyperlinks Within the Presentation

As you view your presentation, you determine that it would be beneficial for parents to be able to link to the Parent Resources slide when viewing any of the cyber dangers. You already know how to hyperlink within a presentation, but this time, you will make a textbox the hyperlink.

1. Select **Slide 3, Cyberbullying**.
2. Insert a text box (use a small font) directing parents to the resources

3. Place it at the bottom of the slide.
4. Select it and insert a hyperlink to the last slide, **Parent Resources**.
5. Now, you can copy the text box to Slides 4 and 5 so parents can easily access the resources.
6. Create a **Back** action button on Slide 7 to take viewers to previously viewed slide.
7. Create a link on Slide 2 to go to Slide 6 and create a link on Slide 6 to go to back to Slide 2.

Textbox

Parent Resources

Inserting Hyperlinks to the Web

Basically, you will follow the same procedure in linking to the Internet as you did linking within your presentation.

1. Click the last slide, **Parent Resources**.

2. Select (highlight) the first parent resource, **StopCyberBullying.org**.

3. With the word **StopCyberbullying.org** selected, click the **Insert** tab and then on the **Hyperlink** command.

The Insert Hyperlink window opens displaying the slides by title and presenting a slide preview.

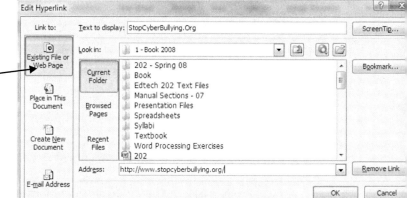

4. Click the **Existing File or Web Page** command.

5. Click in the address box and type:
    http://stopcyberbullying.org

(You can also just click Internet Explorer and go to the address and it will automatically be inserted in the **Address** box.)

6. Click **OK.**

Now hyperlink the remaining 3 parent resources on the Parent Resource slide. The URLs are listed on the following table.

Parent Resources	
These Websites are provided for your Cyber Dangers PowerPoint Presentation	
StopCyberBullying.org	http://stopcyberbullying.org
Microsoft Online Predators	http://www.microsoft.com/protect/family/guidelines/predators.mspx
Cyber Citizenship	http://www.cybercitizenship.org/
NBC Internet Safety	http://www.msnbc.msn.com/id/11030746/

Presentation Software Exercises

Exercise 1: Collaborative Curricular Presentation

Required: ISTE NETS-T Standard 1

This technology exercise was adapted from *Educating Teachers* (2007) – Pollard, C., VanDehey, T., & Pollard, R.

In this collaborative exercise you will be designing a lesson using Google Docs software with another partner or small group. You will also be creating a Google Docs Presentation to augment and support your lesson. You may choose any topic in the elementary curriculum or in your secondary subject area. It may be helpful to use the same topic area you used for a previous assignment.

Why use Google Docs Presentation instead of *PowerPoint*?

Your students can access your presentation at any time, from any computer, to review the lesson/information.

Students can logon to your presentation and make comments/ask questions during your presentation.

You can share your presentation easily with other teachers.

You can easily embed your presentation on other websites or course management systems.

✓ There will be four components required for this exercise:

1. **Lesson plan**: Foundation and justification for the lesson (Google Docs).
2. **Concept Map:** Image created from collaborative concept mapping tool, bubbl.us.
3. **Presentation (Slide show):** Slides containing the curricular content necessary for meeting state and/or national standards (Google Docs Presentation).
4. **Technology Teaching Portfolio:** Insert all components on a webpage on your Technology Teaching Portfolio.

1. Google Docs Simple Lesson Plan

1. Your lesson plan will be created using Google Docs, the **Simple Lesson Plan Template** you used earlier.
2. Name your Google Docs file **CurricularPresentation_YourLastName**
3. Share your document either through a shared Google Doc folder or by sharing the document directly with your classmates.

✓ After selecting the curricular topic area, include the following components:

1. Name of Lesson: (Make this a catchy title!)
2. Grade Level:
3. Subject:
4. Prepared by:
5. Overview and Purpose: Brief description of what the lesson plan is about and its purpose.
6. Educational Standards: Obtain these from your school district's website or national standards, whatever your instructor advises.
7. Objectives: Specify what students will be able to do, using verbs from Bloom's Taxonomy for the Cognitive Domain or language directly from your school district's performance standards.
8. Materials Needed: (Included in this would be your Google Docs presentation)
9. Other Resources: (websites, videos, books, etc.)

10. Information: This would be an outline of your lesson plan steps, with enough detailed information that it could be taught by a substitute teacher.
11. Verification: Provide assessment/procedure to check for student understanding.
12. Activity: Describe activity that students will complete to practice/reinforce the lesson.
13. Notes (Optional)

✓ As with all artifacts you complete for your Technology Teaching Portfolio, make sure that your lesson plan follows Standard English, has no spelling/punctuation/grammatical errors, and is professional and attractive.

2. Concept Map

✓ You will be responsible for designing a concept map of your presentation.

(A free and easy to use tool is bubbl.us https://bubbl.us, which is browser-based. Create a free account and start building your concept map. You can share and collaborate on your concept map with your group.)

✓ Make sure you export your concept map as an image file.

3. Presentation (Slide Show)

✓ Use Google Docs Presentation to create your slideshow.
✓ When you create a new presentation in Google Docs, you will want to rename it, like you do with Google Docs word processing. Click the title to rename the presentation to **Curricular Presentation_YourLastName**
✓ Share your Google Docs Presentation in the shared folder or directly with your classmates.
✓ **Presentation Criteria:**

1. Each slide covers only one concept.
2. 6-7 words per line and approximately 3 to 6 lines per slide.
3. Slides not crowed with graphics and/or text.
4. No more than 3 different fonts in a single presentation or slide.
5. Legible text
6. Accuracy of information
7. No slide number minimum, but enough to support/teach your topic
8. Hyperlinks to URLs if needed
9. Relevant, meaningful graphics that add to the instructional message

4. Insert on your Technology Teaching Portfolio

Tip: Use the two-column format and copy and paste your lesson plan in Google Docs lesson plan to your Google Sites page you have either already created or link to the page and create it at the same time (instructions for this in Appendix A).

✓ Attach your concept map image to this same page.
✓ On the right-hand column insert your Google Docs presentation (**Insert>Presentation**), which creates a gadget that embeds your presentation. (Make sure you publish your Google Doc and Presentation.)

*Required artifact for Standard 1.

Exercise 2: Class or Student Review

ISTE NETS-T Standard 2

This exercise features the use of *PowerPoint* to help your students review information. You will be using the custom animation capability of *PowerPoint* to design an electronic review to be used with a class or given to an individual student as electronic flashcards.

✓ Save the file as **YourLastName Review**

✓ Create your review slides as follows:

1. The question part of the slide will not be animated.

2. The possible solutions (as in a multiple choice question) will be presented after the question.

3. The answer will be presented after the student has an opportunity to think about the question.

Example

The question is not animated.

The possible responses are animated and appear when you click the mouse.

The student or class would have time to consider the possible responses and then could click the mouse one more time (#4) and see the correct response.

✓ Prepare a review for your class or for individual students to use as electronic flashcards.
✓ Design Criteria:

1. Accurate Information
2. Minimum of 10 Slides
3. Animation works correctly

✓ Upload your PowerPoint file to the File Cabinet page on your Technology Teaching Portfolio, create a new page called "Student Review Flashcards" and link to your PowerPoint file.

Tip: Save your PowerPoint as a PDF file and upload this file also to your File Cabinet. Viewers who do not have PowerPoint on their computers will be able to view your presentation in this format.

*Could be used as an artifact for Standard 2.

Exercise 3: Review Games

ISTE NETS-T Standard 2

You can create review games using PowerPoint. One site that provides instructions on PowerPoint games is listed in the table below.

You might also want to explore other online game creation options, such as Sploder. If you create a game using Sploder you won't have it saved on your computer, but should embed it on your Technology Teaching Portfolio.

✓ If you are using PowerPoint, save the file as **YourLastName Game** in an appropriate folder.

✓ Create your game using a template from one of the websites listed below.

PowerPoint Games http://jc-schools.net/TUTORIALS/PPT-GAMES/
Sploder: Where games come true http://www.sploder.com/free-game-creator.php

*Could be used as an artifact for Standard 2.

Exercise 4: Back to School Presentation Using Prezi

Required: ISTE NETS-T Standard 5

✓ Create an innovative and visually attractive presentation using an online tool, Prezi, for your parents who visit your classroom on "Back to School" night. Prezi presentations can be embedded on any website, too.

1. Visit the Prezi site http://prezi.com/ and create a free account.
2. Review the tutorials and practice using Prezi.
3. View some of the Prezis on the website and become inspired!
4. Instead of creating a linear presentation, start with your main idea (Back to School Night) and then create nodes or branches. Include the following in your presentation:
   • Short introduction and picture of yourself (i.e. professional information)
   • Class expectations
   • Standards
   • Class Highlights
   • Parent Involvement
   • Other
5. Create a new page on your Technology Teaching Portfolio and post a reflection about this artifact and how it meets the Standard. Link to your Prezi presentation and check to make sure it works!
6. **Optional:** Look for embed code and embed Prezi presentation on your blog. Include a reflection about using this tool and other ideas you might have.

*Required artifact for Standard 5.

Throughout your work in this book, you will continue to build and add to your Technology Teaching Portfolio. In this Appendix, you will learn how to create this portfolio using the Google web page building application tool known as **Google Sites**. You will use this tool to create a free public website to showcase examples of your technology teaching artifacts. You will create pages, upload and manage files, add media, create Web links, leverage **Google Docs**, and organize other information relative to demonstrating your proficiency as an effective Digital Age teacher.

A Google Site is more powerful than a standard website in a few ways. One feature that makes Google Sites desirable is the ability to share a site with others. You can easily collaborate and build a website together.

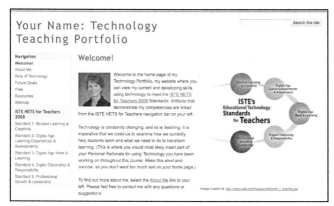

Another powerful feature of Google Sites is the ability to revert back to previously edited pages. This is called **Revision history** and can be found in the **More actions** dropdown box.

Also, if you are skilled in HTML, you can always edit your Google Sites pages using HTML code. Of course, another reason for the popularity of these new websites is the ability to create and edit pages without knowing any HTML code. This is called WYSIWYG (pronounced "wizziwig"), "What You See Is What You Get."

The **Google Sites** tool is part of the standard Google account and is free to all registered Gmail users. (Your school does NOT need to have Google Apps on their domain in order for you to use the various tools included in this suite of applications.) If you already have a Gmail account, then you will automatically have access to Google Sites. If you do NOT have a Gmail account, it's easy to set one up.

Setting up a Gmail (Google) Account

1. Go to http://gmail.com and click **Create an account**. You will need to decide upon your email name and set your password.

2. You will then need to activate your account by going to your email and clicking the link sent to you from **accounts-noreply@google.com**. Click the link in the email and you will have successfully set up your account.

IMPORTANT: Decide which Google account you will be using for all of the Google Apps exercises and activities in this textbook and **use that one exclusively**. Using one Google account will allow you to use all of the Google Apps tools in a seamless, integrated, and fully functional way.

Creating a Google Site From Our Template

Creating your **Google Site** from our template will help you get started more quickly and easier. We recommend if you have never used Google Sites before to construct your site from our template.

Once formatted and published, you can continue to update your site as more information, artifacts, and reflections are added.

It is best to build your Google site over time. Constructing it in one sitting is far more difficult than building a framework and adding to it as you go.

NOTE: The following procedure for setting up a Google Site assumes you are using your own personal Gmail account, NOT one associated with a school domain. However, if you are using Google Apps through your school, the differences are negligible, so these instructions should be easy to follow.

1. Log into your Gmail account (http://gmail.com)

2. Navigate to https://sites.google.com/site/techportfoliotemplate (our template) and click the **Use this template** link.

3. You will be directed to a new page, where you will see the "Technology Teaching Portfolio" template highlighted and selected.

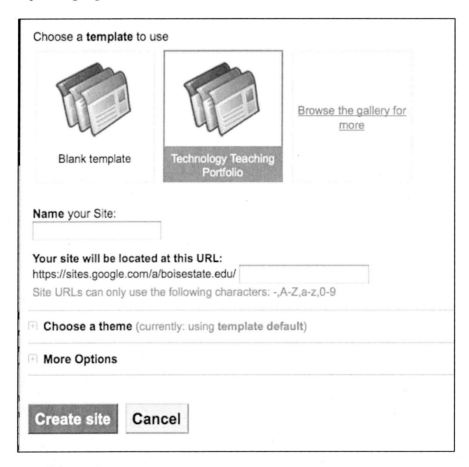

Follow the next set of instructions carefully as the name, description, and permissions you select for your Google Site will affect how others will be able to interact with it.

4. **Name** your Site: In this box, enter your lastnamefirstname, or other identifying name. This will also be the final part of your site URL, so **do not use any spaces**.

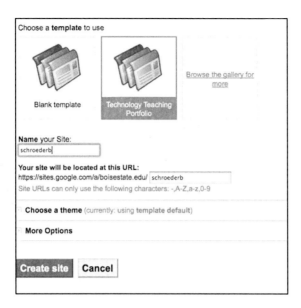

5. Expand the **More Options** section and include site categories (separated by commas) and a site description "Technology Teaching Portfolio for yourlastname firstname."

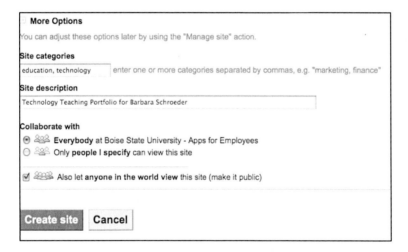

6. Select **Also let anyone in the world view this site (make it public).**

7. Click **Create site**. You are ready to begin!

IMPORTANT! Google Sites is constantly changing and improving, so some of these instructions and screenshots may be outdated by the time of publication. Your instructor is your best resource for help.

Modify Your Site Name

You named your site your last name first initial so the URL would not be too long. Now, you will modify the site name to reflect your site's purpose.

1. Click the **More actions** drop down box on the upper-right hand side and select **Manage site**.

2. You will be directed to a new page. On the left-hand side, select **General** under the **Site settings** category.

3. A new frame will open, where you can change your Site name. Remember, the URL of your site will still end with **YourLastName** (or whatever you selected when you created the site), but now you are naming it to reflect what it actually is.

4. Click in the text box and change your Site name to: **YourFirstName LastName: Technology Teaching Portfolio**. When anyone visits your site, they will know it is yours by your first name appearing at the top of your site.

« Return to site
Site content
Recent site activity
Pages
Attachments
Page templates
Apps Scripts
Deleted items
Site settings
General
Share this site
Monetize
Web Address
Site appearance
Site layout
Colors and Fonts
Themes

Removing the Default Logo

Depending upon your Google Apps account, you will either have a domain name logo in the upper left-hand corner or a Google logo. You will probably want to customize your Google Sites heading, so know that you can change this logo. However, if you want, you can also remove the logo.

1. Click **More actions>Manage site**

2. Then **Site Layout**

3. Click the **Change logo** link

4. Select **No logo** and click **OK**.

Page Types

Select a template to use (Learn more)

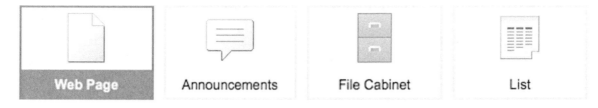

Web Page   Announcements   File Cabinet   List

- The **Web Page** is a traditional unstructured text page with the ability to create tables, embed images, video, links, and embed other objects including Google Docs, spreadsheets, and presentations. Like traditional web pages, you can create bulleted lists, numbered lists, and quickly and easily link to other pages on your site or on the Internet. The majority of pages you will need to create for your portfolio will use this **Web Page** template.

- An **Announcement** page makes it simple to post chronological information. This page allows you to display news, updates, project updates, interesting links, or even as a simple blog. The **Announcement** page template leverages RSS (Real Simple Syndication) to notify subscribers of new posts and updates on existing posts.

- The **File Cabinet** page allows you to upload documents and files to your Google site. This will allow safe storage and access of your artifacts using a simple FTP (file transfer protocol) interface. Once uploaded, you can create links from other pages to those files. The Google sites **File Cabinet** allows you to put all of your important documents in one place. Because they are stored on the Google server, it's not necessary to carry around a jump drive or other portable memory device. These files are also accessible anywhere you have Internet access. The **File Cabinet** page also allows subscribers to be notified of new, updated, or deleted files.

- The **List Page** template allows you to track different types of information. Each is customizable and has advanced sorting features.

Creating New Pages in Google Sites

You may want to create additional pages from our template. To create a new page for your site, click the create page button at the top of your site. (You will need to be logged in, of course, to make any changes to your site).

Select the type of page you want to create, name it, and decide where you want it to be located in your navigation.

You can always delete a page, rename it, or change where it is located in the sitemap.

Editing the Navigation Bar

The **Navigation Bar** contains links to your pages in Google sites. It serves as a structure for organizing key areas of interest to the visitors of your site and helps you and those who view your site find information quickly and easily. Google Sites offers flexibility in the design and organization of this tool.

The following instructions provide information on how to edit the sidebar or add sidebar items:

> **Creating New Pages in Google Sites: Our Recommendation**
>
> When you are creating new pages, you can name them one word, such as "about" with no spaces and all lower-case letters. Then, when you edit that page, change the title to the full title, such as "About Me." Your URL will be short, with the ending "/about," which will make it easier to navigate directly to the page using the web address.

1. In the bottom left hand corner (beneath **recent site activity**) you'll find the **Edit Sidebar** link. Click it to open the **Customize your site layout** controls. On this page you'll find controls to personalize the header, sidebar menus, and site layout.

2. Under **Sidebar** and **Navigation**, choose the **edit** link to modify your navigation bar. This opens the **Configure Navigation** window.

3.   You can now add a page or a URL from an external website. Choose **Add Page** to add additional pages to your navigation bar. This brings up a menu of all pages you have created so far. It also has a search field to add other links and documents.

4.   Remember to **Save Changes** before selecting the link to **Return to Site**.

We recommended that each time you complete an assignment you either upload it to your **Files** page, or copy and paste it on a web page. Similarly, each time you're introduced to a new resource or web page, add that item to your **Resources** list.

Continually adding to your **Technology Teaching Portfolio** will make it easier to build and provide a better example of your proficiency, knowledge, and skill.

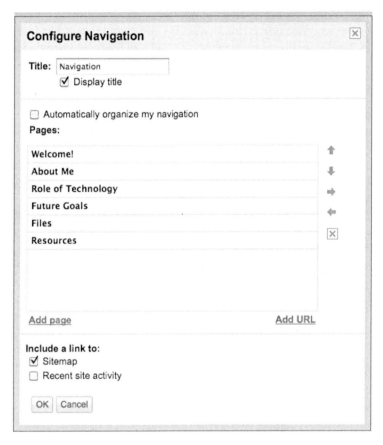

Move title up
Move title down
Increase indent
Decrease indent
Delete entry

Content pages

About Me

The **About Me** page introduces viewers of your site to you, the author. While this Technology Teaching Portfolio shows what you know, have done, and are able to do, it also needs to include information about your background, special skills, and talents. Please include the following information:

1.   a picture of yourself (remember, this is a professional portfolio, so please use tasteful, appropriate pictures)
2.   preferred grade level and/or subject area
3.   expected date of graduation
4.   a brief personal history

5. Optional: Include a short video (or audio) describing any experiences that would qualify you as a teacher. Include how you envision your classroom, learner expectations, and what approaches you might consider technology integration in the classroom.

Role of Technology

One element that defines effective Digital Age teachers is the ability to quantify the role of technology in the classroom. This page will illuminate the reader as to how you plan to implement technology for learning and engagement. Using a minimum of three to five paragraphs, answer the following questions in a well-constructed essay.

1. What technology tools will you employ?

2. How will the students interact with technology?

3. What special skills will be important in students working with technology?

4. How will you use technology to facilitate and inspire student learning and creativity?

5. How will you design and develop digital age learning experiences and assessment?

6. How will you model digital age work and learning?

7. How would you promote and model digital citizenship and responsibility?

8. How will you use technology to engage in personal growth and leadership?

Feel free to use language and writing that you've already created. This can include blogs, discussion boards, assignments, and artifacts. Use only your own original writing. If it is effective or necessary to quote someone else, give appropriate credit.

My Future Goals

As a pre-service teacher, it's a valuable exercise to think about and quantify any personal or professional goals you might have. In three to five well-constructed paragraphs, answer the following questions in essay form.

▪   What are your future professional goals? (i.e. masters, doctorate, administration, counseling, coaching, etc.)

▪   What types of school are you interested in teaching? (Inner city, rural, online, etc.)

▪   What personal goals do you have?

▪   What other information about your personal and professional plans can you offer that help the reader know you?

ISTE NETS for Teachers

This section of your Technology Teaching Portfolio is the most complex. It combines your knowledge of the national standards and artifacts you have created to meet those standards. You will construct an additional five pages, each one representing a different ISTE NETS-T standard. Each page will be a combination of the standard and its performance indicators, digital documents and artifacts you have created, and your reflections about how each artifact meets a given standard.

Each ISTE NETS-T web page will include:

1. the name of the standard;
2. the verbatim description of the standard (from the ISTE website);
3. the performance indicators (from the ISTE website),
4. the names of the required and additional artifacts (minimum of three total for each standard);
5. and a three to five paragraph reflection about how EACH artifact meets the standard and demonstrates your proficiency.

These additional pages are titled as follows:

1. Standard 1: Facilitate and Inspire Student Learning and Creativity
2. Standard 2: Design and Develop Digital Age Learning Experiences and Assessments
3. Standard 3: Model Digital-Age Work and Learning
4. Standard 4: Promote and Model Digital Citizenship and Responsibility
5. Standard 5: Engage and Professional Growth and Leadership

From these pages you will link to individual artifacts that meet each Standard.

Linking To and Creating a New Page In One Process

There are times when you need to create a link to a page that is not yet created. You can do this all at the same time (In other words, you do not need to create a page first, save it, and then link to that page.) Here is how you link to and create a new page in one process:

1. Select the text on your page that you want to link to a new page you have not yet created.

2. Click the **Link** button on your menu bar.

3. A **Create Link** dialog box will appear. Click the + **Create new page** at the bottom of this dialog box.

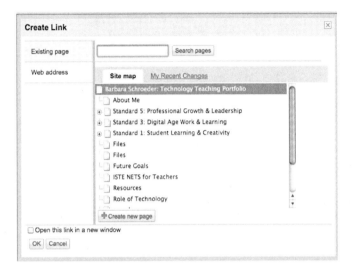

4. Another box will appear.

5. Enter your new page title (remember, you have the option of giving your page a short name, with no spaces, all lower-case, and then change it when you edit the page), decide upon the type of page you want (web page, list, file cabinet, etc.) on what level you want to place the page, and then click the **Create page** button at the bottom of this box.

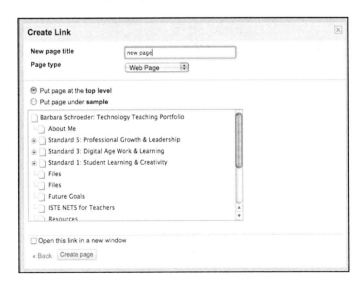

199

In the example image, we have created a page called **new page**, which will be a web page at the top level. (You can always move pages to other locations on your website by navigating to the page, clicking the **More** actions button and then **Move**.)

6.   After you click **Create page** at the bottom one more dialog box will appear. Your new page you created that will be linked from the text you entered shows in yellow.

7.   Click the **OK** button at the bottom of this box and then you will be sent to your original page with the link to this new page. Check out the link to see how it works!

Appendix B: Google Docs Word Processing Basics

Google Docs can be used to create, collaborate, share, and publish documents. It offers most of the word processing tools you need, is browser-based (meaning you don't need any specialized software to use it), free, offers a revision history, easy to use, secure, and allows you to access, edit, and collaborate on a document from any computer with an Internet connection. It also integrates well with Google Sites, the free website software that is part of the Google Apps Suite.

It makes sense to know how to use it, to show your students how to use it, and to include it as an essential technology tool. This Google Docs Basics tutorial will help you get started. After that, you have the opportunity to complete the Parent Newsletter using Google Docs. You might want to compare completing the newsletter in Word and Google Docs, discussing the advantages and disadvantages of both tools on your Teaching with Technology blog.

> Google Docs Getting Started Guide: For more help with Google Docs, visit their online Help/Getting Started Guide: http://bit.ly/d738Zt
>
> You might also want to subscribe to their blog, to stay updated on new updates and improvements: http://googledocs.blogspot.com.

Create a Gmail Account

(Skip this if you already have a Gmail account)

1. Go to http://gmail.com and create a free account. By creating a Google email account (Gmail) you will have access to all of the Google Apps tools: Calendar, Contacts, Sites, etc.)

2. Click the **Create an account** button to sign up with Google.

3. Fill in all of the required form fields to sign up for the account, read through the Terms of Service, and click **I Accept. Create My Account**.

4. You will need to verify your email address you used to create the account by signing into it and clicking the link that Google sends you. By doing so you will be taken to your new Gmail account. Now you are ready to start using all of the features of Google Apps!

Open Google Docs

From your Gmail account, click **Documents** at the top left of your page.

Create a new document, save, rename, and copy

1. Click **Create New** on the Google Docs Menu bar and select which type of file you would like to create.

2. Google Docs will open a new window that will allow you to create a document.

3. To enter text, simply enter the document window, just as you would with any word processing program.

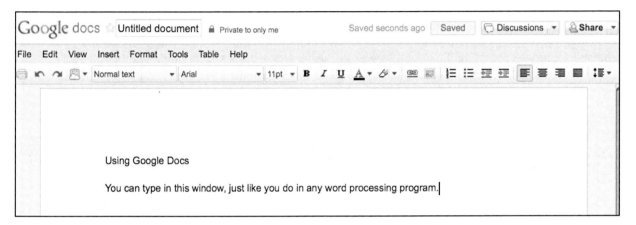

4. **Saving your document:** Google Docs automatically saves your document, but you can always save from time to time by using the keyboard shortcut **Control + S (Apple Command + S).**

5. **Rename a document:** Click the file name at the top left of your document, a popup window will appear, and enter your new name. **IMPORTANT NOTE**: This will NOT save another copy of your document, as is common in most computer programs. It will still be the same file, but with a new name.

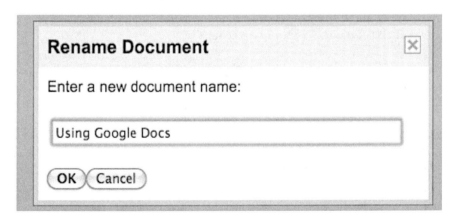

6. **Copy a file:** To make another copy of a file, you will need to rename it. Select **File>Make a cop** from the Google Docs menu bar. Remember, unlike traditional word processing programs, renaming a file does NOT create a new copy of that file. **You need to create a new copy to create a duplicate of your file.**

7. **(Export) Download a file:** You can download a Google Doc to a variety of file formats. With the document open, select **File>Download As** and select your format.

Upload a File/Folder

From your Google Docs Home, click the **Upload** button on the Menu bar. Note that you can now upload folders. You can now also drag files right into your document list. For more information on the various options for uploading files and folders and types of media, click the **Learn more . . .** link on this drop-down box.

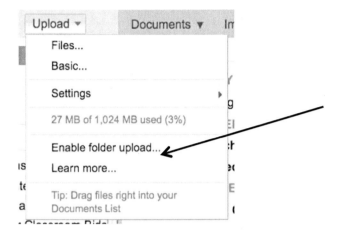

Practice with Google Docs Menu

1. **Main Menu:** The formatting menu and other options should be familiar to you if you've worked with any word processing program before. Most of the shortcuts you are accustomed to using in Word, for instance, work with Google Docs. **Ctrl+S** saves your file, **Crtl+B** makes text bold, **Ctrl+X** is cut, and **Ctrl+Z** is undo. For a complete list of Google Docs shortcuts, go to http://docs.google.com/support/bin/static.py?page=kbshortcuts.html

2. **Insert Menu:** Check out the types of objects you can insert in your Google Doc. Click **Insert** on the main menu and try out some of these items.

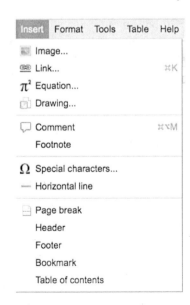

3. **Spell Check:** Yes, Google Docs includes spell check. It is enabled by default. If you wish to turn off the automatic spell check, click View and then unselect **Show spelling suggestions**.

Managing Your Files/Collections

1. Your files are organized in Google Docs according to the most recent ones you've either created or viewed. However, you also have the option to sort by other criteria, by clicking the **Sort by** drop down box.

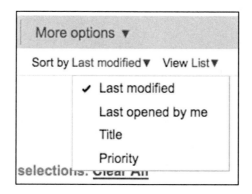

2. Remember, it's important to always name your document something that describes the file so you can easily find it, should you need to search for it. Google Docs provides a handy search bar, where you can usually find what you need. But it's always a good habit to name your files something you will remember.

3. Google Docs allows you to organize your files much the same way you can on your computer.

4. Collections are a combination of labels and folders. A file can have multiple collections. Collections can also be stored hierarchically, like folders on your desktop. In addition, collections can be shared.

5. To create a new collection, click **Create new>Collection** and name it. You can then drag and drop files into any number of collections.

6. Your files are always in **All Items**, but can also be organized into other collections.

7. Collections that you share have a shared icon on them and collections that others share with you are located at the bottom of your folder list.

Share a Google Doc

Google Docs allows you to easily share your work with others, collaborate on a document with multiple editors, and publish your document on the Web. You can revert to previous versions, compare two versions for editing changes, and see what edits each person has made on your document.

Note: To collaborate on a file with you, that person must have a Google Account. Also, there are limits for documents and presentations: 200 combined viewers and 10 people at one time may edit.

Share your collection with others: Click **My collections** in the navigation pane on the left of your docs, select the collection you'd like to share, click **Share** from the drop-down menu, and select **Sharing settings....**

At the bottom of the Sharing settings window, under **Add people**, type the email addresses of anyone you'd like to share the collection with.

Share your document with others: You can share your docs with just the people you want, and you can specify exactly what level of access (view or edit) each person has. Docs start out with a visibility option of **Private** by default, which means that the only people who can view or edit your doc are the people you explicitly share with.

Here's how to add specific editors and viewers:

1. Open the doc you want to share.
2. Click **Share** in the upper-right corner of the doc.

At the bottom of the Sharing settings window, under **Add people**, type the email addresses of the people you want to share with. You can add a single person or a mailing list. You can also choose from a list of your contacts.

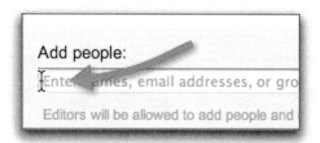

3. To the right of the list of names, choose **Can view** or **Can edit** from the drop-down menu.

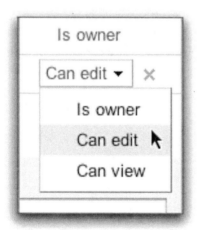

4. Click **Share**

Publish a Google Doc

1. **Publish:** You can publish any Google Doc so that anyone with an Internet connection can view it. You receive a unique URL that will direct anyone to your file. To do this, click the **Share** button at the top right of your document and then select **Publish as a web page**.

2. A new screen will appear and you will be able to publish your document. You have the very handy option of selecting **Automatically re-publish when changes are made**, which means that if you change anything on your original Google Doc, those changes will be reflected on your published document. Copy the URL and provide that to whomever you want to view your document online.

Printing

1. **Print:** To print the document, open it and choose the **Print icon** in the menu bar. Depending upon your computer settings, Google Docs will prepare the file for printing. Another option is to select **File>Print** from the Google Docs menu bar.

2. **Print Settings:** You can adjust how you want your final document to print (such as adding page numbers, page breaks, etc.) by click **File>Print Settings**. Of course, you can also select **File>Print Preview** to see how it will look. From this view, you might want to insert some page breaks to make your document look better.

Revision History

Google Docs has a revision history pane that allows you to view at a glance all changes made to a doc by each collaborator. To find out more about how to access revision history and use it to track changes, go to http://docs.google.com/support/bin/answer.py?answer=190843

Comments and Discussion

There is a new style of commenting in Google Documents. Just like before, you can easily insert comments into a document. With comment threads called **discussions** you also can also keep track of comments, target your comments at specific people, and respond to and follow comments and document updates from your email inbox.

This new type of comments and discussions will only be available on newly created documents, and in the new version of Google Docs. For detailed information on how to use comments and discussion in Google Docs, go to http://docs.google.com/support/bin/static.py?page=guide.cs&guide=1208624

Blog Reflection: Experiment and learn more about cloud-based applications and how they could help solve issues of digital divide and inequality. Post to your blog about your experiences using Google Docs and other web-based tools.

Word Alternative: Creating Parent Newsletter in Google Docs

As an alternative to using Microsoft *Word*, create the Parent Newsletter using Google Docs instead. Share your document with another classmate and have him/her review and make comments as needed.

Follow the instructions for the newsletter, including the required content. On the following page we have provided an example of what the newsletter might look like in Google Docs.

Standards Update

National Educational Technology Standards

The International Society for Technology in Education (ISTE) has recently released the NETS for Students 2007, providing guidelines for student technology concepts and skills in a digital age. ISTE, a professional organization that has provided leadership in technology for over a decade, reports that, "As foundational ICT skills penetrate throughout our society, students will be expected to apply the basics in authentic, integrated ways to solve problems, complete projects, and creatively extend their abilities. *ISTE's National Educational Technology Standards for Students* help students preparing to work, live, and contribute to the social and civic fabric of their communities."

Skills for a Digital Age

A national research study, "Listening to Student Voices," contributed by the Center for Policy Studies reports that today's students are frustrated with the lack of technology in the classroom. The tech-savvy generation that has grown up with technology is disappointed in traditional classroom instruction. The report recommends that technology standards be a focus of K-12 education.

Student Technology Standards

- Creativity and Innovation
- Communication and Collaboration
- Research and Information Fluency
- Critical Thinking, Problem Solving, and Decision making
- Digital Citizenship
- Technology Operations and Concepts

Parents

We are asking for volunteers to help in the computer labs in our after-school technology program. Please write your name in the "I Can Help" column for the days you might be available this semester and send back to your child's school.

Your Name: _____

Phone: _____Email:_____

School	Days/Times	I Can Help
East Elementary School	Mondays (3 - 5)	
West Middle School	Tuesdays (3 - 5)	
Central High School	Wednesdays (3 - 5)	

In an atmosphere of limited school funding and financial support, the burden of raising money for educational excursions, field trips, classroom tools, and other wants and needs often falls on the teacher, parents, students, and school community. While some assistance can be given from the finance office, the responsibility of record-keeping for fund-raising activities, especially those of driven by students, commonly rests on the teacher, coach, or advisor.

Whenever possible, it's good practice to involve multiple leaders in financial administration. This ensures transparency and allows others to share responsibility. When using typical spreadsheet software like Microsoft *Excel* for financial record keeping, it is necessary to save and share the file. This can create a situation where more than one copy of the file exists. If a teacher modifies one financial record, and the booster president modifies another, which file is accurate and up-to-date? The answer is neither.

This concern about accounting, duplication and omission often leads to the burden being placed on just one person. However, if the spreadsheet is shareable in real-time and could allow for multiple simultaneous editors, the responsibility can be shared by many while still keeping the document secure.

Google Docs offers this opportunity.

In this exercise you will:

1. create a new Google Spreadsheet document
2. rename and save
3. create and rename different sheets

Optional Collaborative Activity

This exercise can also be a collaborative activity between two or more classmates. The document can be shared and edited by multiple users. In this setting, participants will need to assign responsibilities, sharing data entry, and collaborate synchronously or asynchronously in the formatting of formula cells.

Note: Web-based applications such as Google spreadsheets are subject to revision. Some of the functionality may change in name or appearance.

Before you begin

Before beginning, it is necessary to have a Google or Gmail account. Since the suite of Google apps comes standard with all North American Gmail accounts, simply accessing or creating your current Google account should suffice.

Creating a New Google Spreadsheet

1. Log into your Google account.

2. Click the **Documents** link in the upper left-hand corner. You'll find it situated with similar global features like Mail, calendar, sites, contacts, and others.

3. Click the drop-down menu **Create new>Spreadsheet**.

4. This new file will be titled **unsaved spreadsheet**, before continuing you will need to rename it.

5. Click the **file** drop-down menu and select **rename**. (Or you can click the name of the file to rename it.)

6. Rename the file **YourLastName _fundraiser**. If this is a collaborative activity, consider renaming the file **groupname_fundraiser**. (Since empty spaces in html and other Internet languages are often replaced by other characters, using the "_" or underscore assures that the file name will not be changed.)

Creating Multiple Sheets

In this exercise it is necessary to create multiple sheets. Each sheet is in individual spreadsheet connected to the larger file. These sheets are organized in a tabbing system, allowing you to quickly move from multiple spreadsheets without creating a new file. You can collect and cull data from one sheet and leverage it in another.

In our example, we will use one sheet to manipulate the costs of our trip, another to account for individual fund-raising efforts, and a third sheet to display student fundraising accounts. While this information could be collected on one large spreadsheet, breaking it up into sheets separates data into categories, allows multiple formatting options, and gives us the flexibility to add or remove fields, columns, and rows without disturbing the appearance or functionality of the entire document.

Adding a New Sheet

1. In the bottom left-hand corner of your screen, you'll find the 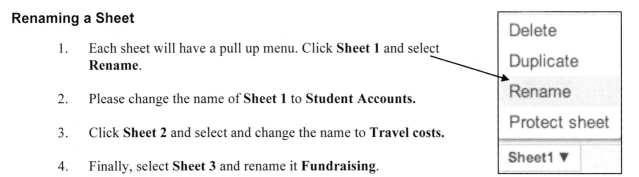 button. Select it. It will create a second sheet titled **Sheet 2**.
2. Repeat step 1 again, creating a third. It will be titled **Sheet 3** and so on.

Renaming a Sheet

1. Each sheet will have a pull up menu. Click **Sheet 1** and select **Rename**.

2. Please change the name of **Sheet 1** to **Student Accounts**.

3. Click **Sheet 2** and select and change the name to **Travel costs.**

4. Finally, select **Sheet 3** and rename it **Fundraising**.

Determining the Cost of a Trip

Many people assume that the cost of a school trip is fixed from the beginning. But the truth is, the cost continues to fluctuate throughout the planning of any large event. Lodging, food, transportation, and activity prices will change over time for a number of different reasons.

Fuel prices, tax, and other factors may cause a change in price between the planning, fund-raising, and execution phases of your trip. In addition, because all of these costs are divided among participating students, chaperones, and faculty, changes in those numbers affects the financial requirements for each. For this reason, it's a valuable to use a spreadsheet to collect these data. When any of these variables change, the spreadsheet can perform the mathematical equations necessary to recalculate the cost of your trip.

The Travel Cost Sheet

This sheet contains all of the information specific to the cost categories for your field trip. This includes transportation, lodging, food, and entertainment. It also includes important variables that affect those categories including the number of days you will be traveling (which affect lodging and food) as well as the number of students attending. Constructed correctly, any of the data can be modified and new trip totals produced.

If academic testing changes the departure date, the number of days can be adjusted and the totals reflected and aggregate throughout the spreadsheet document. If after scheduling the trip the bus company you plan to use changes, the new transportation cost can be modified and disseminated. If a participant changes schools midway through the semester and is no longer able to attend, a well-designed spreadsheet can reflect those changes instantly. The purpose is to develop a fluid, shareable document that will adapt to changes.

Creating the Categories

It is important when creating and organizing a spreadsheet document to make every attempt to include all the categories of information you will need in the design phase. While reorganizing a spreadsheet to include new formulas, labels, and data is possible, it's more difficult to do later.

NOTE: The spaces allow for better visualization of the data and for other labels to be placed at later time.

1. Using the example provided, type the following into the cells of column A:

   ✓ **Travel costs** in cell **A1**
   ✓ **Transportation** in cell **A3**
   ✓ **Lodging** in cell **A4**
   ✓ **Food** in cell **A5**
   ✓ **Fun** in cell **A6**
   ✓ **Days** in cell **A8**
   ✓ **Students** in cell **A10**

2. Then it is necessary to add the column headings:

   ✓ Type **each** in cell **B2**
   ✓ **Per** in cell **C2**
   ✓ **Totals** in cell **D2**

	A	B	C	D
1	Travel Costs			
2		each	per	Totals
3	Transportation			
4	Lodging			
5	Food			
6	Fun			
7				
8	Days			
9				
10	Students			

Formatting Text and Cells

The way you organize and format data helps the user clearly understand what they are looking at and how to interact with it. On this sheet, we will format cells to distinguish them as points of data entry and others as cells that display calculated data.

To give the document an organized appearance you may choose to format text within a cell. One of the simplest forms of text formatting is alignment. You can all line your text to the right, center, or left of the cell by highlighting the cell or cells, column or row and ▦▾ button. It also allows you to align the contents of the cell to the top, middle, or bottom. The options for alignment give the user added flexibility in the visual design of the spreadsheet.

Align your column headings (each, per, and totals) to the center using ▦▾.

You can also change the text or fill color of any cell or cells, roll or column to give a unique appearance.

1. Select cells **D3** through **D6** (also described as **D3:D6**) by selecting cell **D3** and dragging down with the mouse button depressed to **D6** until all are highlighted.

2. Change the **Background Color** by selecting ▦▾. This should change the background color of all cells selected.

3. You can also change the color of the text within a cell by selecting A̲▾.

On our **Travel costs** sheet, we want to be able to modify the number of **Days** and **Students**. It is necessary to design these to make them unique. We will add a cell border, change the background color, as well as change the font size and color. Choose any colors you find complementary and readable.

1. Select cell **B8** and click the **Borders** button on the menu bar.

2. Choose the selection that creates a box, similar to the button itself.

3. Change the **Background Color**.

4. The font size can be modified by selecting 10pt.

5. Finally, change the **Text Color** by selecting.

6. Repeat these steps for cell **B10.**

It is necessary to create a title bar to distinguish the contents of this sheet. A common technique is to **Merge Across** a number of cells to allow larger text.

1. Select cells **A1** through **F1** (also described as **A1:F1**) by selecting cell **A1** and dragging down with the mouse button depressed to **F1** until all are highlighted.

2. Next, select the **Merge Across** button. This combines all of the selected cells into one large cell.

3. Increase the **Font Size** to **24pt** by selecting 10pt.

4. **Align** the merged cell to center.

5. Create a bottom cell border using the **Borders** button.

	each	per	Totals	
Transportation				
Lodging				
Food				
Fun				
Days				
Students				

The costs associated with travel hinge on different factors. Some costs are multiplied by variables while others are divided. The costs of airfare, food, entertainment, and lodging are multiplied by the number of students traveling. For example, if the food expenditure each day is $25, the cost can be determined by multiplying by the number of students and days.

Meal Cost = Food * Student * Days

213

Setting up your Google spreadsheet to account for changing numbers of students or days gives you the ability to track your trip costs as those variables change.

However, some trip costs are divided by the number of students. Bus and hotel costs are divided by the number of students attending. If 45 students were originally sharing the cost of the bus (typically a fixed cost), when three students do not make the trip the transportation cost gets more expensive for the 42 who are still traveling. Your spreadsheet should have the flexibility to reflect these changes.

Bus Cost = Bus Total / Students

Creating formulas to do the math for you allows students, parents, and administrators understand the financial considerations associated with planning a trip. Using formulas also helps you experiment with different scenarios to find a price that fits.

Building your Formulas

The Formula for Transportation

Important: If you have not yet completed a gradebook activity, do not continue. It is important to have a firm understanding of the order of operations, arithmetic operators, and comparison operators to proceed.

The first formula you will create is **Transportation**.

When creating a formula, it's helpful to first build the formula with the names of the variables you plan to use and replace them with the cell coordinates. Use the same operators you would for a traditional formula. Always build it beginning with the equal sign (=). See the example below.

=SUM(~~bus cost~~ /~~#of students~~)
D3   /   B10

There is no reason to include the variable **Days** because in this case the number of days does not affect the cost of the bus. Once you're comfortable with the formula you've created, replace the variable names with the cell coordinates. The correct formula is

=SUM(D3/B10)

Follow these steps to complete the **Transportation** cost formula.

1. In the **per** column, type the word **total**.

2. Enter **2285** in cell **D3**. (Note: it will not be displayed as currency.)

3. In cell B3, enter the formula =SUM(D3/B10). You hit **enter** or **return** on your keyboard.

Immediately you'll notice that something is wrong. Instead of dividing the total transportation cost by the number of students, your cell now displays the following error:

#DIV/0!

This is an important mistake to make early on in the process. This error reminds us that although we have created the formula, not enough information is available to complete the mathematical process.

In this case, we haven't established a number of students. Our formula **=SUM(D3/B10)** only points to one valid number, the total cost found in cell D3.

1. In cell **B10**, enter **24** students and hit **enter** or **return** on your keyboard.

2. Next, format both cell **B3** and **D3** to display the number information as currency by selecting each cell individually and touching the $\boxed{\$}$ button on the toolbar. This will display the contents of the cell rounded to the nearest dollar

3. To choose from other formatting options, click the $\boxed{123 \blacktriangledown}$ button on the toolbar.

4. Take a moment and explore all the formatting possibilities. Some of these options you will use later.

5. To verify you've built the formula correctly, change the number of students. If the value in cell **B3** changes, you have created correctly.

More formatting options

Normal	
1,000	Rounded
1,000.12	2 Decimals
(1,000)	Financial rounded
(1,000.12)	Financial
1.01E+03	Scientific
$1,000	Currency
$1,000.12	Currency
More currencies	▶
10%	Percent rounded
10.12%	Percent
9/26/2008	Date
15:59:00	Time
9/26/2008 15:59:00	Date time
24:01:00	Hours
More formats	▶
Plain text	

The Formula for Fun

Next, you will build the formula for the **Fun** category. Whether you take your students to the museum, aquarium, mall, movie theater, or any other entertaining attraction, budgeting for these activities is important. In the process of planning your trip, these details or costs may change. You may elect to go to the museum instead of the concert. The cost for each student will change as well as the overall cost of the trip. We need to work this flexibility into the overall formula.

In the **per (C6)** column, enter the word **Total**. This tells us that the total cost is flexible. Modifying it cost for fun at each student and the number of students will change the total. Like before, let's begin by building our formula with the descriptors.

$$=SUM(\text{~~Fun Cost~~ * ~~#of students~~})$$
$$\textbf{B6 \quad * \quad B10}$$

This time we are multiplying a fixed cost by the number of students who will be participating. This gives us the flexibility to modify the price of the activities, the number of students, or both and see the new total instantly. Like the previous formula, there is no reason to include the variable **Days** because the number of days does not affect the price of the entertainment or activities budget.

You will begin creating this formula differently than you did the last. Rather than entering the formula, you will use another tool on the menu bar. Follow the next set of instructions.

1. Begin selecting cell **B6** and enter an amount. $50 is a reasonable entertainment budget per student. We can and will change this number, but it's a good place to start.
2. Select cell **D6**.

215

3. Click the **Formulas** or  button.
4. Next, select the **Sum** option from this drop-down menu (right). This will begin the formula for you and place the first parenthesis.
5. With your mouse, touch cell **B6**. Your formula will immediately be reflected.
6. Next, enter your arithmetic operator, in this case the multiplication symbol * found above the **8** key.
7. With your mouse again, touch cell **B10**. The formula will now reflect this.

D6
=SUM(B6*B10

8. Finally, add the last parenthesis to close the formula and hit **enter** or **return**.
9. Using the **Currency** $ button or the **More Formats** 123 ▾ button on the toolbar will allow you to change the way the number is display in your new fields.
10. Change the number of students and fun costs to verify your formula is functioning.

The Formula for Food

For the next two formulas we will have to take into account three different variables. These variables include the cost of the food per day, the number of days traveling, and the number of students.

Food for students on a trip can be approached in a number of ways. Sometimes parent or booster groups will work together to provide food for students. Other times restaurants or food courts may be the best use of your time and resources. Whichever you choose, it is important to budget an amount for the day. These amounts can range from $5-$7 for breakfast, $7-$10 for lunch, and $10-$15 for dinner. Food prices change dramatically by location, so it's important to know what those prices will be. For the purposes of this activity, $23 per day is a good starting figure.

Like before, let's build the formula using the appropriate descriptors and then replace them with the cells containing the actual values.

=SUM(~~Food Cost~~ * ~~#of students~~)* ~~# of Days~~
B5   *   B10   *   B8

Because we are using three variables, an extra set of parentheses is necessary to cover all of the mathematical operators and cell references. Instead the "**=SUM(B5*B10)*B8**" we make sure that all of the operators and coordinates are covered"**=SUM((B5*B10)*B8)**". This discipline becomes more important as the formulas become more advanced.

1. In Cell **B8**, enter **4** for the number of days. Hit enter.
2. In the **per (C5)** column, enter the word **day**.
3. Begin by selecting cell D5
4. Using the **Formulas** Σ ▾ button, select **SUM**

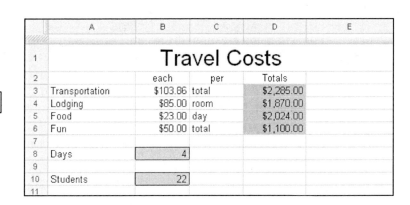

	A	B	C	D	E
1		**Travel Costs**			
2		each	per	Totals	
3	Transportation	$103.86	total	$2,285.00	
4	Lodging	$85.00	room	$1,870.00	
5	Food	$23.00	day	$2,024.00	
6	Fun	$50.00	total	$1,100.00	
7					
8	Days	4			
9					
10	Students	22			
11					

5. With your mouse, complete the following formula =SUM((B5*B10)*B8)
6. Using the **Currency** $\boxed{\$}$ button or the **More Formats** $\boxed{123\blacktriangledown}$ button on the toolbar will allow you to change the way the number is display in your new fields.
7. Change the number of students and fun costs to verify your formula is functioning.

The Formula for Lodging

For this activity, we will assume that your students will be staying at a hotel. In this case, there are four variables. They include the cost of the hotel room, the number of days staying, students participating, and a new variable, the number of students in a room. It's impractical to have each student stay in their own room, it is customary to have students sign up and share rooms with their friends. Schools and hotels have different policies about how students may share rooms. It is important to know what your school or district's policy is regarding student cohabitation. We'll make some broad assumptions for this exercise based on standard practices. They may be different at your school.

Let's begin by creating our formula using the names of our variables and replacing them with their spreadsheet coordinates.

$$=SUM(((\text{students/4.0}) * \text{\#days}) * \text{room cost})$$
$$\quad\quad B10\ /4.0\ *\quad B8\quad *\quad B4$$
$$=SUM(((B10/4.0)*B8)*B4)$$

Because we are using multiple calculations, an extra set of parentheses is necessary to cover all of the mathematical operators and cell references. It is important to ensure the number of parentheses will be balanced on either side of the equation. To include all of the necessary operators, the equation must be spelled =SUM(((B10/4.0)*B8)*B4).

1. In cell **B4**, enter **85**, hit enter.
2. In the **per (C4)** column, enter the word **room** because your room rate is a flexible variable.
3. Begin by selecting cell D4
4. Using the **Formulas** $\boxed{\Sigma\blacktriangledown}$ button, select **SUM**
5. With your mouse, complete the following formula =SUM(((B10/4.0)*B8)*B4).
6. Using the **Currency** $\boxed{\$}$ button or the **More Formats** $\boxed{123\blacktriangledown}$ button on the toolbar will allow you to change the way the number is display in your new fields.
7. Change the number of students, cost of the room, and number of days to verify your formula is functioning.

The benefits of this simple sheet allow you flexibility in planning your trip. Parents, administrators, and students can gain a better understanding of how each individual cost affects the planning a trip. It's through exercises like this that participants can gauge the impact of activity planning and fundraising. Now that the formulas are in place, let's tabulate a trip total.

Creating a trip total

The running total of trip costs will need to be applied to multiple sheets. We will use the SUM function to create this field.

1. Selecting **D7** and **E7** cells, select the **Merge Across** option by selecting the ⊞ key.
2. In that new cell type, **Trip Total**.

	A	B	C	D	E
1			**Travel Costs**		
2		each	per	Totals	
3	Transportation	$103.86	total	$2,285.00	
4	Lodging	$85.00	room	$1,870.00	
5	Food	$23.00	day	$2,024.00	
6	Fun	$50.00	total	$1,100.00	
7					
8	Days		4		
9					
10	Students		22		

3. Increase the **Font Size** to **24pt** by selecting [10pt ▼]
4. **Align** the merged cell to center [≡ ▼]
5. Change the **Background Color** [⊞ ▼] to a color of your choice.
6. Change the **Text Color** by selecting [A ▼] to a color of your choosing.
7. Selecting **D9** and **E9** cells, select the **Merge Across** option by selecting the ⊞ key.
8. Using the **Formulas** [Σ ▼] button, select **SUM**
9. With your mouse, complete the following formula **=SUM(D3:D6)**

	A	B	C	D	E
1			**Travel Costs**		
2		each	per	Totals	
3	Transportation	$103.86	total	$2,285.00	
4	Lodging	$85.00	room	$1,870.00	
5	Food	$23.00	day	$2,024.00	
6	Fun	$50.00	total	$1,100.00	
7				**Trip Total**	
8	Days		4	D9	
9				=SUM(D3:D6)	
10	Students		22		
11					

10. Using the **Currency** [$] button or the **More Formats** [123 ▾] button on the toolbar will allow you to change the way the number is display in your new fields.
11. Continue formatting the cell to give it an attractive appearance (see steps 3-6).

		each	per	Totals	
1		**Travel Costs**			
2		each	per	Totals	
3	Transportation	$103.86	total	$2,285.00	
4	Lodging	$85.00	room	$1,870.00	
5	Food	$23.00	day	$2,024.00	
6	Fun	$50.00	total	$1,100.00	
7				Trip Total	
8	Days		4		
9				$7,279.00	
10	Students		22		
11					

This spreadsheet now gives the user tremendous flexibility. Unlike a traditional paper ledger, details can be modified and effects seen instantly.

The Fundraising Sheet

While some families have the ability to pay for all of their child's activities, others may not. The job of assisting students in their own fundraising efforts often falls on the teacher as trip organizer. As the primary controller of the fundraising effort, it is important to create as open and detailed a record as possible. Utilizing the collaborative tools of the Google spreadsheet, it is possible to create a shared document that helps multiple parties understand and affect the fundraising structure. While it is possible to make the sheets detailed and complex, this **Fundraising** sheet will reflect only five activities.

1. Using the example provided (right), type the following into the cells of column A.

   ✓ **Fundraisers** in cell **A1**
   ✓ **Carwash** in cell **A2**
   ✓ **Carnival** in cell **A3**
   ✓ **Rummage Sale** in cell **A4**
   ✓ **Cookie Dough** in cell **A5**
   ✓ **Wrapping Paper** in cell **A6**
   ✓ **Total** in cell **B1**

	A	B
1	Fundraisers	Total
2	Carwash	475.00
3	Carnival	2,185.59
4	Rummage Sale	1,209.85
5	Cookie Dough	
6	Wrapping Paper	B7
7		=SUM(B2:B6
8		

2. Using the Borders tool, create a line beneath cells **A6:B6**

3. Add cash values to **B2:B4** as indicated.

219

4. In cell **B7**, create a SUM $\boxed{\Sigma \,\blacktriangledown}$ for cells **B2:B6**. Hit **enter** or **return** to calculate. This will give you a total for all of your fundraising.

5. Next, select the entire column by touching the header at the top.

6. Change the format to **Currency** by selecting the **More Formats** $\boxed{123 \blacktriangledown}$ key.

	A	B
1	Fundraisers	Total
2	Carwash	$475.00
3	Carnival	$2,185.59
4	Rummage Sale	$1,209.85
5	Cookie Dough	
6	Wrapping Paper	
7		$3,870.44
8		
9		

It is important to note that no values have been added to the "cookie dough" or "wrapping paper" fundraising efforts. The first three activities, carwash, Carnival, and rummage sale, benefit all students equally. The remaining two fundraisers will be calculated by student on the student accounts sheet and reflect individual effort students have applied toward their own account.

The Student Accounts Sheet

The elements that make collaborative online spreadsheets such a valuable tool will come together. In the next few steps, you will leverage information from all three spreadsheets. You will bring information from the **Trip Costs** sheet into the **Student Accounts** sheet creating new, individual, and flexible totals. You will then leverage those totals in the **Fundraising** sheet.

On the **Student Accounts** sheet, you will create a very important number, the amount of money needed by each student to go on the trip. This will be created by leveraging the cost of the trip from the **Trip Costs** sheet, the amount of group contributions from the **Fundraising sheet**, and the individual fundraising that each student has done. With this information you will create a unique account total for each student. This results in an individualized flexible account balance.

	A	B	C	D	E	F
1	Name	$Needed	$Raised	$Contribution	Cookie Dough	Wrapping Paper
2	Clint Adams					
3	Nancy Baker					
4	Maria Booth					
5	Kelly Cruise					
6	Mark Collins					
7	Alyson Dougal					
8	Ruben Hoffman					
9	Charles Kim					
10	Chris Keaton					
11	Ginger Lane					
12	Robert Lee					
13	Terissa Martinez					
14	Maureen Mahaffy					
15	Steve Peery					
16	Kennedy rian					
17	Joey Ridenour					
18	Any Solberg					
19	Jonas Thompson					
20	Margo Williams					
21	Aaron Zizzo					

You'll begin by populating with the following headers:

1. Using the example provided (right), type the following into the cells of row 1.

   ✓ **Name** in cell **A1**
   ✓ **$ Needed** in cell **B1**
   ✓ **$ Raised** in cell **C1**
   ✓ **$ Contribution** in cell **D1**
   ✓ **$ Cookie Dough** in cell **E1**
   ✓ **$ Wrapping Paper** in cell **F1**

2. Using the Borders tool, create a line beneath cells **A1:F1** to separate and signify the columns.

3. In a **column A**, enter 20 names. You may choose those given or insert your own.

4. In cell **C2**, create a SUM ⟦Σ ▾⟧ for cells **D2:F2**. Hit **enter** or **return**.

5. Next, select the entire column by touching the header at the top. Remember to close with the parentheses. The formula should read **=SUM(D2:F2)**

6. Change the format to **Currency** by selecting the **More Formats** ⟦123 ▾⟧ key.

7. You can now copy the cell to all the cells in the column. By default, all of the cell references are **Relative**. This means, by selecting the small square handle in the bottom right-hand corner of a selected cell, you can copy the formula by dragging it down the column.

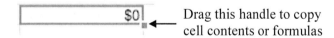
Drag this handle to copy cell contents or formulas

The $Contribution Column

Some of the fundraising efforts selected for this trip are equally distributed between all students. We will collect those data values in column D. Since the data are on a different sheet, we will have to modify the formula to bring in this information.

1. First, select cell **D2** and create a SUM ⟦Σ ▾⟧.

2. At the bottom of the screen, select the **Fundraising** sheet. This will allow you to keep editing the formula in cell **B2** on the **Student Accounts** sheet but view and select any cells on the **Fundraising** sheet.

3. With your mouse, drag and select cells **B2:B4**. These are the cells associated with all of the group fundraisers. Your formula should now read **=SUM(Fundraising!B2:B4.** Please note that the formula is incomplete and not closed.

4. Next, select the **Trip Costs** sheet.

5. Closed first half of your formula with the parenthesis.

6. You will need to add the division symbol / to your formula.

7. With your mouse, select cell **B10** which contains the number of students participating

8. The formula should now read =SUM(Fundraising!B2:B4)/'Trip Costs'!B10

9. Because you planned to copy this formula to multiple cells, it is necessary to apply absolute values to all of the cell references. To do that, it is necessary to add a "$" to each coordinate in the formula. It should read as follows:

=SUM(Fundraising!\$B\$2:\$B\$4)/'Trip Costs'!\$B\$10

Adding a "$" in front of a coordinate makes it an **Absolute Value**. This means regardless of where you drag a cell to copy it, the reference will always point back to that exact column or row.

10. Hit **enter** or **return.**

11. Change the format to **Currency** by selecting the **More Formats** [123 ▾] key.

12. Grab the blue handle on cell D2 and drag it down the column to apply to all students. You should now see the amount in the **row C** and **row D** asked the same amount.

The $Cookie Dough and Wrapping Paper Columns

Since we will be tracking student sales of cookie dough and wrapping paper, these columns on the **Student Accounts** sheet need to be reflected on our **Fundraising** sheet. Google spreadsheets will effectively draw information from one sheet and place it on another. Read the CRITICAL note on the following page before continuing.

1. Begin by selecting your **Fundraising** sheet.

2. Select cell **B5**, cookie dough, and create a SUM [Σ ▾].

3. At the bottom of the screen, select the **Student Accounts** sheet. (Remember the CRITICAL tip offered on the next page.)

4. Touch the header for **column E.** This will allow you to collect the SUM of all contents of **column E.** If you add more students throughout the semester, their totals will be included. (It is also possible to select the sum in cell B7, as some have difficulty making this work.)

5. Close the formula with the parentheses.

6. Hit **Enter** or **return**

7. Change the format to **Currency** by selecting the column header by clicking the **More Formats** `123 ▾` key.

8. To test this formula, return to the **Student Accounts** sheet and enter some values for students ($10, $25, $50, etc.).

9. Return to your **Fundraising** sheet and verify the data is being transferred.

Repeat the above steps modified for **column F** of the **Student Accounts** sheet.

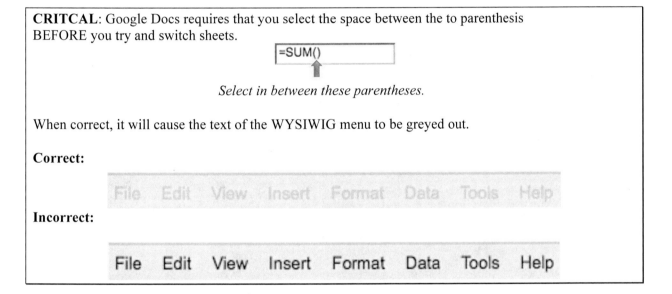

CRITCAL: Google Docs requires that you select the space between the to parenthesis BEFORE you try and switch sheets.

Select in between these parentheses.

When correct, it will cause the text of the WYSIWIG menu to be greyed out.

Correct:

Incorrect:

The $Needed Columns

The final formula you will create for the spreadsheet will display the amount of money needed by each student. **Column B** on the **Student Accounts** sheet will leverage information from the **Trip Costs** sheet against the total money earned or collected.

1. Begin by selecting your **Student Accounts** sheet in cell **B2**.

2. Select cell **B2** and create a SUM `Σ ▾`.

3. At the bottom of the screen, select the **Trip Costs** sheet.

4. Drag your mouse, selecting cells **B3:B6**. This will allow you to collect the SUM of all selected cells, in essence the cost of the trip for one student.

5.   Change those cells to check that references by inserting the dollar symbol ($) into the formula ($B$3:$B$6).

6.   Close this part of the formula with the parentheses.

7.   Then, enter the subtraction (-) symbol after the parentheses and select cell **C2** from the Student Accounts sheet. DO NOT make this an absolute reference. Allowing it to be a relative reference creates a condition where you can copy this formula in **column B**.

The final product is a flexible document for the accounting of trip and student finances. Each sheet allows for the manipulation of multiple variables.

1.   The **Trip Cost** sheet can be modified and the relative costs applied to **Student Accounts**.

2.   The **Fundraising** sheet collects data and leverages some but not all of that information back to the **Student Accounts** sheet.

Using sheet-linking formulas, data can be controlled and collected within their own category but applied in multiple places.

Here is an example of how your final spreadsheet might look:

	A	B	C	D	E	F
1	Name	$ Needed	$ Raised	$ Contribution	$ Cookie Dough	$ Wrapping Paper
2	Clint Adams	$25.93	235.93	$175.93	$44.00	$16.00
3	Nancy Baker	$59.93	201.93	$175.93		$26.00
4	Maria Booth	$60.93	200.93	$175.93	$25.00	
5	Kelly Cruise	$10.93	250.93	$175.93	$55.00	$20.00
6	Mark Collins	$70.93	190.93	$175.93		$15.00
7	Alyson Dougal	$57.93	203.93	$175.93		$28.00
8	Ruben Hoffman	$21.93	239.93	$175.93	$20.00	$44.00
9	Charles Kim	$56.93	204.93	$175.93		$29.00
10	Chris Keaton	-$17.07	278.93	$175.93	$65.00	$38.00
11	Ginger Lane	$35.93	225.93	$175.93		$50.00
12	Robert Lee	$85.93	175.93	$175.93		
13	Terissa Martinez	$60.93	200.93	$175.93	$25.00	
14	Maureen Mahaffy	$52.93	208.93	$175.93	$15.00	$18.00
15	Steve Peery	$75.93	185.93	$175.93		$10.00
16	Kennedy Rian	$73.93	187.93	$175.93		$12.00
17	Joey Ridenour	$71.93	189.93	$175.93		$14.00
18	Amy Solberg	$69.93	191.93	$175.93		$16.00
19	Jonas Thompson	$55.93	205.93	$175.93	$12.00	$18.00
20	Margo Williams	$61.93	199.93	$175.93	$5.00	$19.00
21	Aaron Zizzo	$63.93	197.93	$175.93		$22.00
22						

Mac OS X (Lion) is touted to be the "world's most advanced operating system" (http://www.apple.com/macosx/). It is based upon the popular and stable UNIX framework and includes many tools to increase productivity and creativity. This new operating system will be available in July 2011, and includes many new features: http://www.apple.com/macosx/whats-new/features.html. You will be able to purchase and download this new software from the Mac App store. For more information, visit this site: http://www.apple.com/macosx/how-to-buy/.

If you are a Windows user, we encourage you to view the following Apple video tutorial, which clearly outlines and discusses the differences between the two systems and how to get started using a Mac http://www.apple.com/findouthow/mac/#switcher and other videos featured in the "Find out how" tutorials.

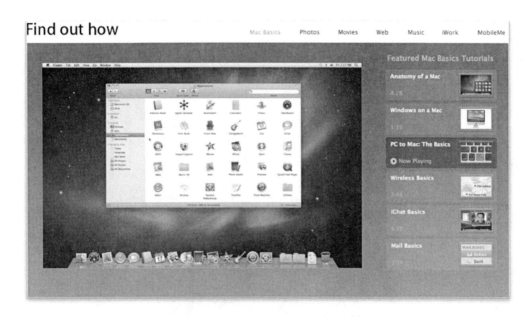

File Management: File or Pile?

Some people prefer to create folders and a structured hierarchy that provides a sense of order to their files. For instance, if you were saving assignments created for an English 101 class, you might create a root English 101 folder, and then embed other folders within this one, organizing them by assignments. However, with Mac OS X this really is not necessary. You could dump all of your files into one folder, as long as you named them something you can remember. With Mac OS X's sophisticated search features, you will be able to find any file very quickly.

Desktop

You will decide on your own system of organization. The desktop is a handy place to keep files you are currently working on. However, if you save everything to your desktop, it can become cluttered in a hurry. Therefore, you may want to clean up your desktop from time to time, just as you clean your physical desktop, especially after working on many active files.

You may want to create a couple of folders on your desktop, called Active and Archive and place files within one of these two files. Or, you might want to put all of your important files in the Mac OS X default Documents folder. Once you start working on a computer, digital files start piling up. Whatever you decide, remember—name your files something that will help you easily identify them.

For more information and ideas on how to organize the structure of your digital files, you might enjoy reading some of these LifeHacker posts on organizing your data: http://lifehackerbook.com/ch2.

Your Mac OS X includes a Dock at the bottom (you can hide this if you want in your System Preferences), which allows you to quickly access important applications and files. The Dock includes the **Documents**, **Downloads**, and **Applications** Stacks. To create a Stack, simply drag a folder to the Dock.

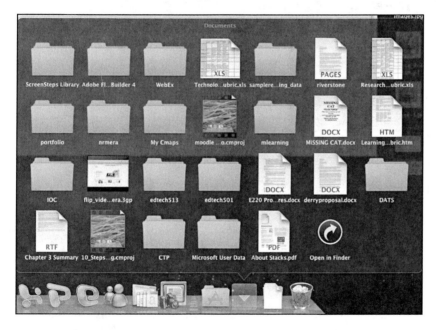

Downloads Stack

When you download items from Safari (Apple's built-in browser), iChat, or Mail, they automatically are saved in the Downloads Stack.

You can customize how you view the Stacks by right-clicking (Control + Click or customize the right-click on your mouse by clicking **System Preferences>Mouse**). Then, select the format in which you would like to view your Stacks. You can also customize and change the Stack's sort order.

Finder

You will use the Finder application in Mac OS X to locate and view drives, files, folders, and other connections to your computer.

Once you click the Finder icon, a window will appear, showing you the current contents of your computer, any other computers you can access on your network, and other networks you may be connected to. Included in the upper right of the finder window is an advanced search feature called **Spotlight**, which quickly and efficiently searches for files and other content on your computer.

You can view full previews of your files in **Cover Flow** and flip through them to view and select quickly and easily. To enable Cover Flow, simply open the Finder window and click the cover flow icon

.

You have a home folder that is indicated by a house icon, an icon for items on your desktop, an Applications folder, and a default Documents folder. How will you organize your digital files so you can find them later? It is up to you, but Mac OS X search features greatly enhance and simplify the ability to locate files. The secret is to name the file something you will remember later on. Also, getting in the habit of naming and saving files to a location before you begin to work on them is a very good idea.

Sidebar

The sidebar in your finder includes information about your computer, starting with the Macintosh HD (hard drive) and any other remote disks, shared computers on your network, folders, and recent searches you have performed.

Spotlight

In your Finder window you can also perform searches using **Spotlight**. Spotlight is in the upper right-hand corner of the Finder window. Enter your search terms, find your file, and view in Cover Flow.

Inserting/Removing a Flash Drive

1. Insert your flash drive (sometimes called a thumb or jump drive).
2. You will notice a drive icon appear on your desktop and also in your Finder window. The drive may or may not have a name.
3. You will also see a little eject icon, which will allow you to safely eject your flash drive.

   (Note: If you have any files open on this drive, you will not be able to eject it.)
4. Mac OS X allows you to eject the device either by clicking this icon or by clicking the drive and using the shortcut **Command + E**. This eject icon or shortcut can be applied to anything you want to eject on your Apple computer, such as a CD or DVD.

Creating a New Folder

You will discover there are many ways of accomplishing tasks on your Apple computer. We encourage you to experiment and see which system works best for you. For instance, there are several ways to create a new folder. Try the two following ways:

Clicking the Cogwheel icon in the Finder Window

1. Double-click the Flash drive icon to open it and view the contents. If your flash drive is new, there may be no files on it!

2. Locate the Cogwheel icon [image] in the upper bar of your Finder Window and click the drop-down arrow.
3. You will be presented with various options. Click the **New Folder** choice, enter your first name, and click **Enter**.

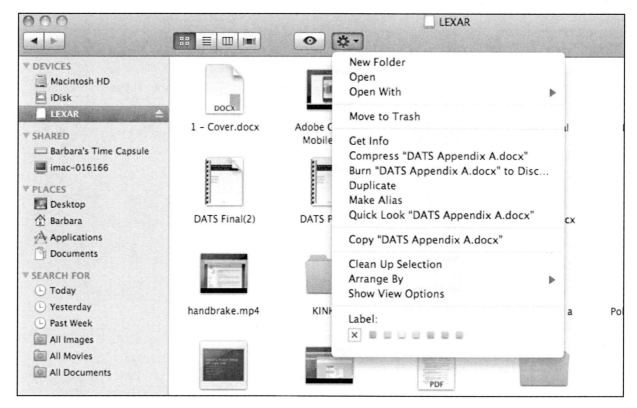

Right-Clicking in Finder Window

1. Double-click the Flash drive icon to open it and view the contents. If your flash drive is new, there may be no files on it.

2. Click the Icon view in the Folder window and right-click within the white space where the folder icons appear (Apple Command + Click or right-click if you have enabled this in the System Preferences>Mouse).

3. Select **New Folder**, enter your first name, and click **Enter**.

Renaming a File/Folder

There are a couple of ways to rename a folder with Mac OS X. Like many of the features and functions you will discover when working on an Apple computer, you will decide which way works best for you.

Rename with the return key

1. Click a file or folder once to select it.
2. Press the Return key and the file name or folder name will be highlighted.

3.   Now, enter your last name, press the return key once more, and the changes are locked in.

Schroeder

Rename with a delayed click

1.   Click a file or folder once to select it.
2.   Wait a second, and click on the file or folder once more. (If you time this just right, the file or folder will become selected, and you can type your new name.)

If you click too fast, the file will open in its default application. Once you get the timing down using this way to rename files and folders, it will become second nature.

Creating Subfolders

To create a folder within a folder (subfolder), simply double-click the folder you want to put another folder in to open it, right-click in the white area of the Finder window, select **New Folder**, name your folder, and select **Enter**.

1.   Double-click your **LastName** folder.
2.   Right-click in the white area of the Finder window.
3.   Select **New Folder**
4.   Enter **Word Processing** in the new folder name box.

Repeat these directions to make seven additional folders for your work files. Use the following titles for your subfolders: **Graphics, Audio, Newsletter, Spreadsheets, Presentations, Internet, and Teaching Resources.**

After you make all of your subfolders, you will want to arrange them. To do this, right-click in the white area of the Finder window where you have your subfolder, select **Arrange By> Name** and your folders will look much neater!

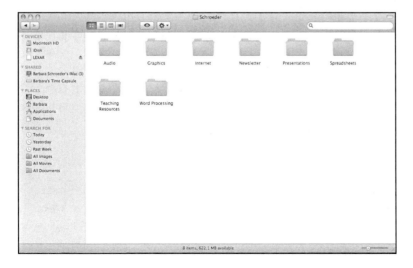

Deleting/Restoring Files or Folders

Mac OS X offers you several ways to delete files and folders. Remember, if you delete a folder, all of the files within the folder are deleted too. However, if you accidentally delete a file or folder, you can restore it from the Trash. Practice doing this with a folder you've created.

1. Select the **Newsletter** folder by clicking it once.
2. Either (1) Drag it to the Trash in your Dock or (2) right-click and select **Move to Trash**.
3. To restore a file you've accidentally deleted, click the Trash to open it, select your file (you can search for it using Spotlight), and then drag it to your desktop. It is now out of the trash and available.

Copying a File or Folder

1. Select **Your Last Name** folder on the flash drive by clicking it once.
2. Right-click the folder.
3. Select **Duplicate**.
4. The folder will be copied to the same location, with the name "Your Last Name copy."
5. Drag the Your Last Name copy to another location on the computer, such as the Desktop.
6. Your Last Name copy will now be on your desktop.

It is always a good idea to make backup copies of your files. Storing files on backup media such as a flash drive is a very quick and easy way to make copies. You can also store any type of file on your Google Docs account, which provides another location for backup copies. There are many ways to backup important files, and Mac OS X provides a software program called Time Machine that works with Time Capsule. We encourage you to make multiple copies and backups of important work, as computer hard drives are not failure-proof.

Copying Versus Moving Using Drag and Drop

With Mac OS X you can drag and drop files and folders to any location. When you drag a file or folder you are moving it, not copying it.

Creating a Shortcut (Alias)

In Mac OS X, an alias is a pointer (shortcut) file that allows you to quickly open the files, folders, servers, or applications used most often. When you double-click an alias, the operating system finds the file it references and opens it.

An alias can be distinguished by its icon, which has an arrow in the bottom left corner. Normally, an alias will remain functional until the original item is deleted, even if the original has been moved or renamed.

You have several options for creating an alias:

1. **Drag and drop:** Click the item you wish to alias and hold down the mouse button. Then, while holding down the Apple Command and Option keys, drag the item to where you want the alias to appear. Instead of moving the original item, this will create an alias at the new location.

2. **Contextual menus:** Hold down the Ctrl key and click the item you wish to alias. From the contextual menu, select **Make Alias**. The new alias will appear next to the original.
3. **Keystroke:** Select the item you wish to alias, and press Apple Command-l (the lowercase L). The new alias will appear next to its original.
4. **File menu:** Select the item, and then from the **File** menu, select **Make Alias**. A new alias icon will appear next to the original.

Use any of the above options and create an Alias for Your Last Name folder, placing it on your Desktop.

Other Features of Finder

Other features are available in Mac OS X Finder that facilitate organizing, viewing, and searching for files and folders. Simply selecting the **View>Arrange By** in the Finder menu will allow you many options to sort and organize your files and folders.

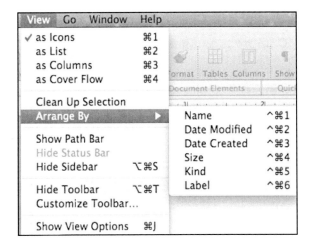

You can view folders in several formats in **Finder**: as icons, in a list, in columns, or with **Cover Flow**:

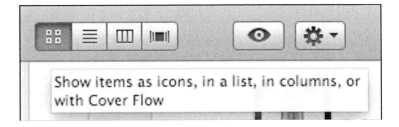

Experiment with the different views in Finder to see how files and folders are represented. For instance, in the column view, the second column provides more information about the file or folder you have selected, telling you the type of file, the size, when it was created, modified, and last opened.

Obtaining File or Folder Data

It's easy obtaining file or folder information on a Mac. Simply click the file or folder once and use the Keyboard shortcut **Apple Command + I**. This will open a dialog box, which will provide you with detailed information about the file.

Why would you need this? Sometimes a file is too large to send as an email attachment or attach to a discussion forum. When you use an image for a website, you will want to make sure the file size is as small as possible. You might need to compress files in order to use them efficiently.

Knowing how to find and analyze information about your files is very important.

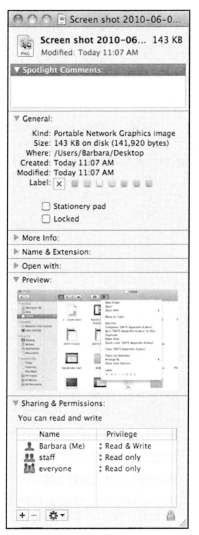

Compressing and Opening Compressed Files and Folders

To compress a file or folder on Mac OS X, select the file or folder, right-click, and select **Compress**. A compressed file (zip) will be made from your original file or folder, with the same file name and extension zip. Therefore, you can turn a folder into a compressed file, enabling you to send just one file to a recipient, for instance. The original folder can be viewed by double-clicking the compressed (zip) file.

Summary

This technology skills section has presented an overview of the Mac OS X file management features. Learning to successfully navigate among windows and use the features of Mac OS X will improve your productivity and your students' performance.

The necessity of introducing file management and an overview of the computer's operating system as early as possible in the school year cannot be over-emphasized. Your students will probably need extra help and direction in the beginning to organize and manage their assignments on the computer.

Next, you will have the opportunity to practice various file management skills and produce an artifact that demonstrates your competency in ISTE NETS-T Standard 3.

File Management Exercise

Exercise 1: Exploring File Properties

In this practice exercise, you will learn how to locate and identify files on an Apple computer and be able to determine file properties including file size and location.

1. Click the **Finder** icon
2. Look for *Word* documents with the extension docx by entering **docx** in the Spotlight entry box.

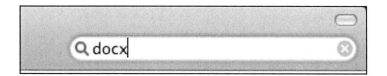

3. You will see all of the files with that extension in the white area of your Finder window.

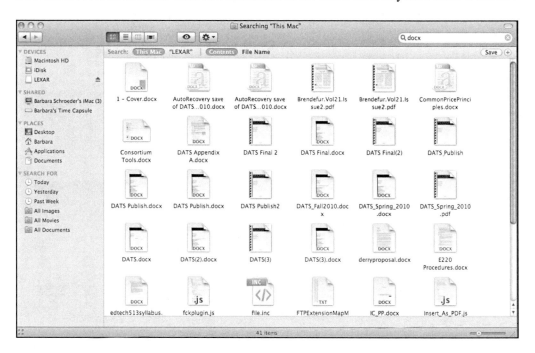

4. Click your flash drive either at the top of the Finder window or in your Finder Sidebar to view all docx files on that device.

Exploring File Properties

1. Select any file and click **Apple Command + I**.

2. A dialog box will appear with information about that file.

3. Click the arrows to the left of the sections to view more information in the section, such as **Sharing & Permissions** to view who can read and/or write to the file.

4. To change permissions, you will need to click the little lock icon in the lower right corner and enter a password as needed.

Next, please return to Technology Skills: File Management and complete the Exercises starting on page 27 or as directed by your instructor.

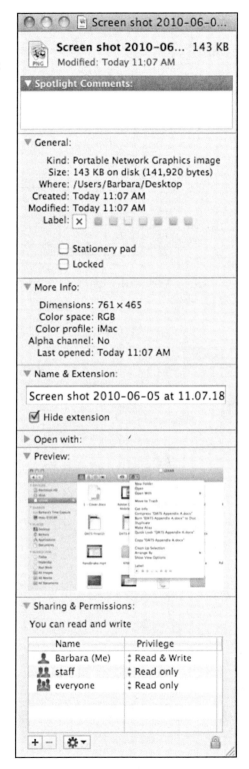

When you open *Word for Mac 2011*, a window opens with a new blank document on your screen. Since word processing is an essential and useful skill, it is important to become familiar with as many of the features as possible and be able to use them in other applications.

The *Microsoft Word for Mac 2011* website offers helpful online tutorials to help you either learn Word for the first time on a Mac or help you transition from Word: Mac 2008. Go to this main link and access any of the tutorials that address your needs: http://www.microsoft.com/mac/word/getting-started-with-word.

Starting Word: Mac 2011

✓ Open your Applications folder, navigate to your Microsoft Office folder, open it and double-click

Word, or click the *Word* icon in your Dock. (This will depend upon how you have your desktop setup.)

The menu bar at the top of your screen includes important functions, such as **Creating a New Document, Opening a document, Saving,** and **Printing.**

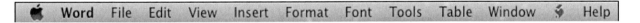

The document window includes toolbars and tabs for various word processing functions along with icons and text.

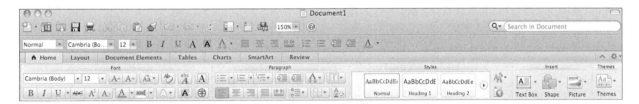

Mac OS X allows you to easily switch between programs you are using. If you cannot view the *Word* main menu bar, simply click one of the documents and it will appear.

Additionally, if you want to close a program, you can right-click it on the Dock and select **Quit** or use the Keyboard shortcut (**Apple Command + Q**). (Open programs will include a small light indicator below the icon in the Dock).

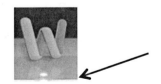

Ribbon

In order to access more of the functions needed for word processing you will want to have the **Ribbon** open, which organizes commends in logical groups under tabs. If you do not see the ribbon

groups, click the down arrow on the right side of the ribbon .

File Menu

Clicking the *Word* **File** menu button allows you to access the menu of commands you use to work with the total document including opening, saving and printing files.

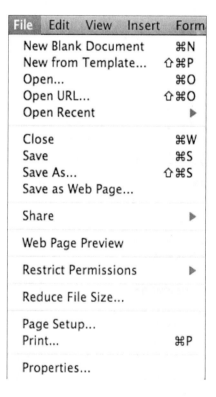

In addition to the basic commands to **Open**, **Save** and **Close** a document, you are able to prepare (security and document permissions), send, and print documents. Using the **Share** command, you can email as an attachment or save to cloud-based Microsoft services.

The **Save As** command is one of the most important commands you and your students need to access each time you start a document. Notice that after clicking the **Save As** command, you are provided with several options for saving the document.

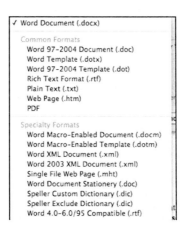

By clicking any of the menu items, you are presented with a functionally related set of commands. For example, click the **Insert** menu and you are presented with a number of common insert commands including inserting graphics, tables, word art, shapes and symbols.

Now that you have had a brief overview of the main elements, open *Word for Mac 2011* and take time to explore the commands available to you.

Viewing Options

Microsoft Word for Mac 2011 offers a number of ways for you to view your document each with specific features to facilitate your task. Views can be accessed by either clicking on one of the icons located on the status bar at the bottom of the document window or by clicking on the **View** menu.

Once selected, commands become available to you related to viewing options including the ability to view windows in multiple modes, show/hide elements on the screen, and adjust the magnification of the document.

Layout Views

You would choose a layout view based on the document you are producing and on your own individual preferences (Note: Most of the exercises in this section are done in the Print Layout View).

1. **Draft** – This view may be preferred when you are working on a draft and want to quickly edit the text.
2. **Outline** – Work in outline view when you are working on a document (such as a book or a long report) and you want to be able to easily organize by headings. This also allows you to use the outline tools.
3. **Publishing** – Create newsletters, brochures, and more using powerful desktop publishing tools.

4. **Print Layout** - Work in print layout view to see how text, graphics, and other elements will be positioned on the printed page. You might choose to work in this view if your document makes use of headers and footers, columns and drawing objects.
5. **Notebook** – Take notes, flag items, and record audio notes in a specialized notebook document.
6. **Full Screen Reading** - Work in full screen reading view for typing and editing text. The layout is simplified so that you can type and edit quickly and easily.

Help Menu

Another feature that will prove to be invaluable to you, and your students, is the **Help Menu**. With the many commands available within the office applications, no one can be expected to know them all. The **Help Menu** provides instant instructions on how to use any and all of the features. A help icon featuring a question mark surrounded by a circle  is located in the right hand corner of the document menu.

Clicking on the **Help** icon takes you directly to *Word* Help Home, making it easy for you and your students to find an immediate answer to queries. You can type in a question or just one word and a list of possible areas is generated.

Using Microsoft Office Help Viewer

1. Click the help icon  and type **deleting shapes** in the help box.
2. Hit **Enter.**
3. The results of the search are displayed with hyperlinks to pertinent information.

Remember, when your students ask how to delete a shape or to perform any other word processing commands, you can simply direct them to the **Help Menu**. In this way, they will become more independent computer users.

Saving Documents

With a blank document on your *Word* screen, you are ready to begin a word processing document. Each time you start a document (or spreadsheet or other application, etc.) you should save it as soon as possible, making sure that you save it in the right directory and folder. This is called a **Save As** command and is one of the most important operations for you (and your students) to perform. Beginning your word processing document by saving it in a specific folder is simply a good file management procedure. It will ensure that the document will be easily located at a later time.

Parent Newsletter

The first document you will prepare is a **Parent Newsletter.** Begin by saving the document on the drive of your choice (if you are working at home, you will probably save in **Documents** on your hard drive; if you are working in a lab, you will want to save on whatever storage device you are currently using).

Optional: Creating Parent Newsletter from Template

Word offers convenient ways to use templates to create professional publications.

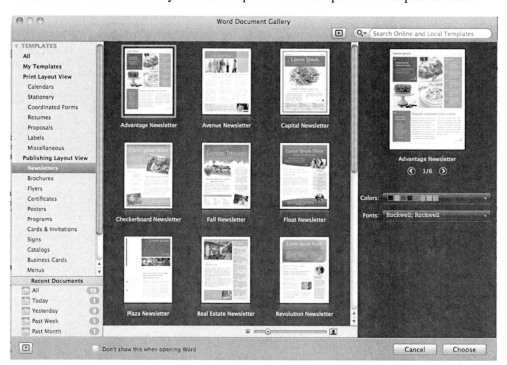

If you are already skilled in using features of word processing programs, your instructor might suggest create the parent newsletter using a *Microsoft Word* template. To begin using a template, follow these steps:

1. On the **Standard** toolbar, click **New from template** .
2. In the navigation pane, under **Templates**, click either **All** or **My Templates**.
3. Click the template you want and then click **Choose**.
4. Include the content required in the Parent Newsletter as described below.

Optional: Creating Parent Newsletter in Google Docs

As another option, review the instructions on how to use Google Docs in Appendix B and create the Parent Newsletter using this collaborative tool. Share your document with another classmate and have him/her review and make comments as needed. Follow the instructions for the newsletter, including the required content. Your Google Doc might look something like the following:

Standards Update

National Educational Technology Standards

The International Society for Technology in Education (ISTE) has recently released the NETS for Students 2007, providing guidelines for student technology concepts and skills in a digital age. ISTE, a professional organization that has provided leadership in technology for over a decade, reports that, "As foundational ICT skills penetrate throughout our society, students will be expected to apply the basics in authentic, integrated ways to solve problems, complete projects, and creatively extend their abilities. *ISTE's National Educational Technology Standards for Students* help students preparing to work, live, and contribute to the social and civic fabric of their communities."

Skills for a Digital Age

A national research study, "Listening to Student Voices," contributed by the Center for Policy Studies reports that today's students are frustrated with the lack of technology in the classroom. The tech-savvy generation that has grown up with technology is disappointed in traditional classroom instruction. The report recommends that technology standards be a focus of K-12 education.

Student Technology Standards

- Creativity and Innovation
- Communication and Collaboration
- Research and Information Fluency
- Critical Thinking, Problem Solving, and Decision making
- Digital Citizenship
- Technology Operations and Concepts

Parents

We are asking for volunteers to help in the computer labs in our after-school technology program. Please write your name in the "I Can Help" column for the days you might be available this semester and send back to your child's school.

Your Name: _____

Phone: _____ Email:_____

School	Days/Times	I Can Help
East Elementary School	Mondays (3 - 5)	
West Middle School	Tuesdays (3 - 5)	
Central High School	Wednesdays (3 - 5)	

Creating Parent Newsletter from Blank Word Document

Save As

You will be doing this a lot, as you open applications, name, and then save the file to a folder/location of your choice. If you are opening *Word* for the first time to create and work on a document, you should get in the habit of naming and saving the file. Here is how you do this:

1. Click **File>Save As** and a dialog box will appear.

2. If your dialog box looks like the one below, you will want to expand it so you can navigate to the folder of your choice to name and save it.

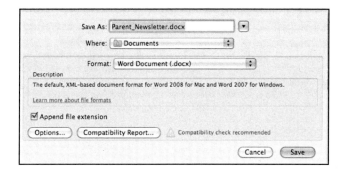

3. Click the blue drop-down arrow at the top to expand your view.

4. Name your file, decide what type of file format you want to save it in.

5. Navigate to where you want to place your file and new folder you will create (You might want to choose the Documents folder or if you are working in a lab, your flash drive.)
6. Create a new folder (click the **New Folder** button).
7. Name the new folder **Word Processing Exercises**. You can save all of your word processing exercises from this book in this folder.
8. Save your file (which will go in your new **Word Processing Exercises** folder).

Now you can save frequently by performing the Keyboard Save shortcut, **Apple Command + S**.

You can also click the little **Save** icon 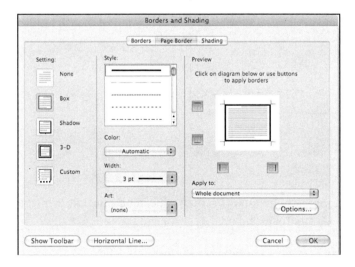 in the *Word* document menu bar. Also note that the title of your document, **Parent Newsletter**, is now displayed in the *Word* title bar.

Planning Your Document

Your next decision involves the actual physical layout of the document. The newsletter you will create will look similar to the one below. You will use **Formatting Palette** to set the size of your document's margins and the physical orientation. This floating palette includes most of the formatting options you will need for a word-processed document.

Page Margins

1. Click the **Layout tab.**
2. Expand the Document Margins by clicking the dropdown arrow.
3. Reduce the size of your margins if necessary to .5 inches on left right, bottom, and top.

In determining the layout of the newsletter, you decide to add a page border.

Creating a Page Border

1. Click the **Border** icon in the Page Background section of the **Layout** tab.
2. Click the borders you want to appear on the entire document.
3. Click the down arrow on the **Width** and select **3 pt**.

4. Click **OK**.

With your margins and border set and your document saved, you begin your parent newsletter by using some of the features of the **Document Elements** tab. Commands available to you include the ability to insert a table of contents, add pages and page breaks, insert text elements and math equations.

The first graphic you will insert in your newsletter is **WordArt** to write the title.

Inserting WordArt

1. Click the **WordArt** icon under the Text Elements section of the **Document Elements** tab.
2. Choose a design from the WordArt Gallery by clicking your choice.
3. Your Word Art choice will appear in your text. You can edit it directly within the text and move it anywhere you want.
4. Enter the title of the newsletter **Standards Update**.
5. You can adjust the layout of your Word Art by clicking the **Home** tab on the **Ribbon** and selecting any of the formatting options.

Your newsletter will be more visually appealing when you add other graphics such as pictures, text boxes and shapes.

Inserting Clip Art

1. Select the **Home** tab from the **Ribbon** and click the **Picture** icon
2. Select Clip Art Gallery.
3. In the **Search** box, type **school**

4. A variety of pictures are presented in the task pane. Double-click the image you want to insert.
5. Click **Close**.

Once you have inserted the graphic, the **Format Picture** tab can be selected, which will include many options for you to customize or format your image.

Select the image and make sure you have the **Format Picture** tab selected.

Positioning Pictures/Graphics

1. Select the **Format Picture** tab in the **Ribbon**.
2. In the Arrange section, click the **Wrap text** and then the **Tight** option.
3. This option allows you to move the graphic closer to the text.

Once the graphic is formatted, it is easier to manipulate by dragging on the handles to resize and holding down the left mouse button and moving it around the page.

Next, you will add a horizontal line to separate the title from the rest of the page.

Inserting Lines

1. On the **Home** tab, under **Insert**, click **Shape**, point to **Lines and Connectors**, and then click the line style you want.
2. In your document, hold down the mouse button and draw the line where you want.
3. To resize your horizontal line, right-click the line, select **Format Shape and Weight** to adjust width.

Now that the banner for the parent newsletter is completed, you will type the text for the first article about the new ISTE National Education Technology standards for students. Type the text located in the box below; the text should go directly below the horizontal line you just inserted.

The International Society for Technology in Education (ISTE) has recently released the *National Education Technology Standards for Students* providing guidelines for student technology concepts and skills in a Digital Age. ISTE, a professional organization that has provided leadership in technology for over a decade, reports that, "As foundational ICT skills penetrate throughout our society, students will be expected to apply the basics in authentic, integrated ways to solve problems, complete projects, and creatively extend their abilities. *ISTE's National Educational Technology Standards for Students* help students preparing to work, live, and contribute to the social and civic fabric of their communities."

You will want to italicize the "*ISTE's National Educational Technology Standards for Students*" text. Applying formatting to text is easily accomplished by using the icons at in the **Home** tab of the **Ribbon** or by using keyboard shortcuts.

Formatting Commands

As you have already seen, most of the formatting commands can be accessed from the **Home** tab on the **Ribbon**. These commands make it easy to change the **format**, the way the text looks on the page, by simply selecting text and then clicking on a formatting icon. There are numerous formatting features available including the ability to change the placement of the text and to add numbering/bullets and borders.

It is a common practice to type your word processing document and then apply formatting features to selected text. You can select text and graphics by holding down the mouse button as you run the mouse over the desired text and/or objects. A word can be selected by double-clicking on the word; triple clicking within a paragraph allows you to quickly select the whole paragraph. You can even select items that aren't next to each other. For example, you can select a paragraph from one page of your document, hold down the Apple Command key and then select a paragraph on another page.

You will be using many of these features to enhance your newsletter. Your article title is **National Education Technology Standards.** Type your title above the article (you may have to hit enter a few times at the top of your text). The article title should be a different font style and size to set it off from the article.

Keyboard Shortcuts you should know for quick formatting
Crtl+B (**Bold**)
Ctrl+I (*Italics*)
Ctrl+U (<u>Underlined</u>)

Changing Font Style and Size

1. Select the title you just entered: **National Education Technology Standards**.
2. Use the options in the **Home** tab of the **Ribbon** to make selections.
3. Click the drop down arrow after the name of the font to view selections.

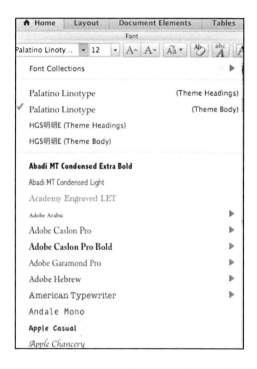

4. Select the font and size (use a larger size for the title). If you want to undo, use the keyboard shortcut **Apple Command + Z**.

Text Alignment

You have several choices for aligning your text: **left justification** (text aligned on the left side); **right justification** (text aligned on the right side); **full justification** (text aligned on both sides); and, **centered** (text centered). The title will be centered and the text of the article will be aligned on both sides. This time use the commands located on the **Home** ribbon to apply the alignment-formatting feature.

1. Select the title **National Education Technology Standards.**
2. Click the center icon under the **Paragraph** section of the **Home** tab.
3. Select the entire article (not the title).
4. Click the full justification icon.

Another formatting feature that will make your newsletter more attractive is the use of columns.

Creating Columns

1. Select the text under **National Education Technology Standards**.

2. On the **Home** tab, under **Paragraph**, click , and then click **Columns**.

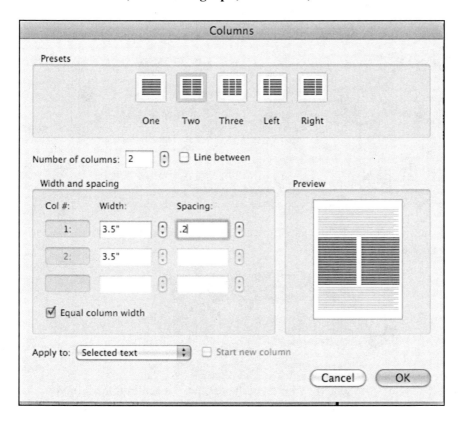

3. Select **Two** columns at the top of the dialog box.
4. Change the spacing to .2"
5. Click **OK**

Inserting Breaks

You can use section breaks to vary the layout of a document. You create a new section when you want to change such properties as line numbering, number of columns, or headers and footers. A section break is a mark inserted at the end of a section, which stores the formatting elements. Placing a section mark at the end of the National Education Technology Standards article will ensure that only the text within the section has two-column formatting.

1. Place your cursor at the end of the paragraph (communities).
2. On the **Layout** tab, under **Page Setup**, click **Break**, and then click the kind of section break you want (**Continuous**).

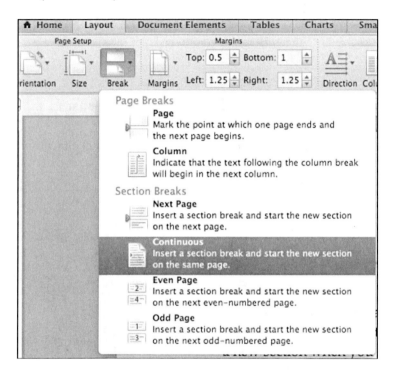

3. If you want to see where breaks are placed, you can click the **Draft View** icon in the lower left of your document.

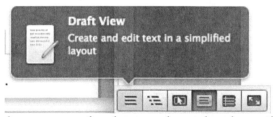

Activating this view will show you exactly where you have placed a section break in your document, which appears as below:

....Section Break (Continuous)..

Now that you have set the section break, let's add a horizontal line below the article with a width of 1.5 pt.

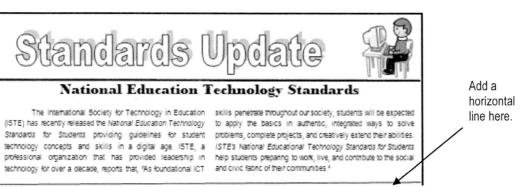

Add a horizontal line here.

The next article to place in your newsletter is a preview of the student technology standards. Type the title **Skills for a Digital Age** in your choice of font and font size. Then type the following article:

A national research study, "*Listening to Student Voices,*" conducted by the Center for Policy Studies reports that today's students are frustrated with the lack of technology in the classroom. The tech-savvy generation that has grown up with technology is disappointed in traditional classroom instruction. The report recommends technology standards be a focus of K-12 instruction.

Inserting a Text Box

With the article already entered, you decide to add a text box and include a listing of the student technology standards for your readers.

1. On the **Document Elements** tab, under **Text Elements**, click **Text Box**.
2. Drag to define a text box on the left side of the page and then click the forward text box link handle.
3. To create a border for the text box, select the text box and click the **Format** tab.
4. Click **Line** and select the line color and size.
5. Enter text in the box by clicking inside the box.
6. Try some of the styles, text, effects and arrangement options for your text box.
7. To move the text box, select it and look for the crosshatch with arrows (the move symbol).

Now that you have formatted the text box, you can move it easily on the page and have the text wrap closely to the text box. Move your text box to the right of the Skills for a Digital Age article.

Inserting Symbols   Student Technology Standards ☑

Enter the title **Student Technology Standards** in the text box with a checkbox symbol at the end of the title (you may have to adjust your box to fit the text and symbol).

1. Click where you want to insert a symbol.
2. On the **Standard** toolbar, click **Show or hide the Media Browser**.
3. Click the **Symbols** tab.
4. Scroll down and select the ☑ ballot box with check.
5. You can move the symbol you just inserted by clicking and dragging it to the location you want.

The Student Technology Standards text box will contain a listing of technology standards for students. You will create a bulleted list of the categories. A **bullet** is a dot or other symbol placed before to text to add emphasis. They are used when there is no specific sequence to the items. If order is important, a numbered list should be used in place of bullets.

Type the following list in your text box (adjust the box borders as necessary):

> **Student Technology Standards** ☑
>
> ✓ Creativity and Innovation
> ✓ Communication and Collaboration
> ✓ Research and Information Fluency
> ✓ Critical Thinking, Problem Solving, and Decision making
> ✓ Digital Citizenship
> ✓ Technology Operations and Concepts

Creating a Bulleted (Unordered) List

1. Select the text you want as a list.

2. Under the **Home** tab, **Paragraph** section, select the bullets icon and the type of bullet you want.

The list is now indented with bullets emphasizing each of the lines of text.

You can adjust the bulleted list and apply formatting features to enhance your text box. Now that you have completed your textbox, adjust the middle section of your newsletter so that the article title is well placed. Add a graphic to enhance the appearance of the article and add a horizontal line to separate this article from the last section of the newsletter.

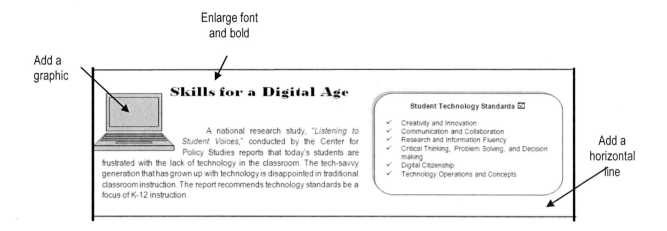

For the last section of your newsletter, you will write a request to the parents to volunteer their time in the after school technology program. To make scheduling easy, you supply a form for parents to complete and return to their child's school.

Type the following text:

Parents,

　　We are asking for volunteers to help in the computer labs in our after school technology program. Please write your name in the "I Can Help" column for the day(s) for which you might be available this semester and send the form to your child's school.

Beneath the text you will create a form by inserting a table. Tables are an excellent means of organizing and presenting information. A table consists of rows and columns of cells that can be filled with text and/or graphics. Your newsletter table will contain three columns and five rows.

Creating a Table

1. Click where you want to insert a table.
2. On the **Tables** tab, under **Table Options**, click **New**, and then click and drag across as many rows and columns as you want.
3. Create 3 columns and 5 rows.
4. The table will automatically be inserted into your document.

Designing a Table

1. Select the table you have inserted and view the options available in the **Home** and **Tables** tabs.
2. Center the titles using the **Paragraph** options in the **Home** tab.
3. To add color to a row, select the row by clicking and dragging across the cells. Then, select a Shading color by clicking the Shading icon in the **Tables** tab.
4. To change the color of the font, select the text and the **Home** tab to access the formatting options.
5. Enter the information in each cell as shown below.

Place your cursor in the top row and enter the column titles. Use your tab key or arrow keys to move from cell to cell.

School	Days/Times	I Can Help
East Elementary School	Mondays (3-5 pm)	
West Middle School	Tuesdays (3-5 pm)	
Central High School	Wednesdays (3-5 pm)	

Columns and rows can be resized by positioning your cursor on the edge of a column or row and dragging the border by holding down the left mouse button.

Resize Columns   Resize Rows

Merging the cells in the last row will provide an area large enough to include parent name and contact information.

Merging Cells in a Table

1. Select the last row in your table (all three cells).
2. Click the **Merge** icon in the **Tables>Table Layout** tab.

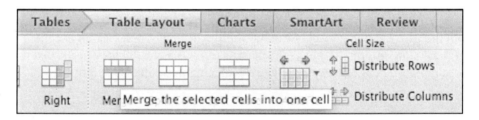

Once the cells are merged, enter the following information:

Name: _____

Phone: _____ Email_____

Table borders can be adjusted and/or eliminated by selecting the table and then using the **Borders** tools in the **Tables** tab. Options include having borders at the top, bottom, outside, and inside as well as having no borders at all.

Printing

As school budgets are limited, it is always a good idea to discuss the school's printing policy with your students and make sure that they know how to print single pages of a multi-page document. Ensuring that students view documents before printing will assist in this process as well.

Previewing and Printing Documents

1. Use the keyboard shortcut **Apple Command + P** or click **File>Print**.
2. Review the many options you have for printing.

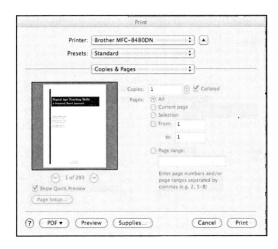

3. You may want to select **Preview** to confirm what you will be printing. You are given an opportunity to change margins, view your document one page or more pages at a time.
4. Make any editing changes necessary before you print.
5. Click **Print**.

You can also print just parts or pages of a document through the **Pages** option. This will save paper, as this option will print the exact pages and/or sections instead of automatically printing an entire document.

Summary

This technology skills section has presented many of the features in *Word for Mac 2011* most commonly used by teachers and students.

Many of the word processing activities and exercises that follow can also be completed using Google Docs, a free, collaborative, online word processing program. Complete details on how to use Google Docs are included in Appendix B.

Word Processing Exercise: Word for Mac 2011

The following practice exercise is provided to introduce you to *Word for Mac 2011* features and ways in which they can be used for curricular purposes. You might try completing them in another application, such as *Google Docs* or *OpenOffice* (http://www.openoffice.org) *Writer*.

Also, your instructor might ask you to go through some of the online tutorials and view videos on the Microsoft Word for Mac 2011 Learning Roadmap: http://bit.ly/byomud This site provides helpful tutorials and other ideas on how you might use *Word*.

Application exercises are provided for you to apply the skills you have learned to create useful artifacts for your Technology Teaching Portfolio.

Exercise 1: Using Word Features

✓ Always begin your document by saving it in the appropriate directory and folder.
✓ Title this document **YourLastName Word Practice Exercise**
✓ Keep your margins at the one-inch default setting.

With your margins set and your document saved, you begin your word processing practice. Type the following words exactly as they appear:

Word Processing Practice
Here is my opportunity to practice the many functions available through word processing. By becoming adept in word processing, I can be a more productive teacher and better guide my students. Word processing skills that I will need to practice include: formatting, editing, and other useful skills.

Copying and Moving Text or Graphics

1. Select a line of text in the word processing practice paragraph you entered. (Click with your cursor at the beginning of the line and then click at the end of the line while holding the shift key down – this selection method works regardless of the amount of text that you want to select).
2. With your cursor in the highlighted area, right-click.
3. Select **Copy**
4. Position your cursor to the spot where you want the text or graphic to be copied.
5. Right-click and select **Paste**.

Now you have copied the text and/or graphic material and placed it in the same document or in another open document. Moving the text can be accomplished using the same procedure, but by choosing **Cut** from the dropdown menu instead of **Copy**. When you cut or copy items, *Word* places them on an Office Clipboard, which can be opened in a task pane while you work. You can paste or delete the items on the Clipboard without going through the copy/cut process. This process will only save the most recent item you've copied to the Office Clipboard. If you want to copy and save multiple items to paste later in *Office: Mac 2011*, use the **Scrapbook**.

Adding a text clip or graphic to the Scrapbook

You store the clips in the **Scrapbook** so you can later add them to any document. For example, you can add an image and then assign a name to the clip. Here's how you use the Scrapbook:

1. On the **View** menu, click **Scrapbook**.
2. In the **Scrapbook** window, click **Add**, and then click **Add File**.
3. Locate the image you want to add and then double-click it.
4. In the **Scrapbook** window, double-click the clip that you added.
5. Type a new name for the clip – **my picture**, for example, and then press Return.

NOTE: The **Scrapbook** accepts the following file formats: GIF, JPEG, PICT, PNG, BMP, PNTG (MacPaint), text, and Unicode text.

The **Scrapbook** allows you to collect multiple items (text and graphics) from any document or other program and then paste them into any document. For example, you can copy data from *Excel: Mac 2011*, a graphic from a *PowerPoint: Mac 2011* presentation, then paste any or all of the collected items in a *Word* document. The collected items stay in the Office Scrapbook until you exit *Office*.

Inserting Comments

The commands available on the **Review Tab** are designed to assist in writing and feature editing and reviewing tools. One tool particularly useful to teachers is the ability to insert comments into *Word* documents. For this exercise, you will insert an editing comment into your Word Processing Practice document.

Inserting a Comment

1. Select the text or item you want to comment on, or click to insert the cursor near the text you want to comment on.
2. On the **Review** tab, under **Comments**, click **New**.
3. Type the comment text in the comment balloon.

The comments can be read and then deleted by your students as they make the suggested corrections/modifications. You can save the electronic document to make sure that you have a copy of your editorial comments as well. To delete a comment, click the circled **X** in the upper right corner of the comment box.

With spelling and grammar tools available, a misspelled word will appear with a wavy red line beneath it. To correct the word, simply place your cursor on the word and right-click with the mouse. A list of possible words will be presented and you need only click the correct word. At this time, you are also able to ignore the suggestions or add the word to the dictionary.

Checking for Spelling and Grammar Errors

1. Type this sentence, **the girl with the books have left the rom with hour pencils.** (Hit **Enter**)
2. Position your cursor on the word with the wavy red underline, rom and right-click it. A drop down list of several choices is displayed. Click **room** (the correct spelling).
3. Position your cursor on the word with the wavy green underline, the and right-click.

4. View the recommendations and decide to either accept or not.

Hyperlinks

One of the most helpful commands available on the **Insert** menu is the ability to insert hyperlinks within the document, to other documents or files and even to the Internet. *Word* allows you to insert hyperlinks within your document through the use of headings and/or bookmarks. Set a bookmark in your Word Processing Practice document so that you will be able to link to that location.

Inserting a Bookmark in a Document (Anchor)

Place your cursor in the last sentence of your Word Processing Practice document directly in front of the "**f**" in formatting. This is the spot you will place a bookmark.

1. Click the **Insert** menu and then select **Bookmark**.
2. Type **Practice** in the **Bookmark name box**.
3. Click **Add**.

Now that you have a bookmarked spot in your document, you will be able to hyperlink to that location.

Inserting a Hyperlink to an Anchor (Place in a document)

1. Select the word **Practice** in the title.
2. Click **Insert>Hyperlink** (or use Keyboard Shortcut **Apple Command + K**) from the Word main menu bar.
3. Select Document tab and locate the Practice bookmark (anchor).
4. Click the **Practice** bookmark.
5. Click **OK**.

Although your practice document is too short to require a hyperlink, you are able to direct your students directly to the practice skills by clicking on the *Practice* hyperlink. Placing hyperlinks to the web or an email address includes the same steps, except you would choose "Web Page" or "Email address" tabs in the Hyperlink dialog box.

Useful Formatting Commands

A common formatting decision is to determine the line spacing for your document.

Setting Line Spacing

1. Select the text where you want to adjust spacing.
2. From the **Home** tab, **Paragraph** section, select the **Line Spacing** icon and then the spacing you want.

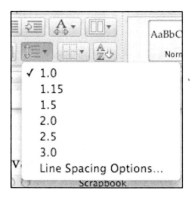

This practice exercise has presented some basic word processing functions.

Please complete the rest of the Exercises in **Technology Skills: Word Processing**, starting with Exercise 2 on page 61 or as directed by your instructor.

These exercises provide opportunities for you to apply the word processing skills you have learned to create artifacts for your Technology Teaching Portfolio.

In this section, you will use the powerful uses of *Microsoft Excel for Mac 2011* to organize, calculate and analyze data by building a worksheet from start to finish. Remember, a spreadsheet helps you answer "What if?" questions, and allows for easy and quick calculations of numerical data. You may also want to use a spreadsheet to track and compare other types of data, too.

A worksheet consists of rows designated by numbers and columns designated by letters. The intersection of a row and a column is called a cell; in the example below, the cell **A1** is the active cell.

A worksheet contains 65,536 rows and 256 columns.

A collection of worksheets is called a workbook.

You can add as many worksheets as you want in a workbook, limited only by your computer's available memory. Although there are many times in the classroom your students will only use a single worksheet in a workbook, multiple worksheets allow you to keep related worksheets in one file and even allow you to perform calculations and use the information among the worksheets.

When you first open *Excel*, you will be presented with information about what's new. Take some time to explore some of the new features. After closing this dialog box, you will be presented with the Excel Workbook Gallery. As with *Word*, you will have some templates available to make your work easier. There are also online templates you may explore for use.

You will want to open an *Excel* Workbook, which is a blank spreadsheet.

After working with *Word 2011 for Mac*, you are already familiar with many of the commands available. There are two new elements in the *Excel* window, a **formula bar** and a **name box**. The name box displays the cell **A1**, which is the name of the currently selected cell. Cell names are also called **cell addresses** or **cell references**.

The new *Office for Mac 2011* suite of tools includes a **Ribbon**, a collection of tabs that includes specific, related functions and features. As in *Word*, *Excel* includes a ribbon with tabs for Home, Layout, Tables, Charts, SmartArt, and Review. There are two extra tabs in Excel: Formulas and Data.

To access the **formula bar**, an important tool in Excel, you will need to make sure the **Ribbon** is expanded. You can expand the Ribbon by clicking any of the tabs. Start by clicking the **Home** tab if you cannot view the formula bar (indicated by arrow below).

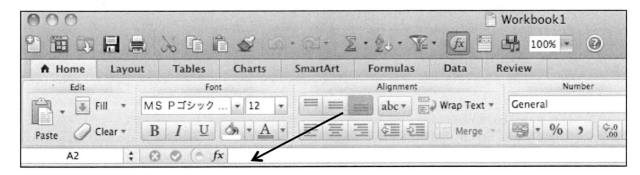

The tab at the bottom of the workbook window is labeled Sheet1; additional sheets can be added by clicking the + icon. Also, you are able to name your worksheets, add or delete worksheets and move the position of the worksheets within the workbook.

Navigating in the worksheet can be accomplished by clicking in a specific cell, hitting the enter key, using the tab key, and/or using the arrow keys. To return to cell **A1**, the very first cell in your worksheet, hold down the Apple Command key and the home key at the same time (**Apple Command + Home**).

Types of Data

The three basic types of data that can be entered into a worksheet cell are labels, values, and dates/times.

1. **Labels:** text entries that do not have a value associated with them. Text is left aligned in the cell.

2. **Values:** numeric entries that can be used in calculations. Values are right aligned.

3. **Dates/Times:** either a time (11:20 AM) or a date (1/1/2003). Dates/times are right aligned.

You are also able to include recorded sounds, graphics and hyperlinks within your worksheets.

Designing A Spreadsheet

The time you take in designing your spreadsheet is well spent. The first step is to determine the information you need and the calculations to be performed. You must decide how to arrange data to determine the appropriate formulas for data analysis. Finally, you will want to use formatting features to make the spreadsheet easier to read and more visually appealing.

The exercise you will complete in this section leads you through the design and development of a class gradebook that will look similar to the one below. In this gradebook, you will learn how to enter values (text, numbers, and formulas), how to format cells, how to add **WordArt** and **Clip Art** to customize your spreadsheet, and most importantly, how to use the power of a spreadsheet to make instant calculations and conduct analysis.

	Student Names	HW-1	HW-2	HW-3	Homework	P-1	P-2	Projects	E1	E2	Exams	Final	Score
3	Possible Points	15	12	17	44	25	35	60.00	55	25	80.00		
4													
5	Engle, Mary	10	7	15	0.73	20	21	0.68	52	24	0.95	0.80	B
6	Garcia, Jose	13	10	10	0.75	23	31	0.90	53	22	0.94	0.89	B
7	Jones, Sally	15	12	17	1.00	25	34	0.98	45	20	0.81	0.92	A
8	Little, Ian	5	5	5	0.34	15	15	0.50	25	13	0.48	0.46	F
9	Smith, John	7	8	11	0.59	18	28	0.77	50	20	0.88	0.78	C
10	Sully, Todd	11	6	9	0.59	18	21	0.65	49	21	0.88	0.73	C
11	Average Scores	10	8	11	0.67	20	25	0.75	46	20	0.82	0.76	
12	Highest Scores	15	12	17	1.00	25	34	0.98	53	24	0.95	0.92	
13	Lowest Scores	5	5	5	0.34	15	15	0.50	25	13	0.48	0.46	

For your class gradebook, you determine that the following elements will need to be included:

- Class title
- Student names
- Class assignments (by category)
  - Homework
  - Projects
  - Quizzes/Exams
- Student performance in each of the assignment categories
- Student performance for the grading period
- Each student's final grade
- Class average for each assignment
- Highest grade for each assignment
- Lowest grade for each assignment

There is another decision for you to make before you begin the gradebook design for your class. You must decide how important each of the assignment categories is in determining your students' overall performance. The actual number of points that you give for any assignment can vary, but you must ask yourself, "How much weight should each assignment category carry in determining a student's final grade?" In this way, you are able to better assess a student's performance and not have to worry about counting total points for a grading period before you are even sure about the number of assignments your students will be able to complete.

For this gradebook, you decide that homework will be worth 20% of the final grade, quizzes/exams account for 40%, and that projects will constitute 40%.

Now that you have determined all of the elements necessary for the gradebook, you will need to plan the layout of the spreadsheet and think about the formulas you will need to use.

Your gradebook will require formulas for determining homework, projects, and exam scores, the average class score, lowest and highest scores, weighted scores, and the final scores for the grading period with the letter grade the student earned.

Optional Online Tutorials

If spreadsheets are entirely new to you, you might also benefit from working through the Learning Roadmap for *Excel* 2011: http://bit.ly/9oQZQp. This series of videos and text tutorials covers the basics and progresses through more advanced functions. Spreadsheets can be very useful tools in math and science classes, as well as for any type of data you want your students to compare and/or calculate.

You might also locate and use some templates to help you get started with budgets, lists, reports, and other types of spreadsheets.

Beginning Your Spreadsheet

Opening Excel for Mac 2011

Click the *Excel* icon in your Dock or open your Application folder and navigate to *Excel*, double-clicking the icon to start the program.

The first step, as you always remind your students, is to save your newly opened workbook on a flash drive, class network drive or on your hard drive (just make sure that you know where you can locate it at a future time). If you do not name your workbook, *Excel* will save it with the title, Book1.

Save As

1. Click **File>Save As** in the *Excel* menu bar. You now need to choose the file format for the saved file.

2. Once you have decided on the format in which to save your workbook, make sure that you are saving it in the right location. If you do not choose a location, your workbook would be saved with the title of Book1 in the Documents directory on the hard drive of the computer you are currently using. As you want to be able to easily locate this in the future, you decide the drive, folder and subfolder in which to save the Gradebook spreadsheet.

3. Click your chosen file format and hit enter. The **Save As** window becomes available.

4. Navigate to the root folder where you want to save your file.

5. Create a new folder by clicking on the New Folder button.

6. Name the New Folder, **Spreadsheet Exercises**. You can save all of your spreadsheet exercises from this book in your folder.

7. Click the **File name** box, and type **YourLastName gradebook**.

8. Click [Save] in the lower right hand corner.

Now you can save frequently by clicking the save icon 🖫 on the worksheet menu bar (or use the keyboard shortcut Apple Command + S) and know exactly where your workbook is located. Also note that the title of your workbook **YourLastName gradebook** is now displayed in the *Excel* title bar.

Although there is more than one way that a gradebook may be designed, this gradebook will feature the student names in the rows with the assignments, scores, and grades in the columns. With your workbook open, you begin your class gradebook.

Entering Labels

1. Click cell **A1** and enter **Student Names**. As you type, note that the entry appears both in the formula bar and in the active cell (**A1**). When you are finished, lock in the entry by pressing **Enter**.

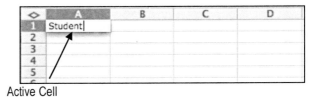

Active Cell

2. To make the cell wide enough to view the full text, put your cursor at the intersection of columns A and B. Hold down the left mouse button as you drag the column to the desired width. (You can also double-click the same intersection and the width will adjust to the student names text).

3. Continue by entering labels for the assignments (homework – HW, projects – P, and Exam – E) labels.

4. Click cell **A2** and enter **Possible Points**, to reflect the total number of points for each of the assignments. Include the total point values for each of the assignments in the corresponding columns.

5. Enter the student names on each of the rows below the **Possible Points** row, along with the values for their assignments. Your spreadsheet will contain the following values:

	A	B	C	D	E	F	G	H	I	J	K	L	M
1	Student Names	HW-1	HW-2	HW-3	Homework	P-1	P-2	Projects	E1	E2	Exams	Final	Score
2	Possible Points	15	12	17		25	35		55	25			
3	Smith, John	7	8	11		18	28		50	20			
4	Engle, Mary	10	7	15		20	21		52	24			
5	Garcia, Jose	13	10	10		23	31		53	22			
6	Little, Ian	5	5	5		15	15		25	13			
7	Jones, Sally	15	12	17		25	34		45	20			
8	Sully, Todd	11	6	9		18	21		49	21			
9	Average Scores												
10	Highest Scores												
11	Lowest Scores												

If you make an error, cell contents are edited by first selecting the cell and making corrections or by selecting the cell and clicking in the formula bar to make your changes. When the correct data have been entered, click the enter key on the keyboard.

Now that you have entered the student names and assignments, it's time to determine their grades. Remember, by weighting the scores, you are able to give any number of assignments and to allocate any number of points to an assignment. Although your imaginary students have three homework assignments and only two projects and exams, the homework will only be worth up to 20% of their final class grade.

Entering Formulas in a Spreadsheet

Once the scores are filled in for each student, you will enter the formulas to determine your students' and the total class performance in each of the assignment. *Excel* uses the following arithmetic operators and comparison operators

Arithmetic Operators		Comparison Operators	
Addition	+ (plus sign)	Equals	=
Subtraction	- (minus sign)	Greater than	>
Multiplication	* (asterisk)	Less than	<
Division	/ (forward slash)	Greater than or equal to	>=
Exponentiation	^ (caret)	Less than or equal to	<=
		Not equal to	<>

When determining formulas for use in *Excel*, be aware that the following **order of operations** will be performed:

Parenthesis
Exponentiation
Multiplication
Division
Addition
Subtraction

> Memorizing this phrase may help your students to remember the order of operations:
> **P**lease
> **E**xcuse
> **M**y **D**ear
> **A**unt **S**ally

You will use formulas, functions, and the fill handle to copy formulas to other cells. First, you will learn how to use the **SUM** function to add a range of cells.

Using the SUM Function to Total Scores

In Row 2, you have the total possible points for each of the assignments. You will want *Excel* to automatically calculate the totals for each of the assignments. The formula, therefore, will calculate new totals should you decide to change or add assignments in a new class, for instance.

1. Select cell E2 and start with the = sign (indicates you want *Excel* to perform a calculation). Enter **=SUM**
2. Enter an opening parenthesis after the word SUM to tell *Excel* you are using a function, **=SUM(**
3. Click cell **B2** and drag your mouse across cells **B2** to **D2** ending with a closing parenthesis.
4. Then click the enter key or checkmark at the end of the formula bar. The formula will look like this: **=SUM(B2:D2)**

(The colon between the cells indicates a range of cells that are included in the calculation. The parentheses indicate this is an *Excel* function. You are telling *Excel* to calculate the sum (addition) of the values in cells **B2**, **C2**, and **D2**.)

You should see the total of 44 in cell **E2**.

◇	A	B	C	D	E	F	G	H	I	J	K	L	M
1	Student Names	HW-1	HW-2	HW-3	Homework	P-1	P-2	Projects	E1	E2	Exams	Final	Score
2	Possible Points	15	12	17	=sum(B2:D2)		35		55	25			
3	Smith, John	7	8	11		18	28		50	20			
4	Engle, Mary	10	7	15		20	21		52	24			
5	Garcia, Jose	13	10	10		23	31		53	22			
6	Little, Ian	5	5	5		15	15		25	13			
7	Jones, Sally	15	12	17		25	34		45	20			
8	Sully, Todd	11	6	9		18	21		49	21			
9	Average Scores												
10	Highest Scores												
11	Lowest Scores												

Do the same procedure for each of the other assignments, the **Projects** and **Exams**. You should have a total for each of the assignments in row 2.

Writing a Formula to Calculate Homework Score

You will write a formula to calculate the number of points for the homework assignments divided by the total points for the assignment. The total homework assignment points possible are calculated in cell **E3** for John Smith, which will include the sum of **B3**, **C3**, and **D3**. The sum function provides an easy way to add up these cells, adding the range of cells, from **B3** to **D3**, indicated in *Excel* by the colon (**B3:D3**).

1. Select cell **E3** (this is where you will type your formula). You want *Excel* to add each of the possible homework points and then divide by the total number of points possible (the calculation you have already done in cell E2), so your final formula will be: =SUM(B3:D3)/$E$2

(The reason for including the dollar signs is to indicate you want the calculation to ALWAYS use the value in cell **E2**, since you will be copying this formula down the column.)

2. To enter the formula, first type an equal sign = (typing an equal sign tells *Excel* that you are about to enter a formula) and then **SUM** (since you want to use the SUM function) and an opening parenthesis =SUM(

3. Instead of typing in each of the cell letters, you will use the **pointing** technique and watch as *Excel* inserts that cell reference in the formula. Point to cell **B3**. You point by clicking in the **B3** cell. Once you click **B3**, you will notice that the formula bar now shows =SUM(B3

4. Continue dragging your mouse across the cells you want to include in the sum (**B3:D3**)

5. Next you need to tell *Excel* you want to divide by the total number of points for the homework category. The divide symbol is the forward slash: /

Since you will always want to divide by the value in cell E2, you will use an absolute cell reference for the row and column, putting dollar signs in front of each to indicate this: **$E$2**

Your final formula in cell E3 should look like this: =SUM(B3:D3)/$E$2

(Remember, when entering formulas you can always point to the cell instead of entering the letters and numbers. The toggle for absolute cell reference on Windows is **F4** and for a Mac is Apple **Command + T**).

◇	A	B	C	D	E	F	G	H	I	J	K	L	M
1	Student Names	HW-1	HW-2	HW-3	Homework	P-1	P-2	Projects	E1	E2	Exams	Final	Score
2	Possible Points	15	12	17	44	25	35	60	55	25	80		
3	Smith, John	7	8	11	0.590909	18	28		50	20			
4	Engle, Mary	10	7	15		20	21		52	24			
5	Garcia, Jose	13	10	10		23	31		53	22			
6	Little, Ian	5	5	5		15	15		25	13			
7	Jones, Sally	15	12	17	1	25	34		45	20			
8	Sully, Todd	11	6	9		18	21		49	21			
9	Average Scores												
10	Highest Scores												
11	Lowest Scores												

The default number format for *Excel* is the General number format, so you see that John Smith earned a 0.590909. The amount of numbers you see will be dependent upon how wide your column is.

Using the Fill Handle to Copy Formulas

The formula you entered in cell **E3** will be the same for the rest of the students in the column. Since *Excel* uses by default a relative cell reference, it knows when you copy a formula to adjacent cells to adjust the cell references. The reason you used an absolute cell reference for the total homework possible points (cell **E2**) is to override the default relative cell reference setting. If this still does not make sense, it will as you continue to work with spreadsheets!

Next, you will be copying the formula you just entered in cell **E3** to the rest of the cells in the column.

1. Click cell **E3** and hold your mouse over the lower right corner. You will see a crosshatch symbol, which is called the **fill handle**.
2. Click your mouse on this fill handle and **carefully** drag the handle down the column until you reach the last student's name.
3. The formula you created in cell **E3** will be copied down the column, automatically calculating each student's score.

◇	A	B	C	D	E	F	G	H	I	J	K	L	M
1	Student Names	HW-1	HW-2	HW-3	Homework	P-1	P-2	Projects	E1	E2	Exams	Final	Score
2	Possible Points	15	12	17	44	25	35	60	55	25	80		
3	Smith, John	7	8	11	0.590909	18	28		50	20			
4	Engle, Mary	10	7	15	0.727273	20	21		52	24			
5	Garcia, Jose	13	10	10	0.75	23	31		53	22			
6	Little, Ian	5	5	5	0.340909	15	15		25	13			
7	Jones, Sally	15	12	17	1	25	34		45	20			
8	Sully, Todd	11	6	9	0.590909	18	21		49	21			
9	Average Scores												
10	Highest Scores												
11	Lowest Scores												

Now, go through the same steps and enter the formulas in John Smith's record for the **Projects** and **Exams** scores. Remember to use the dollar signs (to indicate an absolute cell reference) when you select the cell to divide by the total points for each of the remaining two assignments (cells **H2** and **K2**).

After you calculate John Smith's scores for the Projects and Exams, position your cursor on the fill handle and drag down to copy the formula to the other students.

Next, you will use *Excel* to help you weight the individual assignments, to create a final score.

Calculating the Final Weighted Score (Column L)

You will calculate the final scores using the weighted score for each of the assignments areas (homework @ 20%, projects @ 40%, and exams @ 40%). The weighted score in each of the areas will be calculated to determine the student's final grade.

1. Select cell **L3** (this is where you will type your formula). Notice **L3** shows in your formula bar in blue lettering and the **L3** cell in your spreadsheet is shown as active.
2. You will begin with an equal sign to indicate your want *Excel* to make calculations. You will use the **pointing** technique and watch as *Excel* inserts that cell reference in the formula.
3. Enter the following in the formula bar: **=E3*.2** (Homework is worth 20% or .2)
4. Type a plus sign **+** so that you can add the next two parts of the formula (projects and exams).
5. Click **H3** (the project score) and then enter ***.4** (projects were 40% of the total grade).
6. Type a plus sign **+** and click **K3**. Enter ***.4** (exams were 40%). The formula bar should look like this **=E3*.2+H3*.4+K3*.4**
7. Click **Enter**.
8. John Smith's score should be .77

Remember, since this formula will be the same for all of the rest of the students, you will simply need to select the fill handle at the lower right of cell **L3** and drag it down to copy to the rest of the students' final scores. Do this now.

Calculating the Letter Score (Column M)

John Smith's final score is a .77, but you still need to determine his letter grade for this grading period by using an **IF** formula. Your school's grading scale is as follows:

90% – 100% = A
80% - 90% = B
70% - 80% = C
60% - 70% = D
Under 60 = F

Your **IF** formula will tell *Excel* to give a student an A if he scores greater than or equal to .9, a B if he above or equal to .8, a C if he scores above or equal to .7, a D if he scores above or equal to .6, and an F for any other scores. Each IF statement stipulates a condition.

Type the following **IF** formula followed by the enter key in the cell **M3** to determine your student's letter grade:

=IF(L3>=.9,"A", IF(L3>=.8,"B", IF(L3>=.7,"C", IF(L3>=.6,"D","F"))))

The formula must be entered exactly with close attention to punctuation marks and spacing. Note that there are four closing parentheses **))))** to correspond with the four opening parentheses for the four IF statements.

If your formula does not work, check it carefully as quotation marks and commas must be correctly placed in the formula.

You have included all the formulas you need to determine a student's assignment area score, final score and letter grade. Only one student's grade has been calculated, but you will not have to enter new formulas for each student; you can use the fill handle and easily copy the formulas to adjacent cells. The cell references, called **relative cell references**, automatically reflect the row or column to which they have been copied. Use the fill handle now to copy the letter score formula to the cells below.

◇	A	B	C	D	E	F	G	H	I	J	K	L	M
1	Student Names	HW-1	HW-2	HW-3	Homework	P-1	P-2	Projects	E1	E2	Exams	Final	Score
2	Possible Points	15	12	17	44	25	35	60	55	25	80		
3	Smith, John	7	8	11	0.590909091	18	28	0.766666667	50	20	0.875	0.77484848	C
4	Engle, Mary	10	7	15	0.727272727	20	21	0.683333333	52	24	0.95	0.79878788	C
5	Garcia, Jose	13	10	10	0.75	23	31	0.9	53	22	0.9375	0.885	B
6	Little, Ian	5	5	5	0.340909091	15	15	0.5	25	13	0.475	0.45818182	F
7	Jones, Sally	15	12	17	1	25	34	0.983333333	45	20	0.8125	0.91833333	A
8	Sully, Todd	11	6	9	0.590909091	18	21	0.65	49	21	0.875	0.72818182	C
9	Average Scores												
10	Highest Scores												
11	Lowest Scores												

Using the ROUNDUP Function

One of the most important things you should remember about spreadsheets is that you must review them. It is very easy to accept their results as correct, but sometimes you make a mistake in a formula, copying cells, or any number of errors. That is why it's important to double-check your work.

Take a look at the letter scores in your spreadsheet. Mary Engle has a final letter score of C, but if her final number percentage were rounded up to the nearest two decimal points, for instance, she would receive a B. Mary would probably want to receive a B rather than a C. You will need to tell *Excel* that you want to round up the scores in the Final column so that your letter score calculations are accurate. Therefore, you will use the ROUNDUP function in *Excel* to do this, adjusting your formula in column L. Here's how you do this.

1. Click cell **L3** and change your formula to the following:
   =ROUNDUP(E3*0.2+H3*0.4+K3*0.4,2)
2. Click **Enter**.
3. You are telling *Excel* to round up the calculation of the weighted scores to two decimal points (the number 2 after the comma at the end of the formula).
4. Now, drag the fill handle to the bottom of the student final scores. See how Mary's score has changed from a C to a B?

Using the AVERAGE Function

1. Click cell **B10** to insert the **AVERAGE** function.
2. Type an equal sign.
3. Click the **Formulas** tab.
4. Click the Formula Builder icon.
5. Double-click the **AVERAGE** function.
6. The **Function Arguments** at the bottom of the Formula Builder includes numbers that directly adjoin B8; in this case, **B3:B9**. These are the cells that you want included.
7. Click **Enter**.

Now the formula bar displays the **AVERAGE** function and you see that the class average for the first homework assignment was 10.167. There were 15 points possible so as a teacher you may want to review that assignment to determine if it was clear enough to your students and if they had the prerequisite skills to complete it accurately. Use the Fill handle to copy the average formula in cells **C8** to **L8** to see the class average for each assignment area as well as the class average score.

You can also use functions to calculate the highest score on an assignment (**MAX**) and the lowest score on an assignment (**MIN**).

Using the MAX And MIN Functions

1. Click cell **B10** to insert the **MAX** function and type an equal sign.
2. Enter **=MAX(**
3. Point to the first cell you want to include and then drag across the other cells. In this case, it would be cells **B3:B8**.
4. Here is your function formula you will enter in **B10**: **=MAX(B3:B8)**
5. Click **Enter** or the checkmark and your average highest score will appear.
6. Select the fill handle and drag this formula across the row, through Row L.
7. Click cell **B11** and use the **MIN** function to determine the lowest scores for each assignment which will be **=MIN(B3:B8)**
8. Be sure to select the correct cells for the MIN calculation (**B3:B8**) and use the fill handle to copy them across your spreadsheet. Your spreadsheet should look like the following:

◇	A	B	C	D	E	F	G	H	I	J	K	L	M
1	Student Names	HW-1	HW-2	HW-3	Homework	P-1	P-2	Projects	E1	E2	Exams	Final	Score
2	Possible Points	15	12	17	44	25	35	60	55	25	80		
3	Smith, John	7	8	11	0.590909091	18	28	0.766666667	50	20	0.875	0.78	C
4	Engle, Mary	10	7	15	0.727272727	20	21	0.683333333	52	24	0.95	0.8	B
5	Garcia, Jose	13	10	10	0.75	23	31	0.9	53	22	0.9375	0.89	B
6	Little, Ian	5	5	5	0.340909091	15	15	0.5	25	13	0.475	0.46	F
7	Jones, Sally	15	12	17	1	25	34	0.983333333	45	20	0.8125	0.92	A
8	Sully, Todd	11	6	9	0.590909091	18	21	0.65	49	21	0.875	0.73	C
9	Average Scores	10.2	8	11.2	0.666666667	20	25	0.747222222	46	20	0.8208	0.7633	
10	Highest Scores	15	12	17	1	25	34	0.983333333	53	24	0.95	0.92	
11	Lowest Scores	5	5	5	0.340909091	15	15	0.5	25	13	0.475	0.46	

You have designed your spreadsheet, entered labels, values and formulas; now, you will learn how to use *Excel's* formatting features to format cells, and add color and graphics to your gradebook spreadsheet.

Formatting Spreadsheets

Excel features many formatting commands including the ability to add graphics, sounds, and comments as well as change fonts and use fill colors. You can also modify the size and alignment of cells, insert rows and columns, and add borders. Many of these tools are located on the mini toolbar which can be accessed by a right-click of your mouse. Of course, many more commands are available on the ribbon tabs.

With your Class Gradebook open, let's begin by naming the sheets in your workbook so that there will be a grade sheet for each of the high school English classes you teach. You will then place the students in alphabetical order by doing a **Sort**.

Renaming Worksheets

1. Right-click the **Sheet1** tab at the bottom of the window.
2. Click **Rename**. The Sheet1 tab is highlighted. Type **English 9** in the highlighted tab area. Hit Enter on the keyboard.
3. Right-click the **Sheet2** tab and rename it as **English 10**.

Now, you are ready to modify your gradebook by inserting rows, WordArt, a graphic and a comment. You will format cells so that the text is wrapped and vertically aligned. Your final gradebook will look similar to the one the next page.

Make sure that your English 9 worksheet is open by clicking the tab at the bottom of the *Excel* window. You will be using many of the tools available in *Excel* to make adjustments and enhancements to your workbook. You're already familiar with the Scrapbook and Font commands that are also available in *Word*. Other commands you'll find useful in *Excel* include commands for working with numbers and cells.

Formatting Numbers

Unless you format a cell to display numbers in a particular format, numbers will be displayed in a general format, which is *Excel's* default setting. For your gradebook scores, you will format the cells so that they display only 2 decimal places.

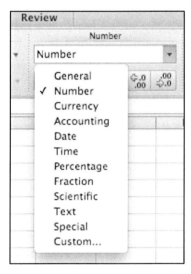

1. Select **Column E**.
2. Open the **Home** tab and click the drop down arrow under the **Number** section.
3. Select **Number**.
4. Click the Increase or Decrease decimal for the number of decimals you want to display.

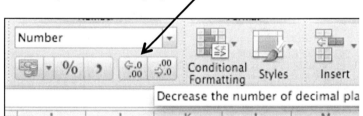

An example of how you might want to format your numbers and decimal points follows:

	A	B	C	D	E	F	G	H	I	J	K	L	M
1	Student Names	HW-1	HW-2	HW-3	Homework	P-1	P-2	Projects	E1	E2	Exams	Final	Score
2	Possible Points	15	12	17	44	25	35	60	55	25	80		
3	Smith, John	7	8	11	0.59	18	28	0.77	50	20	0.88	0.78	C
4	Engle, Mary	10	7	15	0.73	20	21	0.68	52	24	0.95	0.80	B
5	Garcia, Jose	13	10	10	0.75	23	31	0.90	53	22	0.94	0.89	B
6	Little, Ian	5	5	5	0.34	15	15	0.50	25	13	0.48	0.46	F
7	Jones, Sally	15	12	17	1.00	25	34	0.98	45	20	0.81	0.92	A
8	Sully, Todd	11	6	9	0.59	18	21	0.65	49	21	0.88	0.73	C
9	Average Scores	10.2	8	11.2	0.67	20	25	0.75	46	20	0.82	0.76	
10	Highest Scores	15	12	17	1.00	25	34	0.98	53	24	0.95	0.92	
11	Lowest Scores	5	5	5	0.34	15	15	0.50	25	13	0.48	0.46	

Now you will insert rows to your gradebook by using commands located on the *Excel* **main menu.**

Inserting Rows or Columns

To make your spreadsheet easier to read and more visually appealing, you will be inserting two rows – one above your student names and one below the total **Possible Points**.

1. With your cursor on any cell in Row 1, open the **Home** tab and select the **Insert** icon in the **Cells** section.

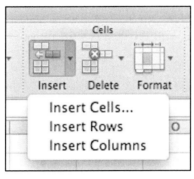

2. Click a cell in **Row 4** and insert a row the same way. Now you have a blank row between your column labels and your first row of students and scores.

Now that you have inserted two rows, you will be merging the cells in those rows, resizing them and filling them with color.

Merging Cells

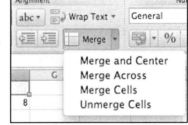

You will be merging the cells in the first and third row of your spreadsheet.

1. To merge the cells in **Row 1**, select cells **A1** to **M1**.
2. Open the **Home** tab and select the **Merge** icon in the Alignment section.
3. Select **Merge and Center.**
4. Merge **Row 4** in the same way.

You now have an area for your class banner (**Row 1**), but it is too narrow for a banner of any size. You want to insert a **WordArt** title and a graphic for your English 9 and will need more space.

Resizing Rows

1. Place your cursor on the intersection line between Row 1 and 2 (the cursor becomes a solid cross).

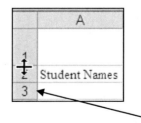

Drag to adjust row height.

2. Hold down the left mouse button and drag the boundary below the row heading until the row is the height you want.

You can easily readjust your row size if it isn't large enough once you insert your WordArt title and graphic. You should also adjust your columns so there is no wasted room on the spreadsheet.

Inserting WordArt and Other Graphics

1. On the **Insert** menu, click **WordArt**.
2. Type English 9.
3. Click your English 9 WordArt graphic, hold down the left mouse button, and drag it to **Row 1**. (If your row is not large enough, adjust either the WordArt graphic or the row).
4. On the **Standard** toolbar, click **Show or hide the Media Browser**.
5. Click **Clip Art** and then on the pop-up menu, select an image. (Or add an image of your own to the Personal section.)
6. Drag the image and place it in Row 1 next to your class title. (You may need to resize it.)

Now that you have a class banner, you can customize your spreadsheet even more by filling cells with color.

Filling Cells with Color

1. Click **Row 1**.
2. Open the **Home** tab and select the **Fill** color.
3. Select your color from the drop down choices.

Use the **Fill Color** feature in other places in your class spreadsheet to create boundaries between categories or make certain rows or columns more visible. You can also change the font of any cell text by selecting the cell(s) and then selecting the font type and size.

Since the column labels on this spreadsheet are fairly long (homework) and the contents of the cells in the assignment rows short (2 - 3 decimal places would be sufficient), change the orientation of Row 2 so that the cell contents are at a 90-degree angle.

Cell Alignment and Orientation

1. Select **Row 2**.
2. Open the **Home** tab and select the **Orientation** icon in the **Alignment** section.

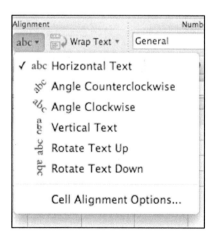

3. Select **Rotate Text Up**.

Sorting Ascending Order

Your class gradebook is looking better, but you notice that student names are not listed alphabetically. *Excel* allows you to sort cells in ascending (A-Z alphabetic or 1-10 numeric) or descending (Z-A or 10-1) order.

1. Select the student names (A4 – A9) and the corresponding data (the entire record).
2. On the **Data** tab under the **Sort & Filter** section click the **Sort** icon.
3. Click the **Sort A-Z** on the worksheet menu bar.
4. Select **Ascending.**

Another *Excel* feature that you will find extremely useful as a teacher is the ability to insert comments into your spreadsheet. In the gradebook spreadsheet, for example, you might want to add a comment in a cell containing a student's score to remember that he/she is planning to resubmit a revised assignment.

Inserting Comments

1. Click the cell **J9** (the second test score for John Smith).
2. On the **Review** tab, under **Comments**, click **New.**
3. Enter **John can retake this test on 3/30.**
4. When you have finished typing the text, click outside the comment box.
5. A red triangle appears on the box and the comment becomes visible when you run your cursor over it.
6. To remove a comment, right-click the cell and click **Delete Comment.**

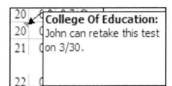

Your final spreadsheet should look similar to the one below:

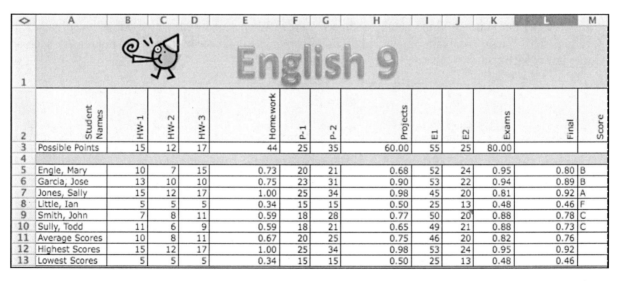

	A	B	C	D	E	F	G	H	I	J	K	L	M
2	Student Names	HW-1	HW-2	HW-3	Homework	P-1	P-2	Projects	E1	E2	Exams	Final	Score
3	Possible Points	15	12	17	44	25	35	60.00	55	25	80.00		
4													
5	Engle, Mary	10	7	15	0.73	20	21	0.68	52	24	0.95	0.80	B
6	Garcia, Jose	13	10	10	0.75	23	31	0.90	53	22	0.94	0.89	B
7	Jones, Sally	15	12	17	1.00	25	34	0.98	45	20	0.81	0.92	A
8	Little, Ian	5	5	5	0.34	15	15	0.50	25	13	0.48	0.46	F
9	Smith, John	7	8	11	0.59	18	28	0.77	50	20	0.88	0.78	C
10	Sully, Todd	11	6	9	0.59	18	21	0.65	49	21	0.88	0.73	C
11	Average Scores	10	8	11	0.67	20	25	0.75	46	20	0.82	0.76	
12	Highest Scores	15	12	17	1.00	25	34	0.98	53	24	0.95	0.92	
13	Lowest Scores	5	5	5	0.34	15	15	0.50	25	13	0.48	0.46	

Creating Charts

A very powerful feature of *Excel* is the ability to create **charts**, which are visual representations of your data. A chart, also referred to as a **graph**, is linked to the worksheet data and is updated automatically when you change the worksheet data. A chart can enhance and simplify your students' understanding of the data. Students are able to see comparisons, patterns, and trends in data.

Using the Chart Wizard in *Excel* makes it easy to construct pie, column, bar, and line charts. Common chart elements include the following:

Title – overall description of the data charted
Labels – specific descriptions of data
Series – set of related data placed in the chart
Legend – contains the labels and identifies the data series

In determining which kind of chart to use to plot your worksheet data, keep in mind that a pie chart can include only one series of data. Each slice of the pie represents only one value from a series. If you were to design a pie chart to give your students a visual representation of the composition of their final grade in your class, it would look like the chart below.

The **pie chart** visually emphasizes the importance of each of the English 9 assignment areas.

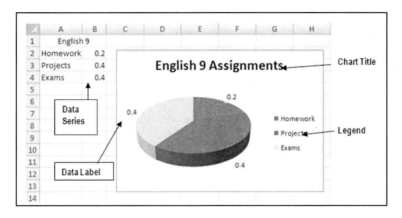

A **bar chart** is useful in visually comparing the differences between values since it can include several series of data. For example, you might use a bar chart to plot the high and low homework scores from your gradebook.

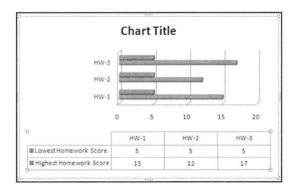

In this chart, two series of data are represented: high and low class homework scores.

Excel can also create a bar chart with vertical bars, which is called a **column chart**. A column chart can include more than one series of data and is useful in comparing differences.

A **line chart** can contain more than one series of data with each line of the chart representing a series. The values in the series are represented by points on a line. An examination of your class performance line chart shows you that your students perform better on exams and in their project activities than on the homework assignments.

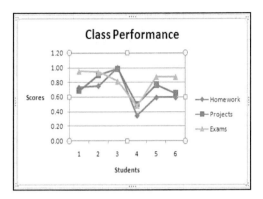

In the rest of this section, you will learn how to create charts from the data in your English 9 gradebook using *Excel's* chart tools. You will need your gradebook open to complete the following practice exercise.

Creating a Pie Chart

1. With your mouse, select the cell containing the data label HW-1. Then, while holding down the **Ctrl key, individually** click cells containing the data labels HW–2 and HW–3.
2. Keep holding down the **Ctrl key**, and click **individually** in each of the data series cells containing the highest homework scores (which were also the total points available for each assignment).
3. On the **Charts** tab select **Pie**.

Data Labels

	Student Names	HW-1	HW-2	HW-3
2				
3	Possible Points	15	12	17
4				
5	Engle, Mary	10	7	15
6	Garcia, Jose	13	10	10
7	Jones, Sally	15	12	17
8	Little, Ian	5	5	5
9	Smith, John	7	8	11
10	Sully, Todd	11	6	9
11	Average Scores	10	8	11
12	Highest Scores	15	12	17

Data Series

As you run your cursor over each pie chart, a text box explains the chart and describes its use. If your pie chart is not correct, check your data range; also, make sure that you click each of the cells individually.

1. Click **Chart Layout>Chart Title** to title your chart.
2. Title your pie chart **Highest Homework Scores**, placing the title at the top.

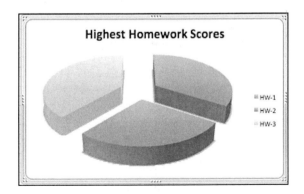

You are able to move your chart by clicking in the chart, holding down your left mouse button and dragging it to a desired location. To size the chart, grab the handles and move your mouse toward the center of the graph (reduce) or away from the center (enlarge). By right-clicking in the chart area, you can access other commands, such as **cut**, **copy**, and **chart options**. To delete the chart, select the chart by clicking in the chart area, and hitting the **delete** key on your keyboard. Now, you will use *Excel's* Chart tools to create a bar chart.

Creating a Bar Chart

1. Hold down the **Ctrl Key** while you select Data Labels – Homework, Projects, and Exams.

2. Keep holding down the **Ctrl key** select the **Data Series – Class average scores** for Homework (.67), Projects (.75) and Exams (.82).

3. Go through the same steps as above, only this time select bar chart.

4. Choose an appropriate bar chart.

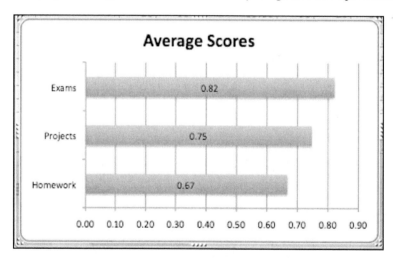

Homework	P-1	P-2	Projects	E1	E2	Exam
44	25	35	60.00	55	25	80.00
0.73	20	21	0.68	52	24	0.95
0.75	23	31	0.90	53	22	0.94
1.00	25	34	0.98	45	20	0.81
0.34	15	15	0.50	25	13	0.48
0.59	18	28	0.77	50	20	0.88
0.59	18	21	0.65	49	21	0.88
0.67	20	25	0.75	46	20	0.82

Data Labels Assignment Areas

Data Series Assignment Averages

Designing your chart layout and formatting it is easily accomplished using the Chart tools that are available when your chart is selected.

Try customizing your chart, giving it different colors and changing the layout by selecting the chart and having the Design tab selected.

Charts can provide compelling arguments by their design and enable quick visualization of data. Following is a chart representing the data selected from your gradebook spreadsheet:

Check out the other options available for your chart layout such as data labels, legends and gridlines in the Formatting Palette.

Creating a Line Chart

1. Hold down the **Ctrl Key.**

2. Select the **Data Labels – Homework, Projects** and **Exams** (be certain no additional cells are selected).

3. Keep holding down the **Ctrl Key** and select the **Data Series – Ian Little's final score** in Homework **(.34)**, Projects **(.50)** and Exams **(.48)**.

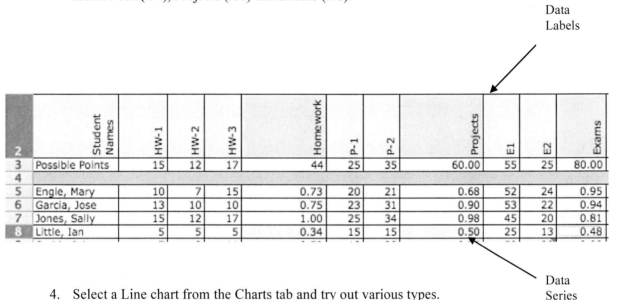

4. Select a Line chart from the Charts tab and try out various types.

5. Make a chart title and call it **Ian Little's Scores.**

6. Provide appropriate names for the horizontal and vertical axes.

7. Provide formatting of your choice.

Take some time to modify the three charts you created and become familiar with the design, formatting, and layout options available for charts. Change the data within your spreadsheet and view how those data change on the corresponding chart.

Now that you have completed your spreadsheet, create a header so that when you print it, pertinent information will be at the top of the spreadsheet.

Creating a Header

1. On the **Layout** tab, select **Header & Footer** in the Page Setup section.
2. Click **Customize Header** and another dialog box will open, allowing you to format it the way you want it to look.
3. Headers and footers in a spreadsheet will only show up when they are printed.

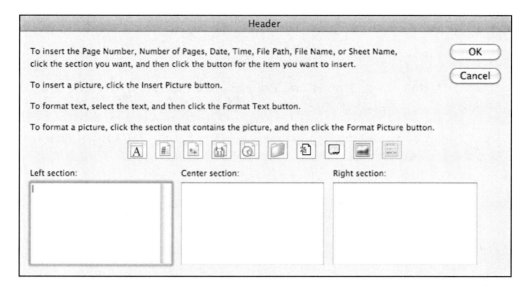

Printing

If your worksheet and charts are too large to print on a single page, you will need to adjust the page setup before printing. *Excel* also provides options for you to print one or all of the worksheets in a workbook or just a selected area of a worksheet. A recommended practice is to always preview before printing.

Printing Worksheets

1. Click **File>Page Setup** in the *Excel* main menu to decide how you want your spreadsheet to look once it is printer. (You will see that you have many options, so play around with them and select **Print Preview** to see how it will look before printing.)

2. You can also move page breaks in your spreadsheet, which are designated by dotted lines in the normal view. Simply click and drag these dotted lines to move the page breaks.

If your worksheet contains too many columns of data, you can change the page orientation to landscape.

You then need to decide the number of copies to print, what you want to print and the print range. You can print the entire workbook, a selected area (one you have highlighted on the spreadsheet, or only the active sheet. Always remind your students to use print preview and select only the page(s) or area(s) that they want to print.

Summary

In this technology tools section of the manual you have become familiar with some of the features of *Excel for Mac 2011* that you can use to improve teaching, productivity, and student engagement. The gradebook you completed can be used as an artifact for ISTE NETS-T Standard 2.

Please return to page 95 and complete the spreadsheet exercises. In Exercise 1, you will learn how to use absolute cell references; Exercise 2 helps you to discover other useful spreadsheet features. In Exercise 3, you will learn how to design interactive learning spreadsheets to help reinforce curricular concepts and skills. More exercises are provided to help you discover ideas for using the spreadsheet as a curricular tool.

✓ Begin by opening Microsoft *PowerPoint for Mac 2011* by either clicking the icon on your dock or opening your Applications folder and double-clicking the program icon.

✓ Select a White background. You can always change this later.

✓ The default title is **Presentation1** so you will want to save your presentation in an appropriate location and title it **YourLastName Cyber Dangers.**

Save As

✓ Click, **File>Save As** from your *PowerPoint* main menu bar and name/save your file in the location of your choice or as directed by your instructor.

✓ You can decide what file format to save it in. (Default file extension is pptx).

While **Normal View** is used in creating the presentation, **Slide Sorter View** is used to determine the final arrangement of the slides in the presentation. In this view, you are able to easily reorder slides. Clicking the **Slide Show View** displays your slides as they would actually be displayed for your audience.

As with the other new *Office for Mac 2011* applications, PowerPoint includes a **Ribbon** with tabs: Home, Themes, Tables, Charts, SmartArt, Transitions, Animations, Slide Show, and Review.

View	Insert	Format	Arrange
✓ Normal			⌘1
Slide Sorter			⌘2
Notes Page			⌘3
Presenter View			⌥↵
Slide Show			⇧⌘↵
Master			▶
✓ Ribbon			⌥⌘R
Toolbars			▶
Message Bar			
Media Browser			^⌘M
Toolbox			
⭐ Custom Animation			
🖼 Scrapbook			
📖 Reference Tools			
🔧 Compatibility Report			
Header and Footer...			
Comments			
Ruler			
Guides			▶
Zoom			▶

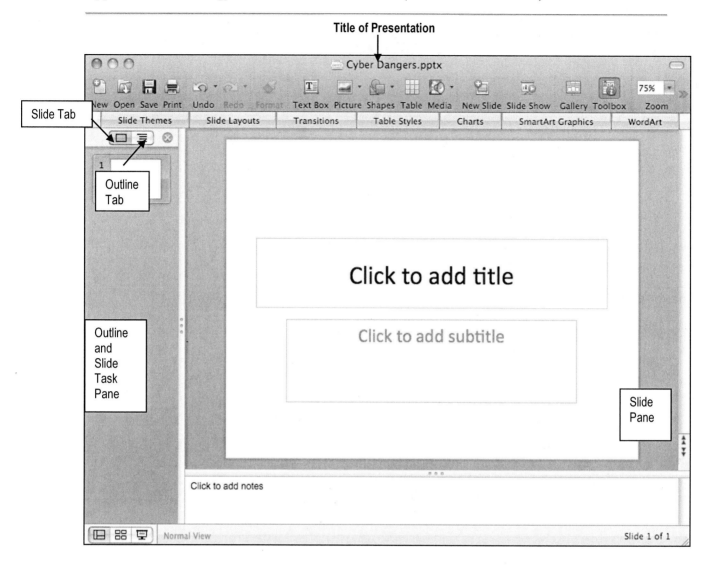

The Title Slide

Notice that your opening screen presents the first slide with layout for providing a title and subtitle. Although you could change the layout, starting a slide show with a title slide is customary.

1. Click in the area **Click to add title** and enter the title of your presentation: **Cyber Dangers**
2. Click in the **subtitle** textbox and enter **YourName** and **School**

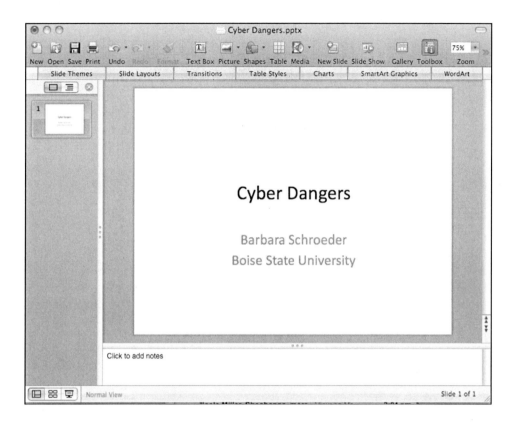

Adding New Slides

1. Click the **New Slide** icon located in the Home tab.
2. To change the layout of the slide, click the icon to the upper right of the **New Slide** icon.

3. Type the title and bulleted list as shown in the next slide image. You can choose the bullet style you wish for the slide.

Slide 2 – Normal View

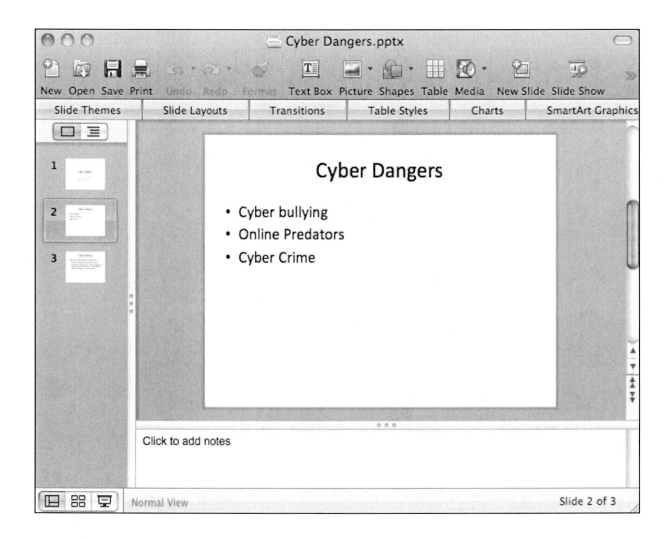

Continue adding new title and content slides for each of the next five slides with the following information on each slide:

Slide 3 – Normal View

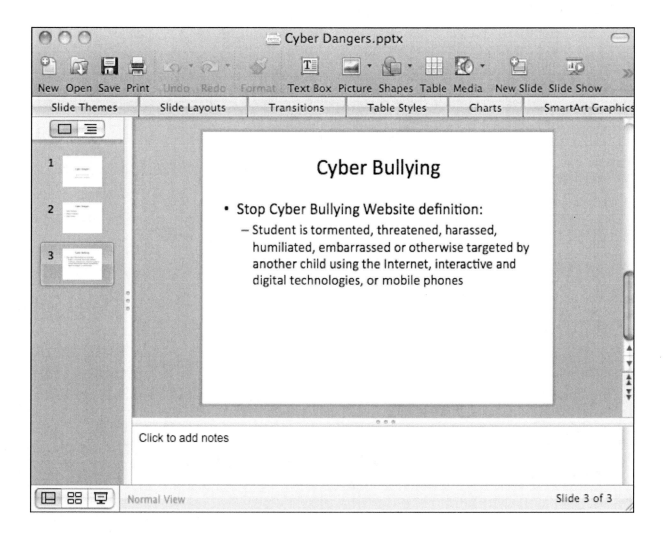

Slide 4 – Normal View

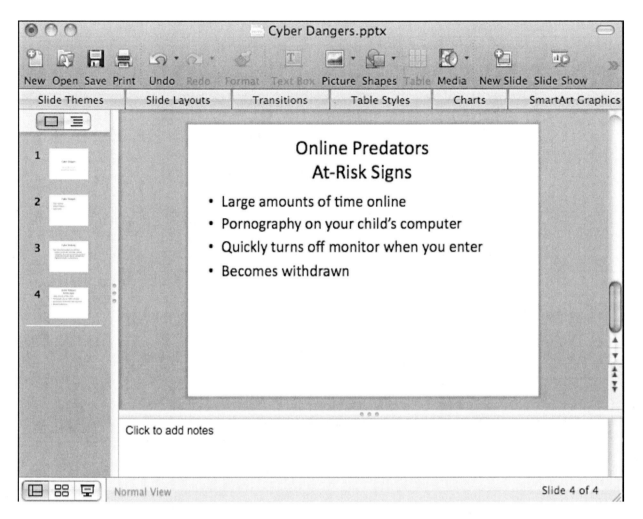

Slide 5 – Normal View

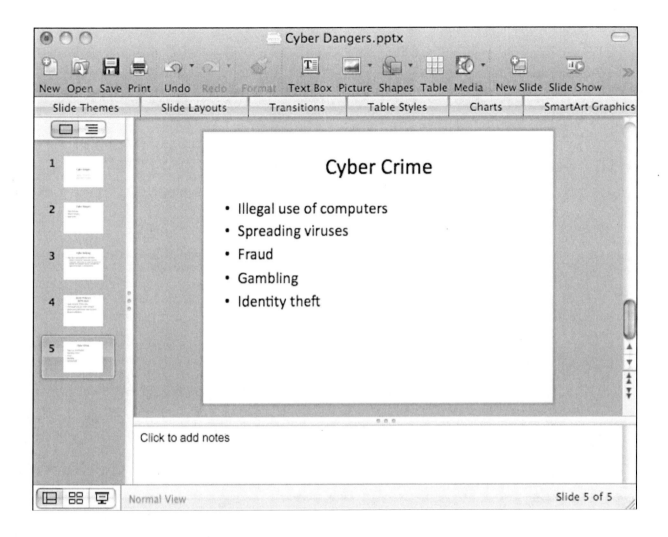

Slide 6 – Normal View

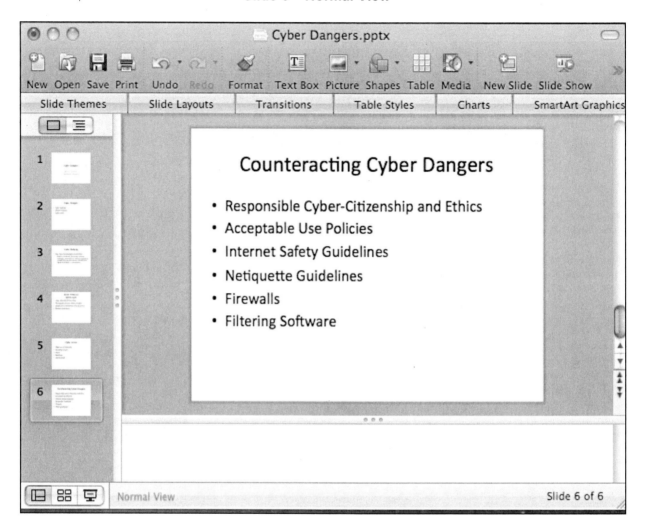

Slide 7 – Normal View

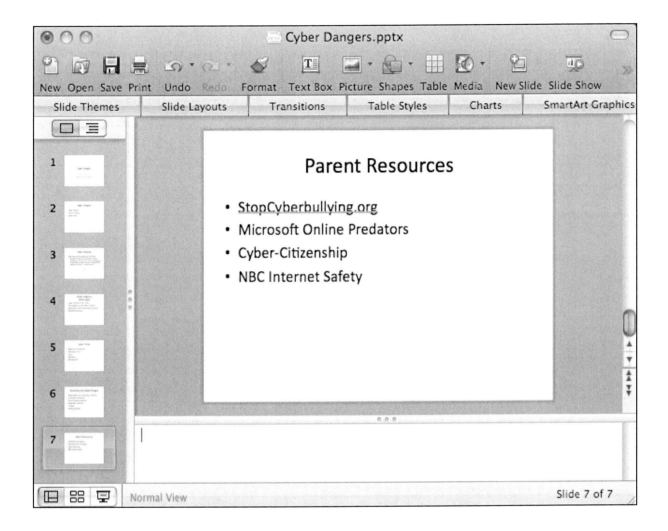

You now have a 7 slides slide show and are ready to add other elements such as graphics, background, fonts, and hyperlinks. Click the **Slide Sorter** icon located at the bottom of the screen to view all 7 slides and to easily rearrange your presentation.

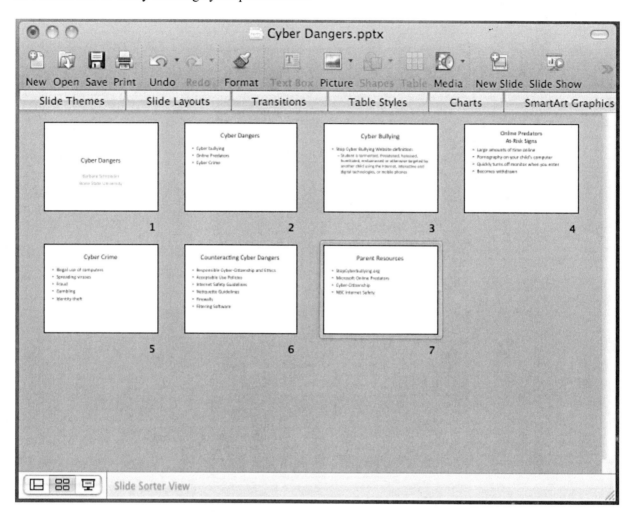

Inserting Graphics from Clip Art

1. In **Normal** view, select Slide 2.

2. On the **Home** tab, select the Insert **Image** icon.

3. Select the **Clip Art Gallery** and search for images, clipart, or images on your computer.

4. Drag the image you want to appear on your slide directly to the slide.

Inserting Graphics from Other Sources

Inserting graphics you have saved is also easily accomplished. Navigate to the Textbook Data Files link on our companion website (http://dats.boisestate.edu) to locate the required files or locate and save an image file of your choosing to a location on your computer.

Tip: it's very handy to save an image to your desktop so you can easily drag and drop it right on your slide. You will see a little green + icon, indicating the image is being added.

1. In **Normal** view, select Slide 3.

2. Locate an image using Google image search (http://images.google.com), click to navigate to the online location of the image, and drag it to your desktop. (Do an Advanced Search and make sure you are selecting an image labeled for reuse!)

3. Drag the image to your slide. (You may need to decrease the size of the image, so click the image and drag the handles toward the center. If you want to maintain the aspect ratio of the image adjust the size holding down your Shift key at the same time you are using the image resizing handles.)

4. Following is a example of what your slide might look like:

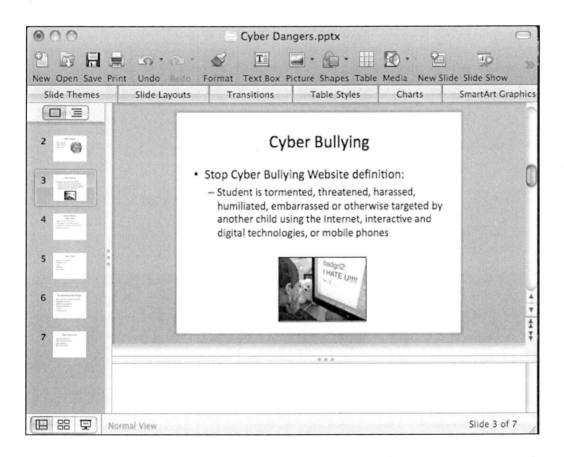

Applying Themes and Backgrounds

Applying a theme to your Cyber Dangers presentation is easy with plenty of pre-existing themes readily available in *PowerPoint for Mac 2011.* (Make sure you don't use a theme that will distract the viewers from your message, however. Since you are using images to represent your main concepts, you will want to keep the design simple and straightforward.)

1. In **Normal** view, select any slide.

2. Click the **Themes** tab to access themes on slide menu bar.

3. You will see various themes, which you can scroll through using the arrow on the right.

4. To apply the theme, click the thumbnail.

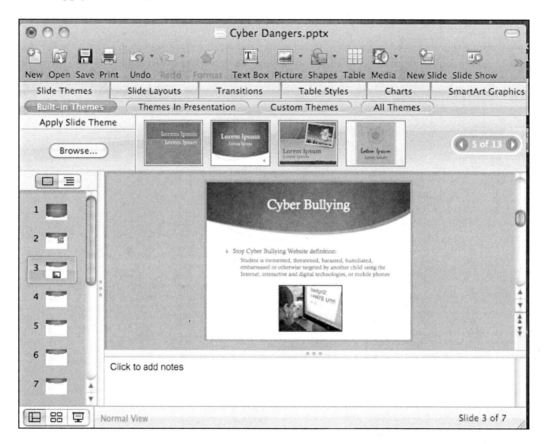

Take a few minutes to try some of the themes offered in *PowerPoint for Mac 2011* and a color, background and font change to determine your preferred presentation design.

Next, you will learn how to add movement to your slide show. Slide transitions refer to movement from one slide to the next while animation refers to the movement of the elements on the slide.

Applying Animations to Text and Objects

A variety of animations is available in *PowerPoint for Mac 2011* that can be quickly applied to either single slides or to the entire presentation. You can animate text and objects in your presentation to give them visual effects, including entrances, exits, changes in size or color, and even movement. You can use any animation effect by itself or combine multiple effects together. **Note**: Transitions are another way to add visual effects when moving from one slide to another in a slide show.

1. Click the part of your slide you want to animate (such as text or image).
2. Select the **Animation** tab.
3. Add the effect you want from the list of choices. Experiment with all of the options!
4. Click the little play button at the left of the **Animation** tab to view how your animation will look.

If you are animating text, note that you can have text animations occur all at once or as one object. Click the **Reorder** icon to customize how you want animations and the timing.

Applying Transitions

Transitions can help your viewer better understand any transitions in content and create a sense of animation to your slideshow. However, they can also be distracting.

Here's how you apply transitions in *PowerPoint for Mac 2011:*

1. On the **Transitions** tab select the transition you want.
2. You can apply transitions to all slides or selected slides.
3. View how your transitions look by clicking the **Play** button in the left side of the **Transitions** tab.

Inserting Sound and Video

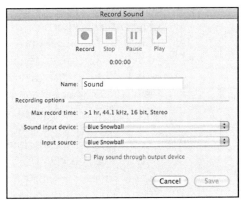

You are also able to insert sounds and video into your presentations. These can be sound clips you have saved to your computer or you can record directly in *PowerPoint*. The ability to record in each slide enables you to record your presentations and make them available to students/parents who were not able to attend your class or presentation. If you decide to make a presentation available online, you should definitely write your narration and record it.

Tip: Use the **Notes** feature in each slide to write your narration. It is much easier to record your narration this way, will save time, and will sound much more professional. Additionally, you can save your *PowerPoint* file as a PDF including the notes, for viewers who might be hearing impaired.

To record your voice, make sure you have a microphone available and select the slide in which you would like to add a recording.

1. In the navigation pane, click the slide you want to add sound to.
2. On the **Home** tab, under **Insert**, click **Media**, and then click **Record Audio**.
3. To start recording, click **Record Audio**.
4. When you are finished, click **Stop**.
5. To listen to the sound you just recorded, click **Play**.
6. In the **Name** box, type a name for the sound, and then click **Save**.
7. An audio icon appears on the slide.
8. For more help with audio, click the **Help** button on PowerPoint and do a search for "record." Select "Set the play options for audio."

Uploading a Narrated PowerPoint to Online Services

There are many free online tools that will enable you to upload a narrated PowerPoint for parents and other to view. One excellent tools is AuthorStream: http://www.authorstream.com. Another is SlideBoom: http://www.slideboom.com.

You can also upload presentations to YouTube (http://youtube.com) through AuthorStream. Your instructor might ask you to narrate a presentation, upload it to an online service and embed it on your Technology Teaching Portfolio. Always be aware and think of ways you can increase communication and collaboration with your students, parents, and community by using new and freely-available online tools.

Creating Hyperlinks Within a Presentation

In **Normal** view, select Slide 2, **Cyber Dangers**, which lists the 3 dangers to be explored in the presentation. You will be using slide 2 as a table of contents, linking the 3 dangers to the individual slides that discuss each of them.

1. Select (highlight) the word that will be used as a link. For this slide, **Cyber bullying**, will be the link. Parents need only click Cyber bullying and be taken to the slide that defines the term.
2. With the word **Cyber bullying** selected, click the Insert hyperlink icon on the **Home** tab (shortcut is **Apple Command + K**).
3. The **Insert Hyperlink** window opens.
4. Click the **Document** tab.
5. Click the **Locate** button next to Anchor.
6. Click the little triangle next to Slide Titles that will display the individual titles of the slides.
7. Select the Cyber bullying slide and click **OK**.
8. You will return to the **Insert Hyperlink** window to verify that the slide you have selected is correct. If it is, click **OK**.
9. You will see the underline hyperlink, but when you click it in **Normal** view, it won't go anywhere. To view it as a hyperlink (it will go to the slide), you will need to select **Slide Show** View.
10. Test it now in **Slide Show** view.
11. Link the other two dangers to the appropriate slides and check to see if they work.

When you return to **Slide Show** view and click the hyperlinks, you discover that you now need a link to come back to Slide 2. Let's insert an **Action Button**, which works as a navigational hyperlink.

Inserting Action Buttons (Navigation Buttons)

As you want to be able to go back to Slide 2, which lists the 3 main presentation topics, you will add navigational action buttons to the three slides that you hyperlinked to earlier.

1. Select **Slide 3**, Cyber bullying, for the first slide to have an action button.
2. On the **Home** tab, click the **Insert Shapes** icon and select **Action Buttons**.
3. Select Back Arrow Action Button.
4. Place your mouse on the slide and you will notice a crosshatch appears. This allows you to draw the **Action Button** right on your slide.
5. Drag it and draw the button. You can move it like an image and resize it, too.

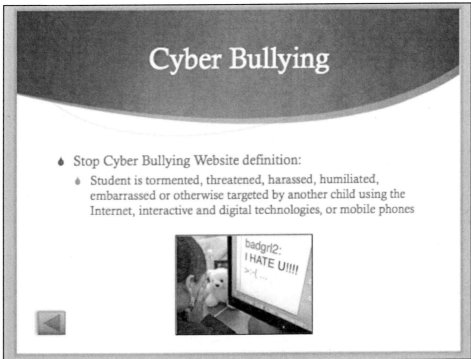

6. After you draw the button, the **Action Settings** dialog box appears. Since you will be copying and pasting this button to other slides, you will want the button to go to a specific slide, slide number two.

7.   Under **Hyperlink to**, select **Slide**. You will be presented with a choice of options.

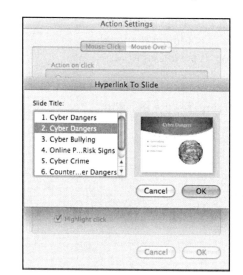

8.   Select **Cyber Dangers** (Slide 2) and click **OK**.

9.   The Action Settings dialog box will appear again, confirming that you want the Action Button to link to Slide 2. Click **OK**.

As with your previous hyperlink, you will need to click the **Slide Show** view to see that the Previous Action Button will take you back to Slide 2.

Now that you have an action button that takes you to Slide 2, you can copy and paste that button on any slide, and once clicked will go to Slide 2.

10.   Copy and paste the action button on slides 4 and 5 so that it is easy to return to the main contents slide (Slide 2).

Inserting More Hyperlinks Within the Presentation

As you view your presentation, you determine that it would be beneficial for parents to be able to link to the **Parent Resources** slide when viewing any of the cyber dangers. You already know how to hyperlink within a presentation, but this time, you will make a textbox the hyperlink.

1.   Select Slide 3, **Cyber bullying**.
2.   Insert a text box (use a small font) directing parents to the resources
3.   Place it at the bottom of the slide.
4.   Select it and insert a hyperlink to the last slide, **Parent Resources**.
5.   Now, you can copy and paste the text box to Slides 4 and 5 so parents can easily access the resources.
6.   Create a **Back action button** on Slide 7 to take viewers to previously viewed slide.
7.   Create a link on Slide 2 to go to Slide 6 and create a link on Slide 6 to go to back to Slide 2.

Inserting Hyperlinks to the Web

Basically, you will follow the same procedure in linking to the external web sites as you did linking within your presentation.

1. Click the last slide, **Parent Resources**.
2. Select (highlight) the text: **StopCyberBullying.org**.
3. With the text **StopCyberbullying.org** selected, use the keyboard shortcut **Apple Command + K**.
4. Click the **Web Page** tab.
5. Enter the URL of the website you want to hyperlink to http://stopcyberbullying.

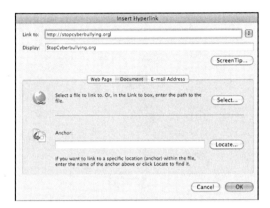

6. Click **OK**.

Now hyperlink the remaining 3 parent resources on the Parent Resource slide. The URLs are listed on the following table.

Parent Resources	
These Websites are provided for your Cyber Dangers PowerPoint Presentation	
StopCyberBullying.org	http://stopcyberbullying.org
Microsoft Online Predators	http://www.microsoft.com/protect/family/guidelines/predators.mspx
Cyber Citizenship	http://www.cybercitizenship.org/
NBC Internet Safety	http://www.msnbc.msn.com/id/11030746/

Tip: Whenever copying and pasting websites, select the URL in the browser window and use the shortcut command **Apple Command + C** to copy and **Apple Command + V** to paste. This way, you will avoid errors in copying URLs.

This concludes the section on *PowerPoint for Mac 2011* skills.

Please return to page 187 to complete the Presentation Software Exercises in your text or as directed by your instructor.

Instructional Context: Creating an Annotated Video Playlist with YouTube

One of the criticisms of YouTube (http://youtube.com) and other web-based video outlets is that the content is "not very educational." On the surface, the thought has merit. The vast majority of the hundreds of millions of YouTube videos were not designed to supplement traditional classroom instruction. They were created by the general public to share personal events, sporting feats, political perspectives, tragic events, and anything else we, as a culture, have captured on video. In essence, these video resource sites constitute society's photo album. Some content is amazing, some offensive. It is largely for this reason that most schools avoid using YouTube as a supplementary tool for education and sometimes prevent students from accessing content through filtering software.

So, what do water balloons, marshmallows, and dead pigs have to do with formal education?

Add the magic ingredient—context—and you have the ability to use the water balloon to teach about the lungs in a music class, the marshmallow to teach the laws of air pressure, and fetal pigs to support instruction in biology. All it takes is context.

The primary responsibility of the teacher in such instances is to provide this context. In much the same way that water balloons would have a detrimental effect on a classroom without appropriate context, some web-based video resources would fail to have the educational impact unless properly applied.

An annotated video playlist allows us to utilize the benefits of Web 2.0 and repurpose videos designed and deployed for one reason to meet specific educational goals within our classroom. In essence, we can reuse videos that, on the surface, do not seem to align with educational standards by adding meaning, direction, and context.

In the following exercise, you will create an **Annotated Video Playlist** using YouTube.

Create an Account

1. Navigate to http://youtube.com and click on the **Create Account** link. (Note: this may require you to log out of any instances of Google or Gmail that you may currently be using.)

2. Complete all of the required account creation information and click the **I accept** button.

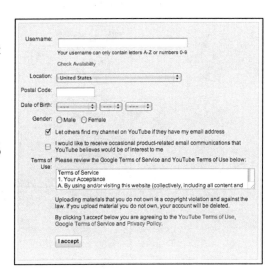

It is recommended that you select an account name (also known as Channel name) that is easy to remember and identify. Also, select a password that you will remember and write it down in a location where you can access it easily.

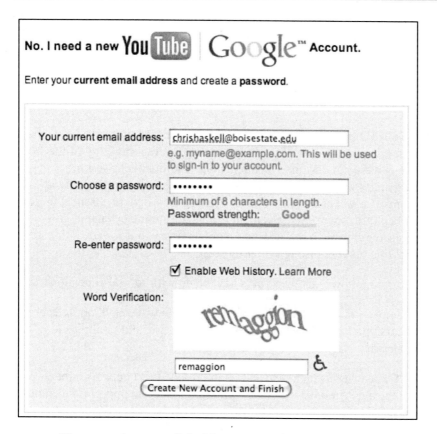

You may choose to link this to your existing Google account or create a new Google account specifically associated with this YouTube channel. It is possible to have multiple YouTube channels for different purposes (i.e., school, family, sports, etc.)

Browse for Videos

Once you have created and logged into your account, you have the ability to add videos to personalized Playlists and flag videos as Favorites. These are valuable tools in organizing web-based video resources. Begin looking for videos within your content area.

Add a Video to a Playlist

Select the "Add to" Option

When you have located a video you like, add it to a new playlist. This is done by selecting the **Save to** option and selecting **Create a new playlist . . .**

Name Your Playlist

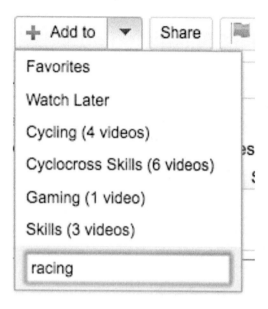

Give your playlist a name that will be easy to recognize later.

Add More Videos to Your Playlist

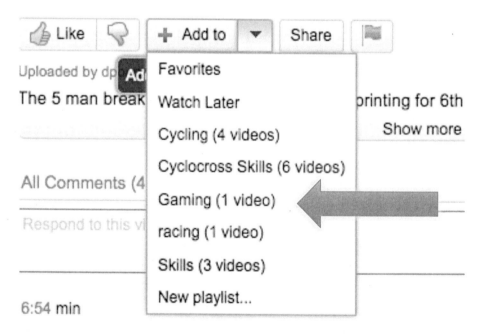

Add several more videos to your playlist

Take a Look at your Playlist

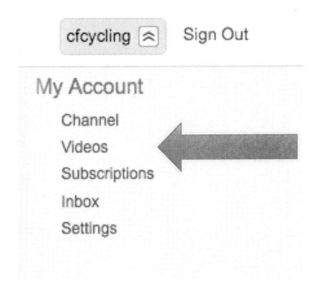

In the top right-hand corner of any YouTube page you will find your account name. That account name opens a menu, which will allow you to view your channel, inbox, account details, subscriptions, videos, favorites, and more. Selecting that button will open a pull-down window.

You can access your playlists by selecting **My Videos** or **Favorites**.

View Your Playlist

Reorganize Your Playlist Order

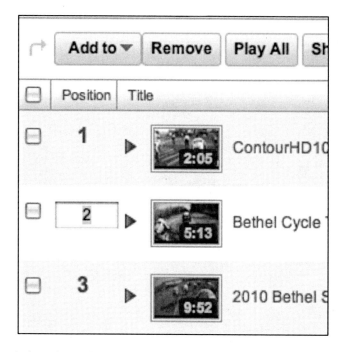

Select the ordered number of the video to change its position. Simply select the number and replace it with the desired new position and the remainder of the list will move to accommodate it.

Add Your Own Videos Using the Upload Button

Upload

To add context to the videos you've selected, it is necessary to insert videos that will help the viewer understand what you want them to look for, what is important, what questions you might hope the videos would answer, or any other context that would make these videos meaningful to the over-arching message of the lesson. It is this context that makes otherwise unrelated videos valuable in the scope of formal instruction.

(Students could also complete this process demonstrating their knowledge by selecting videos and adding their own annotations to the timeline.)

Choose Your Method of Upload

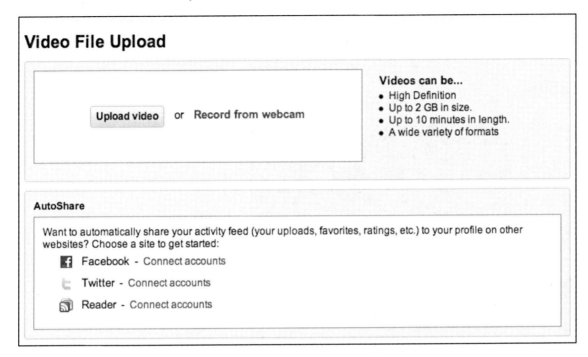

Videos can be high definition, up to 2 GB in size, up to 10 minutes in length, a wide variety of formats. You can record videos using personal video cameras, cell phones, desktop cameras, and even standard digital cameras. If you use any of these tools, you will need to transfer them to your computer to allow upload to YouTube. Some cameras and cell phones have built-in apps that will upload directly to YouTube from the device.

You can also record directly to YouTube using a computer's integrated video camera.

(Optional) Record from Webcam

YouTube will recognize and use (with your permission) any integrated video camera. Without using any special software, the site will upload your video directly to your YouTube account.

Record Your Annotation

Add any important context or commentary worth including in your video playlist by recording short video clips of yourself or students.

Review Your Recording

After recording, press the stop button. If you are unhappy with your video, select **Re-record**. If you like it, select **Publish**.

Add Video Information

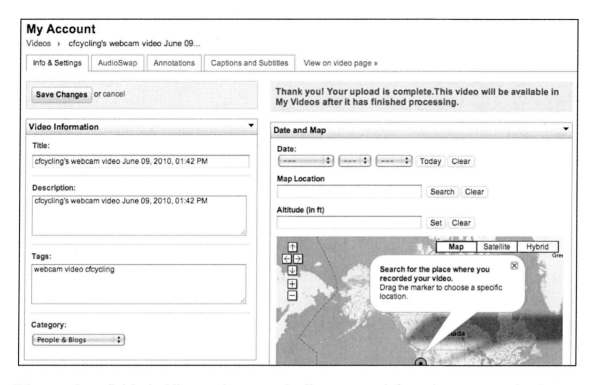

When you have finished adding any important details, tags, map information, etc., save the changes.

Add Your Video to the Playlist

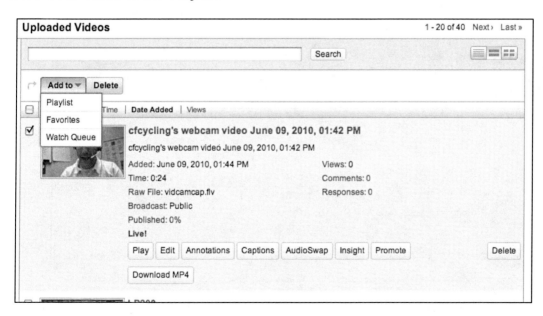

In **My Videos**, select the checkbox to the left of your video and touch the **Add to** button to add it to your playlist.

Select the Playlist

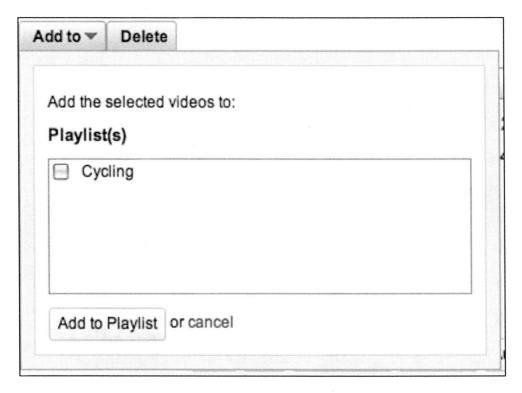

Select the playlist you'd like to add it to, and choose **Add to Playlist**.

Reorder Your Playlist

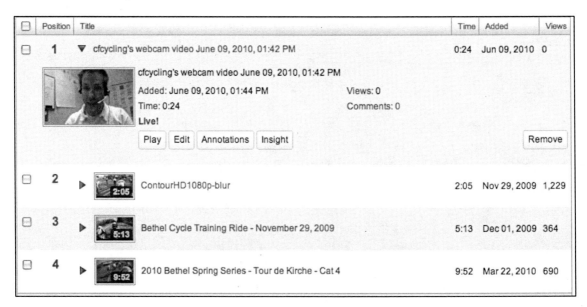

As before, utilize the position number buttons to achieve the correct play order of your videos and those that you added to your playlist.

Link or Embed Your Annotated Video Playlist

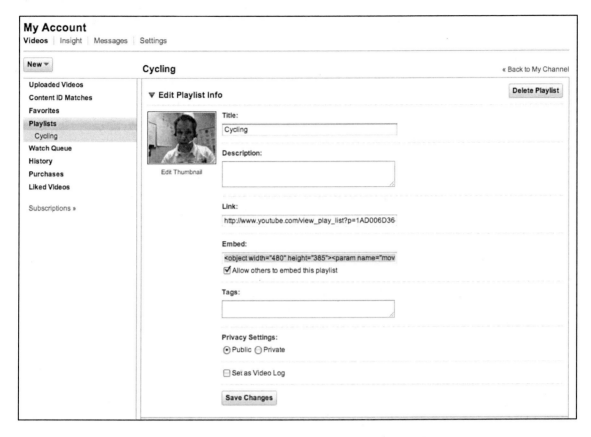

While viewing your playlist, select the **Edit Playlist Info** button above your playlist to expand the details. Within this area you will find both the URL for the direct link to the playlist and the embed code which will allow you to place that playlist in a blog or HTML enabled webpage.

Once you have completed your playlist, please return to Exercise 7, page 144.

✔ = Represents primary standard, ✧ = also meets standard

Appendix I: Artifacts Table

Artifact (Primary artifacts are highlighted)	Page #	Standard 1	Standard 2	Standard 3	Standard 4	Standard 5
Research Technology in Education, Ex. 1	14					✔
Teaching File Management, Ex. 4	29			✔		
Jigsaw Activity, Ex. 1	36	✧	✔	✧		
Vocabulary Cards, Ex. 2	61	✧	✔	✧		
Class Centers Schedule, Ex. 3	61	✧	✔	✧		
Back to School Newsletter - Ex. 4	62	✧		✔		
Correcting Papers, Ex. 5	63	✧		✔		
Fund Raiser Flyer, Ex. 6	63	✧		✔		✧
Special Event Brochure, Ex. 7	64	✧		✧		✔
Technology-Supported Lesson, Ex. 1	69	✧	✔			
Spreadsheet: Gradebook (Skills chapter)	73	✧	✔	✧		
Technology Review Interactive SS, Ex. 3	98	✔		✧		
M & M Spreadsheet, Ex. 4	106	✧	✧	✔		
M & M Charts, Ex. 5	107	✔		✔		
Curricular Interactive Spreadsheet, Ex. 6	107	✔		✧		
Problem Solving Spreadsheet, Ex. 7	108	✧	✔			
Field Trip, Ex. 8	110	✧	✧	✧	✔	✧
Curricular Spreadsheet Lesson, Ex. 9	111	✧	✧	✔		
Team Story Problem, Ex. 10	112	✧			✔	
Analyzing Data with Google Squared, Ex. 11	112			✧	✔	
Creating a Test Answer Sheet, Ex. 1	117	✧	✔			
Creating a Rubric, Ex. 2	119	✧	✔			
Providing Parent Feedback, Ex. 3	120	✧				✔
Online Survey Tools: Google Forms, Ex. 4	124			✧		✔
WebQuest, Ex.1	138	✔	✧	✧		✧
Scavenger Hunt, Ex. 2	140	✔	✧	✧		
Internet Search, Ex. 3	140	✔	✧			
Assistive Technology, Ex. 4	141	✧		✧	✔	
Class Blog, Ex. 5	141	✧	✧	✔		✧
Teaching with Technology Blog, Ex. 6	143	✧		✧		✔
Digital Story, Ex. 7	143	✧	✧	✧		✔
Annotated Video Playlist, Ex. 8	144	✧	✧	✧		✔
Addressing Digital Inequality, Ex. 1	152	✧			✔	
Digital Inequality Websites, Ex. 2	152	✧			✔	
Plagiarism and Citing, Ex. 3	153	✧		✧	✔	
Internet Safety, Ex. 4	153	✧		✧	✔	
Netiquette Guidelines, Ex. 5	154	✧		✧	✔	
Creating a Creative Commons License, Ex. 6	154	✧			✔	
Critiquing an AUP, Ex. 7	154	✧			✔	
Professional Websites, Ex. 1	167	✧		✧		✔
Shared RSS Page, Ex. 2	167	✔	✧	✧		✧
Curricular Presentation, Ex. 1	187	✔	✧	✧		
Class or Student Review, Ex. 2	189	✧	✔			
Review Games, Ex. 3	190	✔	✧	✧		
Back to School Prezi Presentation, Ex. 4	190	✧		✧		✔